This Thing of Darkness
A Sociology of the Enemy

This
Thing
of
Darkness

A Sociology of the Enemy

James A. Aho

UNIVERSITY OF WASHINGTON PRESS

Seattle and London

Library of Congress Cataloging-in-Publication Data

Aho, James Alfred, 1942–
    This thing of darkness : a sociology of the enemy / James A. Aho.
      p. cm.
    Includes bibliographical references and index.
    ISBN 0-295-97355-2. – ISBN 0-295-97386-2 (pbk.)
    1. Social conflict. 2. Hate – Political aspects. 3. Enemies.
  I. Title.
  HM136.A324 1994
  303.6—dc20   94-12015
                                                    CIP

Contents

Acknowledgments

One of the great pleasures accorded an academic writer is the opportunity to acknowledge his debts. In the case of *This Thing of Darkness* a major one is owed to Vilho Harle, senior researcher at the Tampere Peace Research Institute in Finland. Half the papers in this volume were prepared for TAPRI projects under Vilho's artful, diplomatic direction. The first such project was a workshop held in 1988 in Helsinki, entitled "European Values in International Relations" (subsequently published in London by Pinter, 1990); the second, in 1990 in Tampere, was entitled "Overcoming the Enemy." It is out of the second project that the idea for this collection arose. There is no little irony in the fact that driving to the airport on August 2, 1990, to deliver my paper, then entitled "Who Shall Be the Enemy in a Post-Communist World?" (chapter 6 herein), I turned on the radio and heard the news that Iraq had just invaded Kuwait, signaling the onset of Desert Storm.

The hospitality of the Finns was remarkable. The give-and-take of peace scholars from across the globe, stimulated by TAPRI's steady encouragement to always seek intellectual honesty, was humbling and challenging – truly a process offering an excellent example to all who crave a just peace. These essays are dedicated to the fellows and associates of the Tampere Peace Research Institute.

I would also like to acknowledge the encouragement of Naomi Pascal, editor-in-chief and associate director of the University of Washington Press, and the work of her capable staff; the incisive criticisms of earlier versions of the manuscript by both Michael Barkun of Syracuse University and Patrick McNamara of the University of New Mexico; and my poet wife, Margaret, who suggested the title.

Portions of *This Thing of Darkness* have been previously published, as noted below:

"Heroism: The Construction of Evil and Violence," first appeared in

European Values in International Relations, edited by Vilho Harle (1990), and is reprinted here by permission of Pinter Publishers of London.

"Reification and Sacrifice: The Goldmark Case," first appeared in the *California Sociologist,* 10 (Winter 1987): 78–95, and is reprinted here by permission of The California Sociologist.

"A Library of Infamy," first appeared in the *Idaho Librarian,* 41 (Oct. 1989): 86–88, and is reprinted here by permission of the Idaho Library Association.

"Out of Hate: A Sociology of Defection from Neo-Nazism," first appeared in *Current Research on Peace and Violence,* 11 (1988): 159–68, and is reprinted here by permission of the Tampere Peace Research Institute of Finland.

This Thing of Darkness
A Sociology of the Enemy

This thing of darkness I acknowledge mine.
— *William Shakespeare,* The Tempest, *V.i.755–56*

Introduction

This *Thing of Darkness* continues a long-standing effort on my part to link sociologically humankind's highest aspirations with its basest appetites – spirituality with materialism – without reducing either potentiality to the other and therefore trivializing the enigma of existence. Initially, my efforts took the form of an examination of the dialectic between religion and violence as expressed in the primary texts of selected civilizations.[1] While the product of that study is for the most part satisfactory academically, its design reveals a reluctance, perhaps an incapacity, to engage those mysteries intimately. Whatever else the present collection says about this author psychologically, it documents a conversion in research style, out of the library and into the field: not with the abstraction called "respondents" in controlled questionnaire surveys, even less with those known as experimental "subjects," but with human beings in what is jargonistically called their "natural setting," including their infinite complexities, quirks, and passions. This is for me a rediscovery of what in my professional training I had somehow lost sight of, a fascination with people.

This reknowing can be dated exactly: December 1984. At that time I inaugurated a several-year study of right-wing extremists and extremism in the Pacific Northwest.[2] While my initial inclination was to distance myself as far as possible from those I deeply feared and from ideas I loathed, I found that to adequately comprehend the movement I had to mingle with my enemies. All the chapters in this volume grew out of my study of right-wing extremism.

I went into the field with a typically objective scientific question: What causes people to join hate groups? In the course of my research, not only was I compelled by my findings to revamp the tone and direction of this question, but many other questions arose: one as a result of an unexpected phone call at night from a disaffected neo-Nazi; another from an opportunity to interview a racist skinhead through the recommendation of his analyst, whose wife was in a class I taught; another from a chance request to aid a county prosecutor prepare a murder trial brief; another from a chamber of commerce invitation to relate the "other side" of the story – a community's response to hate; and still another when the granddaughter of a founder of a major neo-Nazi group decided, upon her grandmother's death, to give me her entire library of hate tapes and pamphlets.

At the time, I put such questions aside as distractions from the main research project. Here each is examined in depth. This book may therefore be read as a sequel to the original study. Chapter 3 analyzes the case of a Seattle family of four murdered by a distant associate of the very people I was studying at the time. Chapter 4 recounts a tragic shoot-out deep in the Idaho wilderness several years later involving one of my original interviewees. Chapter 5 deals with the "literature" routinely consulted by these people, which has inspired their Manichaean world view. Chapter 8 studies how individuals have been able to gravitate from hate to acceptance of their onetime enemies, and chapter 9 examines a specific example of this process in the rapproachment between a Jewish cantor and his personal antagonist, a self-acknowledged Nazi. Chapter 10 provides a sociological account of how a group of ordinary Pacific Northwest citizens, taking up arms against hate in their own town, found themselves unwittingly thrust into an even more perilous confrontation. They were forced to ask the existential question upon which this anthology rests: Can I struggle effectively against evil without becoming tainted myself?

This Thing of Darkness is in two parts, each comprising a theoretical introduction and several cases. The first part details what I call the construction of enemies, and the second deals with their deconstruction, although it is understood that neither of these subjects can be addressed adequately without alluding to its complement.

This is a sociology of enemies. Some preliminary observations on what I mean by this term should help readers locate themselves in the vast literature of war and peace studies. Unlike sciences such as biology or physics, sociology does not represent a single viewpoint. While all sociologists are concerned with group life as opposed to individual behavior, there are many professionally recognized ways to interpret what people do together: structural-functionalism, critical theory, exchange theory, Marxism, and symbolic interactionism, among others. Nor is a sociologist restricted to one of these theories, but is permitted (in some cases required) within the bounds of internal consistency to borrow from any that seem to elucidate a problem. Although the reader will find evidence of eclecticism in the following pages, my theoretical preference will also become obvious. I call it humanistic phenomenological sociology. The principles of this approach will become clear in the course of the book. Here, the following brief comments should suffice.

Phenomenological sociology first of all concerns itself with our experience of the world in general.[3] With its duties, privileges, groups, classes, and institutions, this world ordinarily presents itself to us as objectively found in the nature of things themselves. This is reflected in the way we typically speak about worldly matters. For example, we say, "I *have to do* certain tasks," or "I *must* meet that appointment," or "my obligations *force* me" to do such and such. Or we say, "I *know* my perception of the world is shared by all rational people and therefore is the *correct* way of seeing." Or, finally, we insist that certain social arrangements like wars, prisons, and inequality have "always been with us" due to our "nature" as territorial, hierarchical beasts.

Phenomenological sociologists characterize this way of talking about the world as the "natural attitude." But the natural attitude, we believe, is a mistaken attitude – a kind of false consciousness. For even a moment's reflection reveals that what I see as trash some other person might well see as food, what I experience as pleasure someone else may see as pain, what I call a duty may in reality be a choice; and thus the social institutions we commonly hold to be inexorable, necessary, and unavoidable are in fact our own collective creations, hence not inevitable at all. In other words, human beings reside in worlds they themselves have fashioned. Our worlds are cultural "art-facts," not natural affairs. However, we tend to forget this truth, attributing responsibility for our world instead to some other thing, event, or Person independent of us: our genes, Fate, the Will of God, "the way I was raised," and so forth.

One of the pivotal dimensions of any human world is the enemy, that which is held responsible for the bad things in life. The position taken in these pages is that as factual and "natural" as the enemy appears, in reality it is (at least in part) our very own creation. It is not important here to detail the steps in the production of enemies; these will be introduced later. The important fact to emphasize is that the enemy is a *joint* production. It is rarely a phenomenon achieved by any one person alone, but is something done socially, by all of us together.

Recently two books have appeared dealing with enemies,[4] filling a gap one of the authors decries in these words: "Look in any library and you will find books that deal with every imaginable aspect of war except one – the enemy."[5] I am not going to review these books now, although I have occasion to mention them later. Suffice it to say that as brilliant as they may be, and as persuasively written, they remain psychologies of the subject. In focusing attention primarily on the individual or the individual in its social environment, they overlook, except in an anecdotal way, what I take to be the most important tools used in building enemies: courtrooms, mythologies, schoolhouses, pulpits, altars, and the media.

As a matter of practical policy, it may seem more helpful in reducing hatred to attend to individual attitudinal change rather than try to reform large-scale institutions. Scientifically, however, the social factors bearing on hate reduction cannot be ignored. For if it is true that enemies are socially assembled, then they must also be socially disassembled. Chapters 7 through 10 examine the tactics and difficulties involved in collectively deconstructing enemies. At the same time chapter 7 questions the workability of individual counseling and therapies in solving the enemy problem.

Sociology originated in the Enlightenment dream that with increased knowledge human beings could eventually conquer nature, including *human* nature – the chthonic swamp, the Id, the It, as Freud called it, of lubricious sexuality and savagery, ready to erupt at the slightest provocation. Given events since 1914, we have had to renounce the most extreme variants of this presumption. We now speak of the far less ambitious goal of accommodating ourselves to nature in a life-enhancing way. Among other things, this means that the enemy object can probably never be annihilated. The best we can hope for is to become more conscious of how Evil uses us as its instruments, and in so doing get some control over our lives.

This limited aspiration reflects the belief that to justify itself sociology must have a moral purpose beyond simply satisfying intellectual curiosity.[6] This is why I add to my title – phenomenological sociologist – the adjective "humanistic." For the point of this book is not to pretend ethical detachment about matters of the enemy, but to gain a semblance of objectivity while remaining morally engaged with the subject. Intellectual gymnastics of this sort can give rise to considerable tension. But tension can be rewarded by morally elucidating insights. It is these insights that constitute the ultimate point of this book.

1

The Problem of the Enemy

In the question 'what are the common values that the Europeans share?' is also the following question, which originally made me feel quite a bit of uneasiness: 'What or who are the victims that the Europeans sacrifice?' " By asking such questions in his playfully bitter analysis of the essence of the "(W)est" (*est* means "it is" in Latin), the Finnish sociologist Jussi Vähämäki reaches the conclusion that to be European (or North American) means gathering around the object that is killed, an action that "gives Being, language, understanding to the (W)est," thereby keeping it together. "It is astonishing," he writes, "how blind we are to our own history. Our past is full of accidents, full of accidentally dead people, people who just happened to be there, as it is said. No one had any intention to kill them, suddenly they were lying there in front of us. But they gave us our life, some of them were even 'sacrificed' so that we could live. Read Roman history! It is full of these accidents."[1]

Vähämäki amplifies his musings by citing the Latin infinitive from which "Occident" derives: *occido,* which means to fall down, to perish, to die by one's hand (from *ob* "to," *cado* "fall").[2] In polite circles, of course, the "falling down" implied here is said to refer to the setting sun and approach of evening. However, the darker semantic resonances to which Vähämäki directs our attention are worthy of examination, considering the evident march of the West, noted by contemporary European observers of Occidental history, toward "militarization," "thanatocracy," "exterminism," and "pure war."[3]

European-American mythology equates modernization with social progress: better health, longer life, domestic security, freedom from ignorance and personal liberty. In its simplest form the myth goes like this: Primitive societies – warlike, susbsistence-based, grounded on magic and superstition, and ruled by tyrants – must and will evolve into scientific, peaceful, industrialized democracies, or they will disappear altogether. Granted, there is a price to be paid for taming nature and its savage inhabitants ("accidents," to use Vähämäki's term). There may even be momentary "deviations" from the linear impetus of progress as countries such as Germany, China, the Soviet Union, and Japan, for example, move through "transitional" stages of development. But totalitarianism and state-directed mass murder cannot be considered essential features of modernization. They are, if anything, "obstacles" to it.[4]

The suspicion has begun to dawn that this arrogantly optimistic philosophy of history is fundamentally mistaken. It appears that the industrialized democracies of the civilized West with their scientific bureaucracies – not crudely dressed, wand-waving savages – constitute the gravest threat to life on earth today. Furthermore, far from being accidental deviations from or obstacles to modernization, human and environmental death alike appear somehow inextricably bound up with it. As logistical and organizational "achievements," human holocausts and their environmental counterparts are technically possible only in societies well on their way to adopting an Occidental outlook. As one critic says, mass death must be seen as *the* significant "history" of our period, the central moral and material fact of American and European civilization in full flower.[5]

In the forty-three interstate wars that have each produced at least 100,000 deaths in this century, conservative estimates are that a total of 84 million people have died. European nations have been directly implicated in over four-fifths of these engagements. This does not include wars in which they have figured only as weapons dealers or sponsors.[6] Apart from the obvious biological waste, there has been a cultural cost for this. The spectacle of mass death has occasioned for the Occidental citizen a breakdown in his inherited constellation of death meanings. For regardless of how it is experienced by the victim, to those of us who witness it, death by battlefield slaughter, massacre, siege, or concentration camp is public and statistical. Having neither personal name, face, nor reason with which to identify, it has little existential focus. Thus is undermined the traditional *artes moriendi* of Western culture, the doctrine of the "good death," a slow natural mortality, a dignified death confronted in full consciousness, courageously worked with, artfully staged in the midst of loved ones, which reflects on and amplifies the authenticity of one's life. To accommodate the reality of public mass death, a new necrological vocabulary has emerged: "engineered public death," "technologically produced macro-death," "industrialized machine-death," "death breeding," "death event," "death nation," "death world," "total death."[7]

One of today's death machines is the Poseidon submarine. Honoring the sea god of the Greeks, it carries in its hold nuclear weaponry with an explosive power three times that detonated by *all* parties in World War II. The most recent addition to America's arsenal, the Trident submarine, named after Poseidon's forked spear, has a destructive capacity nearly three times greater than Poseidon's. Even with the end of the cold war the United States is going ahead with plans to deploy a fleet of twenty such vessels. It is estimated that this arm of America's retaliatory triad alone has half again the capacity to incinerate every city and town on earth.

Beyond calling for a new language of death, modern warfare has accomplished something more sinister. It has thrust into doubt the entire Occidental doctrine of progress, and with it the corollary of unending individual advancement. If the first has legitimized the project of European conquest since A.D. 1500, the second has been the overarching directive of a fulfilled and significant individual existence. As the plausibility structures undergirding the twin myths of progress and upward mobility have collapsed, prophets have announced the obvious in their own bloodthirsty imagery: This is the end of the world, our world, the only world we know and have known. The response to this disquieting news has been predictable: the creation and use of an armory of consciousness-deadening tools; battle against those presumed to be at fault for the apocalypse; and the critical examination of our own cultural inheritance for a way out of the crisis. This book ventures modestly on the third and what I consider only responsible path.

In contemplating the possibility of annihilation, the issue of life preservation assumes extraordinary urgency. But the issue of human survival is the essential concern of social theory: How can human affairs be structured without risk to human security? Is there a truly life-engendering politics? Questions like these inevitably call for a reexamination of our nature as communal animals. And this, in turn, leads to analysis of the perennial themes in political rhetoric. What is distributive justice? our duty to the state and its to us? our obligation to the past, to future generations, to each other? Of these themes, perhaps the most important, at least one of the most beguiling, concerns the Enemy, the human other who threatens community life and against whom the polis takes up arms. How are enemies made possible? What is to be done with them? Can the enemy be overcome?

This book concerns the enemy: how the enemy is constructed socially, how it is destroyed, and, finally, how it can be *de*constructed or transcended. No claim is being made that having answered these questions we will have solved the crisis of our times. I am convinced, however, that until we become conscious of the central role enemies play in our lives and then undertake some effort to deal with this fact, we not only will continue to be victimized by our illusions but will blindly persist in victimizing others.

This chapter undertakes a preliminary exploration of what I call "enemy territory." This is best viewed as consisting of a series of paradoxes – notions that at first appear unbelievable or even absurd, but nonetheless prove to be true. These paradoxes are traps of sorts into which the unwitting may stumble, compromising their own safety and that of others – traps avoidable only by means of well-exercised mental agility. The three paradoxes are: evil grows from the quest to defeat the enemy, however understood; the latent function of such struggles is harmony; the enemy harbors a dual nature – living both "out there" and also deeply inside ourselves.

The First Paradox: Evil's Inseparability from Good

The subject of violence becomes challenging ethically and intellectually when *I* feel justified in acting violently. But I sense that my violation of you is vindicated when I grasp profoundly my own victimization: when I not only see you as my enemy but viscerally *feel* it. This is the first paradox: My violation of you grows from my yearning to rectify the wrong I sense that you have done me. Violence emerges from my quest for good and my experience of you as the opponent of good.

This paradox has an added turn which magnifies its tragedy: what we have said also applies to our enemies. They, too, violate out of a sense of victimization. Take the prototypical Nazi. Apart from how we personally perceive it, to him the world is "overrun" by Jewish Communists and Freemasons who secretly plot his destruction. It is primarily as a victim of "persecution," not as an aggressor, that he understands his military posturing. Like those of people everywhere and always, his is a "just" war, carried out in "self-defense," engaged in "reluctantly" and only as a

"last resort." These are the words of Adolf Hitler taken from the concluding sentences of his discussion of "My Years of . . . Suffering in Vienna"
in *Mein Kampf:*

> Blood sin and desecration of the race are the original sin in this world, and the
> end of a humanity which surrenders to it. . . . Thus I believe that I am acting in
> accordance with the will of the Almighty Creator: *by defending myself against
> the Jew I am fighting for the work of the Lord.*"[8]

To dismiss this exhortation as deluded and fantastic may be comforting, but to do so prevents us from grasping with any profundity the
meaning of Nazi vengeance, and thus also cripples attempts to work
against it effectively. Moreover, it inhibits us from understanding and
controlling our own capacity to harm others.

But, the reader may object, surely some persons "sincerely" believe in
their delusions. Is this not the very symptom of insanity? True. With the
subject of enemies we stand before what seems to be a form of collective
psychosis. My argument is that if we choose to describe outbursts of hate
in medical terms, then this "illness" is not limited to Nazis, but is familiar to people of all conditions, races, places, and doctrines.

Let us examine this paradox in the context of America's armed engagement against Iraq in the spring of 1991, Desert Storm. I begin with a
comment by the renowned sociologist W. I. Thomas. Situations defined
as real, he says, are real in their consequences.[9] As difficult as it is for us
to hear them, Iraqi ravings about Western "imperialism," American "duplicity," and the "violations" of Muslim women and sanctuaries are in a
pragmatic sense probably as "realistic" to Iraqis as is the following creed
expressed so baldly by American officials and repeated like cant by the
American public: Saddam is the "greatest peril" today to freedom, security, and the American way of life, a "ruthless tyrant" who has committed "outrageous acts of genocidal barbarism" that "surpass" even those
of Hitler in their brutality.[10]

Read sympathetically, these counterclaims by two typical antagonists
enable us to grasp the fundamental tragedy of violent conflict – that *all*
parties do wrong out of a sense of right. This is the kind of seeing called
for by a sociology of political violence. It is a kind of perception that
throws one off cognitive balance, but is nonetheless essential for healing
illumination.

The sociological comprehension of political violence contains a grave risk, the danger of becoming demonic oneself. For it can, if taken incorrectly, be considered an apology for moral relativism, nihilism, and ultimately for cynicism of the sort congenial to fascism ("fascism" defined here as a style of thought that prides itself on its "courage" to see politics as nothing but a struggle for power, and where all claims to morality are viewed "realistically" as masquerades for mass consumption). In fairy tales, this is the reason behind the warning given the hero not to inquire too persistently into evil, as Marie Louise von Franz has discussed in her writings.[11] So, too, the reverence routinely accorded the chthonic gods of antiquity: "People turned away and covered their faces, and when they prayed to Hecate [queen of Hell and patron of witches] they put on a black veil *not* to see her – in order not to become her."[12]

Granted, there are dangers in approaching the first paradox of the enemy too closely, but to blind oneself to its truths is equally hazardous morally. For the consequence is not likely to be innocence, but unconscious complicity in the death potlatch that is so much of history. Consider the following case of a "theologian," as he is called, of the "nuclear priesthood."

Col. Joseph P. Martino (ret. USAF) is a weapons development specialist and systems analyst. I cite his example not because it is unique, but for the opposite reason. It typifies not only American techno-strategic discourse but the thinking of the ordinary man in the street.

Martino is a Christian husband and father of two, a man of obvious ethical sensibility. Nevertheless, with the equanimity of a medieval casuist, he recommends the military destruction of innocent people by nuclear weapons when deemed "morally appropriate." According to the Just War principle of Double Effect, says Martino, an evil effect such as the mass homicide of innocents is permitted if it is incidental to a military action intended to produce a morally licit effect. This is true even if these innocents are themselves victims of the enemy government: "It is, after all *their* government, not ours."[13]

How many innocents it is morally permissible to kill is a relative matter, Martino continues. However, a just war requires that the values sacrificed must always be proportionate to the values preserved. But insofar as democratic Christians "know" (the word is his) their values "*are* better than others,"[14] then killing even a million innocents in defense of these values may be acceptable: "When we consider how many of its own people the Soviet government has killed and is killing through official terror, a discriminating attack that permits a million deaths but weakens the Soviet government . . . [may] be morally justified."[15] Nor can the deaths of even one million innocents be considered an upper limit to violence: "If the values at stake are important enough, the loss of *millions* of lives may be a proportionate cost."[16]

This example illustrates how easy it is for good people, people like ourselves, to do the dirty work of mass murder. To paraphrase Ernest Becker, human beings pile up horrors around themselves not out of a perverse lust to wreak havoc, at least not ordinarily, but, like Martino, out of a clear-sighted yearning to do good; not to destroy the world, but heroically to save it.[17] It is this dark truth that must be faced if we are ever to come to grips with what I call the crisis of exterminism.

This is not to say that the killing of designated enemies or the putting of oneself or one's family at risk in doing so is ever easy. We can imagine the Martinos of the world agonizing about the harm they advocate, wondering if perhaps they have come to mirror the enemies they destroy. But as Becker again reminds us, the hallmark of "true heroism" is the capacity to persevere in the face of doubt, to choke down what is distasteful.[18]

The Second Paradox: The Unifying Function of Enemies

Even a cursory observer of the 1990–91 mobilization of thousands of all political persuasions to animosity toward "Saddam" (or in Iraq and Jordan, toward "Bush") is tempted to grant that we were witnessing a hysteria, for want of a better term, of massive proportions. Just days prior to this collective "effervescence," as Émile Durkheim might have called it, Saddam Hussein was being courted as a stalwart defender of "civilized values" against Iranian fanaticism and Syrian terrorism. Iraq now lies in smoking ruins and anarchy, witness to American fickleness and technological might; the United States treats Syria, its recent "implacable foe," as a long lost prodigal child; Iran, meanwhile, obsequiously curries favor with the late "great Satan," America; and America in turn finds itself allied with the former "evil empire," Russia. The capacity of entire populations to shift radically their allegiances and hatreds virtually overnight betrays what seems to be an unplumbed depth of hostility in the human psyche. This leads to consideration of a second paradox in the sociology of enemies.

Popular legend teaches that culture and ideology – the so-called ideational realm – serve only to legitimize society's goings-on after the fact, the political-economic substructure of social life, "the *real* world." Technically, they are said to be causally "dependent" rather than "independent" variables in social conflicts. Without engaging the veracity of this legend directly, in these pages I assume the opposite position. I argue that political and economic activities serve "ideal," "spiritual" ends. It is not simply because Saddam threatened our oil resources that American parents embraced so enthusiastically the state's call to offer their children on the shrine of Mars. It is also that Americans had in the prior months been deprived of an idea that for half a century had bound them as a people – anti-Communism – and thus they *needed* an enemy. Without one there could be no heroic community with which to identify.

In the months immediately preceding the Persian Gulf war such issues as illiteracy, the greenhouse effect, acid rain, the trade imbalance, Daniel Ortega, and "Panamanian strongman" Manuel Noriega had all momentarily captured the public's interest, but none sustained it. This evidently was because they did not contain the exact mix of non-Caucasian racial type, alien language and confession, "uncivilized" life-style, and suitably dangerous – "battle-hardened" – but not insurmountable armed force required for credibility as a bona fide American enemy. Although admittedly this is an overdrawn claim, it may be argued that America needed a petty Hitler, and thus set about manufacturing one to meet its specifications. Its name: Saddam.

This is not to say that Saddam Hussein, out of his own stupidity, greed, and treachery, did not freely stumble into the strobe projected by the American psyche, thereby becoming archdemon in a reenactment of the American drama of world redemption. Nor am I saying that American military, industrial, and petrochemical elites did not have their own financial and political interests at stake in a Persian Gulf crisis. But this hardly explains why the common folk, who paid with their lives, children, and property to enhance those interests, seized upon the possibility of fighting with such evident jubilation.

The second paradox of the enemy: There can be no harmony without chaos, no peace without war. While groups ostensibly fight only to secure their own short-term interests at the expense of others, the latent "function" or unintended end of such fights is social solidarity.[19]

That the Persian Gulf war served a socializing function, at least among Coalition Forces, is unassailable. Not only was a semblance of unity achieved between unlikely candidates for alliance – prior to Desert Storm, for example, Kuwait refused to acknowledge Israel as a nation, preferring the frighteningly ambiguous title "Jewish entity" – but even grizzled American Marine generals were quoted as speaking openly to their men of their "love" for each other.[20] More than this, American strangers rediscovered a bond transcending their petty domestic differences. As the headline of one article read, "What a Wonderful Time To Be American!"[21]

"Old Glory is still glorious – and fashion-forward. It goes so well with yellow ribbons these days," the article states. To display "our everlasting patriotism," the writer recommends purchasing a "Home Sweet U.S.A." cross-stitch kit or a yellow slap-on wristband imprinted with "Support Our Troops." After all, singer Janet Jackson, the Rolling Stones, and the actor Lou Gosset, Jr., all wear them. Furthermore, "for a classic and timely memento" of the war, Bulova is marketing a limited edition "patriot watch." It features an eagle with outspread wings and an American flag with leather band for only $150.

The indicators of war-generated solidarity in the United States alone were prolific. A nationwide Military Family Support Network was established to counsel and aid families whose loved ones were overseas; children of every race and region were photographed ceremoniously tying yellow ribbons to schoolyard trees and participating in letter writing campaigns with soldiers they'd never met; athletic teams sewed American flags on uniforms; and fashion designers pushed not only red, white, and blue skirts and blouses, but facsimiles of desert camouflage combat outfits, complete with gas masks, epaulets, and brass buttons; nursing homes were reported to have positioned pasteboards in TV rooms with photos of grandchildren stationed in the desert ("Labor supplied by the staff"); newspapers printed full-page color American flags "suitable for taping to walls"; and state legislatures organized Operation Gratitude, proposing to grant tax and hunting privileges, separation bonuses, tuition-free college educations, and free employment assistance to returning troops.

Of course there was dissent. But credible private polling services independently documented support for the Gulf War at anywhere from 80 to 90 percent. Indeed, nearly half the voting population verbally advocated the use of nuclear weapons if the ground battle stalled. Besides this, what dissent there was took a revealing turn. Dressed in the same costumery and symbolic accoutrement of the prowar side – Old Glory and yellow ribbons – it was directed exclusively against the "government," not toward "our boys" in the field. That is to say, it did not attack the national consensus as much as it implicitly celebrated it through civility and good humor. As one sign advertising an upcoming peace rally promised, "No ideology checks." Tolerance was equally characteristic of the prowar crowd. While it may have disagreed with the antiwar folks vehemently, it acknowledged their "right" to disagree, and used the fact of its tolerance as "proof of America's democratic grandness and still another reason to fight."

The Third Paradox: The Duality of the Enemy

All social sciences share at least a perfunctory interest in the enemy; but they approach the subject in different ways. Economists, for example, consider enemies to be rational, hedonistic competitors for scarce resources. Political scientists emphasize the relative power of enemies and the inequitable distribution of resources issuing from their struggles for preeminence. Sociology, the perspective employed in this book, views the enemy as a metaphor and conflict as a ceremonial rite. Formulated syllogistically: The enemy represents evil; the ultimate evil is death. *Ergo* to expulse the enemy is to "kill death."

The annihilation of the enemy expresses mankind's perennial yearning for immortality. In this sense all armed combat against the enemy is sacramental. All civilizations (including our own, as testified by the appearance of a nuclear death cult) charge with sacred meaning both the protagonist and his victim, as well as the instruments and "arts" of human violation.[22]

The enemy has all the elements Rudolf Otto has attributed to the holy (in its negative form) in his classic study of the religious experience.[23] The enemy is a *mysterium tremendum,* to use Otto's phrase, a paradoxical duality that simultaneously revolts and attracts us.

We are horrified and appalled by tales of Nazi brutality yet can't seem to put them aside. Their very awfulness allures us in some perverse manner. What is the basis of this fascination? Nazism most certainly exists as an objective phenomenon "out there," and I want to return to its facticity momentarily; but Nazism is also a potential each of us harbors in ourselves. This is the source of its never-ending enchantment; for as clinical psychologists have long recognized, what fascinates us most is our very own self. Hence the gossipy obsession of puritans with "disgusting" sexual goings-on; of dishonest businessmen with "international banking conspiracies"; of corrupt political leaders with how their opponents "plot" against them; and of the 1991 Coalition Forces with Iraqi weapons capabilities and Saddam's crimes against the aboriginal Kurds. In each of these cases the protagonists have unconsciously identified their *own* forbidden fantasies and actions – their *own* diabolism – in the enemy.

This is why it can be said that protagonists "constitute" enemies from their own substance. The enemy, in other words, is the protagonist's own projection, his own creation. But – and here we return to the issue momentarily ignored above – the enemy is more than this. After all, some sexual practices *are* heinous in themselves regardless of the opinions of Victorian prudes. Some international bankers and commodity brokers *are* corrupt. Iraq *did* commit atrocities against the Kurds and Kuwaitis; it *did* build a chemical and bacteriological arsenal; and it *was* working on deliverable nuclear bombs when attacked. The enemy is not simply a subjective creation; in many cases it is also an objective reality. Ignoring its facticity condemns us at best to paralysis; at worst it prepares us for being victims.

In *A Distant Episode*, Paul Bowles writes of a highly cultivated, liberal French professor researching linguistics in the Moroccan desert. Headstrong in the pursuit of data, enthusiastically open to the shadowy exotica of nomadic life, he ignores his own vague intimations of impending danger, and accidentally stumbles into a cave of robbers. He is summarily beaten, stripped, and his tongue ripped out. He is then sewn into a camel leather pouch, starved for ten days, and transported to an oasis in the next province, where he is sold to provide entertainment for its residents. There, attired in a costume of tin can remnants attached to rags, which produces tinkling sounds with every movement, the good professor ends his days, dancing and grunting for food to the delight of his audience.[24]

Of course this is fiction, but fiction with a warning for romantics who tend to lose sight of an objective reality apart from their theories – a reality that can be overlooked only at risk of imperiling themselves.

Emmanuel Lévinas is celebrated today for radically reorienting Occidental ethical thought.[25] Although this is not the place to thoroughly review his work, its general flavor can aid us in illustrating that there is more at stake in the third paradox of the enemy than appears at first glance.

The task of ethical philosophy, Lévinas insists, is to overcome the destructive and peculiarly Western habit of speaking of other people (and of nature) as if they are objects – objects constituted out of aggregates of sense impressions, thus things to be utilized, managed, or exploited. To avoid this habit, Lévinas proposes that the other be written of as immediately present to oneself, as a corporeality in its own right, as a "thou," not an "it." After all, if the other were merely an object, it would not be worthy of the pronoun signifying its very otherness, "You."

Your alterity "overwhelms" me, Lévinas continues, "overloads" my consciousness. Your face "defies" signification; it ruptures the coherence of my world, making "holes in the walls of my house." Your presence awakens in me a response; I respond to you; I become "responsible to you," "infinitely responsible." Here Lévinas introduces his radical altercentric ethics.

You are "already there," prior to my interpretation and understanding of your presence, Lévinas insists. You are my "prior," my superior, my "before me," my "form-er." You form me, hence I am "beholden" to you. In these words, Lévinas places the characteristic French stamp on his ethics. The familiar Anglo-Saxon precession of me to you is inverted. The ghost of August Comte and the French socialists who coined the term "altruism" is resurrected. This is the same Comte who recommended that the well-known biblical injunction be rephrased to read, "Love thy neighbor *more* than thyself."[26]

Lévinas refuses on principle to reduce his altruistic ethics to a list of categorical imperatives. Such rules would be as arbitrary, he believes, as the inevitably partial and exclusionary definitions of "man" upon which they might be based. Nevertheless, he is willing to point to an ethical style appropriate to the priority of the other. It is expressed in such phrases as "letting the other be," "hearing the other out," "attending to the other," and "willing the freedom of the other." I should "give voice" to the excluded dimensions of existence in any epoch (sexuality, death, the body in general), says Lévinas, to those without tongues, or to whom speech is forbidden (women, slaves, and minorities). I should "give ear," without judgment, when "you" speak, and allow you to disclose yourself to me.

The openness and vulnerability prescribed in these recommendations, as attractive as they seem in the abstract, also appear, at least to me, to betray a dangerous romanticism regarding human beings. How far, we might ask, should one go in "letting the other be?" Should I "will the freedom" of a mass murderer? Should I "give ear" to the ravings of every madman and self-proclaimed prophet? To what extent should I be, *can* I be, "infinitely responsible" for the other "who," says Lévinas, "is in need of everything necessary for a human life?"

It may be that Lévinas can answer these questions satisfactorily. Undoubtedly as a Jew he has had to confront the reality of Nazism, and as a Zionist the presence of the Palestinian in Israel. However, it is possible that on taking the preceding recommendations to heart, those with less subtlety than Lévinas can be the occasion of considerable havoc. For the reality is that in advocating a duty to others prior to discrimination, altercentricism seems to render problematic the possibility of being ethical. This is because to engage others "rightly" I must first discriminate, and discrimination requires that I give your pesence some kind of meaning, that I understood who and what you are. True, unconscious signification is arrogant, and the unconscious attribution of evil to others is often a precursor to murder. But indiscriminate vulnerability to others is at least as harmful. For it ignores the possibility that if encounters with otherness are often pleasant, the other can also be a repository of unspeakable horrors.

The steps in the production of enemies are enumerated in the following chapters. By grasping the details of how we construct an enemy, we are positioned to see that many of our battles are gigantic jousts with our own illusions. This can be a painful realization, particularly when the costs in treasure and human lives are counted. But the pain may be seen as a necessary injection to inoculate us against a particularly virulent plague, political anthrax, carried by hate mongers – a plague that respects no nation, race, or religion. Having said this, however, we should never forget that the enemy is a mysteriously paradoxical phenomenon. It has both a subjective and an objective face. While failing to acknowledge our own culpability in creating enemies puts us at risk of becoming executioners, being blind to the objective facticity of evil contains the danger of rendering us its victims. As Albert Camus said, our task as human beings is to be neither victims nor executioners.[27] This requires the courage to renounce both the extreme of punctilious rectitude that perceives only those evils external to itself, and the extreme of romanticism that reduces evil to an internal and solely subjective event.

Part I

The Enemy Socially Constructed

2

Heroism, the Construction of Evil, and Violence

"Imagine 'the enemy' as conceived by the man [who would reform the world]," wrote Nietzsche, "and here precisely is his deed, his creation: he has conceived 'the evil enemy,' 'the evil one' – and indeed as the fundamental concept from which he then derives as an afterimage and counter-instance, a 'good one' – himself."[1]

Warfare is an occasion of calculated mutual violation. The violation of human beings requires their social construction into certain kinds of things – enemies, embodiments of evil. The sociology of reification elucidates the procedures that groups use to manufacture evildoers. The sociology of heroism explains why groups undertake such an enterprise in the first place. Together, they constitute an emerging, comprehensive theory of collective violence.

The Sociology of Heroism

The general theory of heroism and its relationship to violence was first articulated by the late Ernest Becker.[2] Its axioms can be stated succinctly: All organisms want to "feel good," to maximize pleasure and minimize pain. But human needs are more than just biological; they are also symbolic, spiritual. Human beings yearn to "feel good about themselves." They need to know that their existence is somehow significant in the cosmos, that they are justified. To use Becker's phraseology, human beings need to know themselves as heroes.

The tactics used throughout history to publicly display and solicit acknowledgment of human greatness constitute a thesaurus of cultural anthropology. They vary from accumulating riches to having numerous progeny (who, as they extend one's life germ, symbolically extend one's self), from earning degrees and honors to completing projects and expeditions, from ascetic denials of one's biological appetites (including, as in *hara-kiri* and *sati* [suttee], the denial of life itself to obtain greater life), to what interests us here: redemption of the world.

The cultural motif of heroic world redemption is not unique to modern Europe. The Islamic *jihad* (the struggle for righteousness) and the armed pilgrimage (*peregrinatio pro Christi*) to the Holy Land to cleanse it of the Antichrist can both be understood as elaborate, violent ceremonies conducted in the service of order and sanity; so too can the Aztec *guerra florida* or "flowery war," Hinduism's "conquest of regions" to preserve the world from moral anarchy (*apattikala*), and even the sublime martial arts of China and Japan.

Nevertheless, it is also true that social order and the heroic labor to save it have been conceived differently in various civilizations.[3] In the Orient, anomie is experienced as a rupture in the unchanging impersonal cosmic order – let us call it *Tao* – and world redemptive gestures typically take the form of egolessly realigning private and public affairs with this eternal Way. As Confucius teaches: To "hit the mark" in archery is not the same as to go through the leather target. That, he says, is a measure of brute strength, and that is the "old way" of the barbarian. The goal is to shoot stylistically but effortlessly in accordance with the ceremonial rules, including shooting in harmony with flute and drum. In this sense the true hero, or "superior man" (*chün tzu*), does not stand out in the manner of the blustering hero of the West who, like Samson the Nazarite (or Rambo), screams his outrage at injustice, and then, in God's name, rips down houses, burns vineyards, and slays sinners by the score. Instead he becomes silent and invisible: he is absorbed into a cycle infinitely larger than himself.

In civilizations that have come under Judeo-Christian and Muslim influence – which is to say, among others, modern Europe and America – chaos is experienced as the product of disobedience regarding ethical duties, not mere ritual infractions, as these have been revealed through prophecy. Here, then, the heroic task becomes one not of passively yielding to the Way but of energetically taking up weapons to reform the world after the personal commandments of the Holy One. The Occidental holy war functions to sterilize the world of an alien darkness or disease, not to reconcile man to its inevitability, particularly its inevitability in himself. It is this type of world-saving effort that is the focus of concern in the following pages.

For adherents of sacred and secular Occidental faiths (such as Marxism, liberalism, or fascism), the world is "fallen" or "problematic," hence susceptible to reform. But no reform movement can make the world over all at once in its entirety. Therefore, each focuses its indignation and redemptive energy on a "fetish" of evil – a despicable act, a heretical belief, a foreign place, an alien people, a criminal person – that is to be fettered, expulsed, or exterminated. Chapter 7 will describe the archetypal features of the enemy. Here it is enough to appreciate that the word "fetish" implies the largely fantastic, sometimes hysterical, almost always capricious nature of bestowals of the title "evil one." Collective fetishism is tragic, says Ernest Becker, "precisely because it is sometimes very arbitrary: men make fantasies about evil, see it in the wrong places, and destroy themselves and others by uselessly thrashing about."[4]

The Dialectic of Heroism

As applied to the work of world redemption, the dialectic of heroism can be seen as comprising three moments. In the first, an ideal is imagined: democracy, equality, peace, love, freedom, racial purity, moral perfection, the conversion of all peoples to the "true" faith, and so forth. In the second moment, the actuality of the real world is counterpoised to the ideal. This is the *Is* in opposition to the *Should Be:* inequality, tyranny, mistrust, cynicism, miscegenation, corruption, the babel of faiths. Out of the experience of contradiction issues suffering, pathos, and *compathos* – compassion for others. To eradicate his own pain and what is suffered for others sympathetically, the hero embarks on the third and decisive moment in his quest: transformative labor, courageous, persistent effort to embody his ideal in concrete. This is the doubt-filled, exhausting, morally risky toil to reconcile "essence" with existence.

To use Hegel's imagery, the successful completion of the heroic task may be spoken of as the realization of the ideal and the idealization of the real. In it the hero reappropriates the alienated object world, making it his own. He reconciles his "insides," his ideals, with what is outside himself, and in so doing experiences a sense of joy in the union of subject and object. But the heroic quest does not always end happily. While the more formidable the contradiction between real and ideal the greater the psychological reward in reconciling it, the greater too are the hazards of compromise and failure. Emotionally the most compelling struggles take place at the very point where fulfillment and tragedy meet. Holy war to reform the world according to a transcendent ideal employs the most craven means. Hence as the Old Testament, the Mahabharata, the Iliad, the Edda, the Sagas – indeed all the world's great mythic literature – understands, it is the preeminent stage for heroic dramatization.

Heroic Violence and Reification

The warrior needs an enemy. Without one there is nothing against which to fight, nothing from which to save the world, nothing to give his life meaning. What this means, of course, is that if an enemy is not ontologically present in the nature of things, one must be manufactured. The Nazi needs an international Jewish banker and conspiratorial Mason to serve his purposes of self-aggrandizement, and thus sets about creating one, at least unconsciously. By the same token, the radical Zionist locks himself in perverse symbiosis with his Palestinian "persecutors," the Communist with his "imperialistic capitalist running dogs," the capitalist with his Communist "subversives."

It would be the height of insipience to deny that there are bona fide conflicts of interest out of which mutual hostilities emerge: fights over scarce food and water, over wealth and power, over "ideal" interests such as prestige and honor. Part of the impetus of peace studies is to reduce international hatreds that threaten war by demonstrating to national leaders that in light of the self-destructive consequences of building and deploying modern weaponry, they share a concrete interest in peace. Without disputing the validity of this program, the theory presented here suggests that groups sometimes fabricate conflicts of interest with convenient others in order to struggle against them.

The way in which the assembly of enemies proceeds was first articulated by Peter Berger and Thomas Luckmann in their ground-breaking classic, *The Social Construction of Reality*.[5] This book rests on the familiar distinction between Being itself (as seen, so to say, by God) and being as it appears to, or is experienced by, man. The idea is that insofar as things in themselves can never be directly known, we should henceforth redirect our attention to "phenomenology" – that is, to our *experience* of things. Berger and Luckmann attempt to describe in detail the contents of the world as presented to differently situated people, and then to analyze how that world has come to be, to use their word, "constructed." We will have more to say about this theoretical approach in chapter 7.

In essence, say Berger and Luckmann, our experience of the world is built up stepwise through what they call reification or objectification.

The Process of Reification

"Reification" refers to the way in which people come to perceive their own creations, incorrectly or falsely, as things for which they have no responsibility, over which they have no power, and which they must passively suffer as victims do their fate. Although any number of phenomena could illustrate this, I mention a particularly striking one, the nuclear bomb.[6]

At the simplest level, of course, the Bomb is merely a product of human labor, organizational skill, and scientific genius. Yet its first blinding manifestation above the Alamogordo desert in 1945 induced in many of those who witnessed it something akin to a profound religious experience: absolute horror coupled with fascination, an ineffable exhilaration, both humbling and exalting. Robert Oppenheimer found that the only words capable of encompassing the experience were those from the Bhagavad-Gita: "I am Death, the all devouring . . . , devouring worlds on every side with my flaming mouths. . . ." To describe what they saw and felt Robert Jungk, Otto Frisch, Isidor Rabi, and Victor Weisskopf, to name just a few, invoked similar imagery. Since that time, a cult of sorts has evolved – elsewhere I have entitled it the nuclear death cult – having its own ritual practices, legends, and priestly structure. In effect, a human product has been rendered into an idol to which both great treasure and thousands of lives, in peace and war, have been sacrificed.[7]

Berger and Luckmann itemize the steps through which reification proceeds: naming, legitimation, mythmaking, sedimentation, and ritual. They make no claim that these steps always occur in this particular sequence or that later research may not find that more than these five steps are involved.

Thus far, variations on reification theory have been profitably used by sociologists to grasp how death and dying are "accomplished" in hospitals, how illness (as opposed to disease) is socially "constructed," how insanity is "manufactured," how criminality, delinquency, addiction, and even incapacitating handicaps are fabricated by the sometimes sincere, sometimes cynical collusion of physicians, court officials, families, and well-doers, at the expense of unwitting victims.[8] The theory has also been applied to the general field of social problems and used to account for the growing interest in the maltreatment of children, the elderly, and women since 1970; it has been used to explain the increase in public concern that large numbers of children are being abducted annually by strangers in the United States; and it has been used to interpret the significance of America's latest war on drugs, the "crack attack." Most recently, reification theory has been employed to better understand the emerging phenomenon of alleged adolescent "satanism."[9] It can easily be extrapolated to the field of evildoers and evildoing generally to include the whole panoply of witches, commies, nazis, terrorists, micks, niggers, japs, gooks, pigs, fags, and slopes selected throughout history to play the role of foil to the world-redeeming hero in the theater of self-glorification.

Naming

Jack Douglas urges: "Our motto must be, 'The world of social meanings is problematic until proven otherwise.' "[10] Phenomenological sociology begins with the observation that aspects of life generally considered unproblematic and absolute – for example, good and evil – are in fact matters of convention. Persons, acts, or situations are in themselves neither good nor evil. They come to be seen as such when, in the course of everyday social life, they are so defined.[11]

A crucial step in social definition is naming, or as it is more popularly known, "labeling."[12] It is not uncommon in public (journalism) and private (gossip) discourse for defamatory labels to be flippantly imposed on persons, acts, or situations that are not what they supposedly "should" be. Sometimes these labels are bestowed on the basis of a loose, intuitive "fit" between the person, as known through his actions and background, and the formal criteria for the label's usage. During crises, defamatory labels are bandied about arbitrarily and may fix on anyone who chances to be in the way.

While "nut," "slut," "fag," and categories of far more dangerous import – "heretic," "terrorist group," "Communist," "soft-core fascist," or "queer" – may be used incorrectly, with the labeler unconscious of any malicious intent, they are more often employed with calculation to destroy careers and enhance political and national causes. The point is that defamatory language rarely, if ever, simply describes things; it also rhetorically "accomplishes" them. And what it accomplishes is an enemy, ready for violation.

Legitimation

It is one thing to malign others; it is another for such labels to "stick." If labels are to adhere to the intended party, they must be validated. One vehicle for effecting this is the public degradation ceremony.[13] This is a formal hearing, trial, inquisition, or tribunal presided over by presumed experts licensed to pronounce disparaging judgments on their fellows. As analyzed by Harold Garfinkel, while such ceremonies may differ in detail, those that actually "work" to reconstitute people into beings appropriate for exile or destruction must meet several conditions: (1) They must be held in extraordinary, hallowed precincts, on sacred ground, at sacred times, with the victim and executioners alike arrayed in special costumery. (2) All the actors, including the victim, must assume an attitude of solemn reverence toward the proceedings. (3) The accusers called to testify against the victim must show themselves to be motivated by patriotic concern for "tribal values," not by private considerations of vengeance, envy, or greed. (4) The tribal values must be made explicit in the course of testimony. (5) The accusers must demonstrate that nothing in the victim's life is accidental, but is part of a uniform gestalt, or action type ("evil"). (6) This action type must be rhetorically counterpoised against its opposite – such as "Christian American" – of self-evident virtue and dignity (and of which the accusers must be examples).

Later we shall see how ceremonies meeting these requirements, *regardless of their formal outcomes,* can have unanticipated, pernicious consequences. Even if entirely innocent, the accused is contaminated – his guilt, insanity, addiction, subversiveness, or apostasy "confirmed" in the eyes of the masses.

Each society, it has been argued, stables poor, uneducated, diseased aliens either within or outside its gates to appear as the accused in rites of degradation. Since they are people of little other utility, their participation in such ceremonies can be viewed as their primary "role" in life. In return for their upkeep, they appear in successive reenactments of degradation during which community values are revivified and the community itself symbolically saved.[14]

Mythmaking

"Mythmaking" refers to the provision of biographical or historical accounts of defamed persons showing why it is inevitable, necessary, and predictable that they act as they do – namely, as evil ones. It is a second way to validate defamatory labels.

Sometimes mythmaking occurs after the "successful" outcome of a public degradation ceremony, as in a pre-sentencing report in legal proceedings.[15] In such instances authoritative jargon must be used, documenting how the victim's case fits the official "scientific" theory of evil in favor at the time: biological, psychological, or sociological. For example, incidents may be selected from the victim's past to "index" his origins from a "broken home," his "abuse" by parents, his "culture of poverty," or that he has a "genetic propensity" for evil as indicated by his body build, facial features, or skin color.[16]

Where there has been no ceremonial judgment passed on the victim, mythmaking may proceed outside official channels, the reconstructions of his background becoming even more fanciful. Every social movement staffs for this purpose fabulists, nowadays trained in a variety of media, including motion pictures and color video.

In Christian civilization perhaps the most notorious example of a fictional literature reifying human beings into malignant objects is that concerning its archetypal enemy, the Jew. Included in this literary corpus are *The Talmud Unmasked* and *Der Talmudjude*, by the nineteenth-century Catholic priests Justin Pranaitis and August Rohling, respectively. These works have been used by subsequent generations of Judeophobes as authentic sourcebooks of "satanist" Jewish belief and folkways. Still another is the infamous *Protocols of the Learned Elders of Zion*, in part a plagiarism of a novel by an obscure German government clerk and an anti-Napoleonic tract by a disgruntled conservative French lawyer. It pretends to detail the tactics used by the High Jewish Council, the Sanhedrin, in its quest for world domination. We will return to this arcane and sinister mythology in chapter 5.

Sedimentation

Once experience has been formulated in word and myth, it can be transmitted from one person to the next or, more significantly, across generations. In this form the experience becomes available to those who have never had it. This is what is meant by "sedimentation," a particularly powerful stage in reification.[17] Through this process, legends come to have lives of their own. Detached from the original act of naming or storytelling, they evolve into anonymous parts of the everyday taken-for-granted "stock of knowledge" of society. What was at first a demeaning label, perhaps nonchalantly thrown out in the course of idle gossip or irresponsible editorializing, becomes with each retelling "common sense" – what everybody "knows" to be true about "them," the enemy.

As the inculcation of defamatory messages in the minds of a new generation proceeds, three things follow: (1) The subtleties and qualifying details are filtered out and the message becomes more concise. (2) The calumniating essentials are sharpened for recall. (3) The message is stylized into a mnemonic cant.[18]

One example will suffice. The celebrated geneticist Theodore Dobzhansky describes with care how genotype and environment jointly influence IQ test scores. He illustrates his argument by pointing to the relatively low mean IQ score for black American conscripts in World War I, emphasizing the pivotal and nefarious influence of a segregated school system.[19] One of Dobzhansky's statements is lifted out of context by University of Alabama racist biologist Wesley George (deceased) in his tract *The Biology of the Race Problem* to support the contention that intellectual ability is not distributed equally among the races.[20] George, in turn, is routinely cited in Ku Klux Klan brochures to validate "scientifically" the inflammatory formula that the "negroidal race" is closer to the ape than to *Homo sapiens*.

Ritual

Human memory is fickle and the lessons taught new minds must be reimprinted continually. The preeminent pedagogy for this is ritual, the vivid dramatization of the myth's principal themes. In its enactment the "truth" of the myth is reconfirmed, and what was momentarily at risk of being forgotten is recognized.[21]

The culminating step in the social construction of enemies is as follows. The "good guys," as they honor themselves, respond "appropriately" to those they have designated as evil – with secrecy, caution, cunning, and, if necessary, cruelty. To act in any other way would be imprudent. After all, it is of their "nature" that enemies prey on the nonvigilant. Any mercy extended them would only invite aggression; any openness would reveal our own mortal weaknesses; and our trust would be repaid with duplicity. But here is the catch: Being rational in their own right, enemies reply to these gestures precisely as expected, which is to say "evilly" – with paranoia, distrust, wiliness, and savagery. In this way the prophecy concerning their diabolism is uncannily fulfilled, the truth of the myth sustained.[22]

Of course, enemies do not always return evil for evil. Some speak of "loving" their persecutors and turning the other cheek; still others disclose their most deep-seated infirmities. But typically these gestures are understood by protagonists in the context of the category into which the enemy has already been cast: as subterfuges, cowardice, *ressentiment* (the sublimation of hatred by the powerless and its neurotic reversal into a facsimile of love),[23] or, in the case of self-confessed disabilities, as displaying real insight into their own virulent condition.[24] In other words, far from disconfirming the ugly "truth," conciliatory gestures by the enemy may actually amplify the sense of his depravity.

If, as often happens, persons are naive about their arbitrary selection and denotation as evil ones, they may internalize self-demeaning legends, feeling compelled to act in ways they themselves would acknowledge as detestable. This is particularly likely if those espousing the legends are "significant others" to the victim, persons whose opinions the victim values or upon whom he is dependent for his well-being. This has been observed with juvenile "troublemakers," being unwittingly groomed by teachers, welfare workers, and probation officers to be the next generation's felons. As Jean-Paul Sartre has demonstrated regarding European Jewry and Frantz Fanon with native African subjects of colonial rule, self-loathing can also take place among entire races and ethnic groups.[25] Where this path in the jungle of psychopathology eventually leads goes beyond our concerns here.

In summary, routine combat against society's internal and external enemies (respectively, the judicial system and warfare) endlessly generates the very evildoers it supposedly is undertaken to protect us against. In trying to engineer an end to this cycle, peace proponents face a formidable obstacle. War, preparations for war, imprisonment, and execution have the effect of validating dearly held myths concerning evil, relative to which we are good. Despite their costs, then, they do provide a perverse sense of security. History reveals that human beings sometimes choose to die in heroic struggles against evil rather than contemplate the unsettling possibility that their stories about it might be fundamentally mistaken.

Conclusion

Fetishes of evil are socially assembled and then destroyed so that the world can be saved and the executioners might sense their greatness. In ancient times this was accomplished ritualistically by placing upon the head of a goat the community's sins and then exiling the goat, with the sins, into the desert.[26] Having the advantage of distance, we see this as a practice in collective delusion. Our first task as devotees of peace is to realize that although we are clothed in scientific garb and armed with nuclear bombs and satellite laser beams, we, like the ancients, are ethical primitives. Our second task is to compose an ethics for our age, an ethics without fetishes. For it is not enough simply to illuminate moral blindness; we must also propose remedies. Chapters 7 through 10 examine several such remedies in detail. Here it is enough to speculate about the nature and sources of nonfetishistic ethical discourse in our times.

First, nonfetishistic ethical thinking is a basic element of what has come to be called, probably incorrectly, "feminist" metaphysics, which rejects hackneyed "patriarchal," absolutist divisions between spirit and matter, mind and body, god and man, us and them. In other words, it begins with awareness of the subtle complementarity of all things. This is not to say that these dimensions are not conceptually distinguishable, but rather that they are not separable ontologically in any simplistic sense.

Second, this new ethics is not the monopoly of a few cloistered academicians, but has evolved into something approaching a zeitgeist in which we all increasingly participate, knowingly or not. It finds expression in both the ecological movement and the world citizenship movement, of which the study of peace is merely an offshoot.

Third, the disavowal of fetishistic ethics is not so novel after all, but is a reappropriation of our own cultural heritage. It is a drinking more deeply from the well of our own tradition of wisdom. Anticipations are found both in the Occidental religious notion of Original Sin and in the pagan appreciation that the opposition between enemies is in part illusory.

In the Indo-Aryan Mahabharata the great battle of the Bharatas ostensibly occurs between diametrically opposed forces, the righteous white-skinned Pandus and the infamous black-skinned Kurus. As the tale unfolds, however, it is revealed that the Pandus have overcome their foes through diabolical means, urged upon them by the Lord Himself, Krishna. In the end, the righteous are shown for what they truly are: blood brothers of evil, with the Kurus offspring of the same father Vyasa, himself son of the daughter of truth, Satyavati. Absolute good and evil, we are taught, is *maya,* an illusion.[27]

Fourth, our recent glimpse of this truth has come to us not in friendly guise, clothed in life and light, but in the most despicable form imaginable: the death and horror of our ultimate technological creation, the Bomb. Again, this should not surprise us. The Pandu brothers are likewise provoked into recognizing their own complicity in evil only when, after a postbattle victory celebration, a hideous apparition visits their camp:

> The warriors in the Pandu camp beheld Death-night in her embodied form, black, of bloody mouth and bloody eyes, wearing crimson garlands and smeared with crimson ungents, attired in a single piece of red cloth, with a noose in hand, and resembling an elderly lady, employed in chanting a dismal note and standing full before their eyes. . . .[28]

Fifth and most important, a nonfetishistic ethics has not come from the logical deduction of normative prescriptions from abstract theoretical principles. Instead, it has grown from a deeply personal, painfully shocking awakening of Europeans and Americans from their ego identification with moral purity. At an individual level, psychologists speak of this kind of awakening as a "psychic wound." Here we may refer to it as a "cultural wound," for it has seared an entire generation – ours – with grief, guilt, shame, and terror that this is the "age of death," to use Tanabe Hajime's phrase, the End Times, brought about not by divine wrath but by our own technological arrogance coupled with moral smugness.

In the Bible this experience is symbolized by circumcision, as in Saint Paul's reference to "circumcision of the heart" (Rom. 2:29). In Indo-Aryan mythology, it is represented by the *vajra,* the diamond-lightning bolt of insight that cuts through even the most obdurate illusion of self-righteousness. Perhaps today's equivalent to the *vajra* bolt is "the light brighter than a thousand suns," the illuminating flash of the Bomb. With the Pandu brothers we cry out, "although victory hath been ours, O Krishna, our heart, however, is yet trembling with doubt. . . . The foe who were vanquished have been victorious! Misery looks like prosperity; and prosperity . . . like misery."[29]

3

Reification and Sacrifice
The Goldmark Case

The dialectic of social reality comprises three moments: externalization, objectification, and internalization. Or, as Berger and Luckmann have expressed it, society is at once a human product, an objective reality, and a cage fitted to human specification; and man himself its creator, sustainer, and victim.[1]

Humanity projects itself into materiality by means of its creative labors, embodying imagination in concrete substance, linguistic expression, and gesture. By sedimentation into human memory, mythical elaboration, and ceremonial legitimation, these projects come to assume lives of their own. They become "very thinglike." To use the term employed in chapter 2, they become "reified."

As autonomous things, humanity's projects return to haunt their authors. Says Ludwig Feuerbach: mankind creates heavenly pantheons after *its* own image and likeness, not the other way around.[2] But then in what must constitute the height of diabolical reversal, these same gods demand of their human makers their own sacrifice in "flowery wars,"[3] armed "pilgrimages" for Christ to cleanse holy lands, and terroristic jihads. Mankind breaks itself on the altars of idols wrought by its own hands because although we see aspects of ourselves in our products – this is the reason for our fascination with them – this recognition is only indirect. We fail to grasp that it is we ourselves upon whom we gaze with such wonder, delight, and horror. Karl Marx called indirect recognition of this sort "alienated consciousness" – alienated because the objects of our devotion present themselves to us as separate from us, estranged from us, things over which we have no power and for which we have no responsibility.

This chapter is a sociological vignette of one destructive consequence of reification and alienated consciousness. It focuses on five concrete actors, these five mimetically reiterating in a single evening the "ceremonial incunabula," as Hugh Duncan once called it, of Christian civilization: redemptive purification of the world through victimization of the

Jews.[4] By expelling the Jew, the Christian *anathema,* the plausibility of the Christian cultural *thema* has been sustained historically. In the specific case we focus on here, involving a tragic misidentification of the Goldmarks as Jewish Communists, we examine the sacrifice of a single American family.

The personae: David L. Rice, an unemployed twenty-seven-year-old transient; Charles Goldmark, a respected Seattle lawyer; his community activist wife, Annie; and their two preteen children, Colin and Derek.

The date: Christmas Eve, 1985, hours before a major feast day in the Christian liturgical calendar.

The rite: The Goldmark Case, as it came to be known in police records. Rice, as self-proclaimed "soldier," forces himself into the Goldmark home with a toy gun. He chloroforms the family, handcuffs them, and proceeds to stab them with a knife and bludgeon them to death with a steam iron.

The outcome: Rice is found guilty of first degree murder and on July 27, 1986, is sentenced to death.

The case's relevance for sociology is as a poignant and vivid illustration of the dangers of reification. A stigmatizing word is flippantly attached to an innocent man and wife. It evolves into a taken-for-granted local truth, and is then transferred to their family, who, as incarnations of the dreaded thing, must be destroyed.

It pictures the maddeningly arbitrary manner in which deadly labels are routinely conferred on ordinary citizens by their neighbors; how such labels have uncanny "stickiness"; how courtroom decisions can paradoxically backfire, rendering those legally vindicated de facto guilty; and how, after repeated telling, popular legend is eventually received as fact.

The Process

The following is not intended as a historical narrative. Instead, it is organized to correspond to the five steps in the reification process described in chapter 2: (1) *Naming.* A mistaken characterization of a family as an instance of an abstract category. (2) *Legitimation.* The validation of this mistaken identification by subversion of a legal finding. (3) *Mythmaking.* The retrospective mythologizing of the mistaken identity. (4) *Sedimentation.* The embedding of the legendary tale in the memory of the next generation. (5) *Ritual.* The termination of the problem family.

Naming

Howard Becker was one of the first to appreciate the possibility of stigmatizing labels being mistakenly conferred.[5] By "mistaken identity," I mean an attribution of meaning contrary to what might reasonably be considered directly observable facts.

John Goldmark was an eastern-bred honors graduate of Harvard University Law School.[6] After serving with distinction in the Navy during World War II, he moved with his wife, Irma "Sally" Ringe, to rural Okanogan County in eastern Washington, there to devote his life to ranching. First elected to the state legislature in 1956, he rose to become chairman of the House Ways and Means Committee.

Although John's father was nominally Jewish (by which I mean a practicing congregant of a synagogue), his mother was a descendant of famed Calvinist minister Jonathan Edwards. Since in talmudic orthodoxy religious affiliation is inherited from the mother, strictly speaking John was non-Jewish. In any case, what formal religious and moral training he did receive was from Quaker schools, including Haverford College in Pennsylvania. A self-acknowledged moderate liberal Democrat – supporter of increased public school appropriations, parks, and higher taxes – John was an equally outspoken anti-Communist.

Sally Ringe was the daughter of a strict Protestant household in Brooklyn, New York. Educated at the University of Wisconsin, she had belonged to a Communist Party study group from 1935 to 1942 while living in Washington, D.C. At the time, she was working as an employee for various New Deal agencies. Political historians refer to this as the period of the so-called Popular Front, when the Communist Party presented itself to the liberal community as "twentieth-century Americanism."

After her marriage in 1942, Sally's interest in the Communist Party ended. Two decades later she would speak of her activism as a youthful indiscretion. "I think I made a mistake," she would insist, and in any case was never "fully committed" to the party.[7] Instead, after marriage her hours as a ranch wife and mother became filled with the PTA, the county fair board, the library board, and the Democratic Women's Club.

John and Sally had two sons, Charles (b. 1944) and Peter (b. 1946). Conventional religion seems to have played little role in their lives. Charles would go on to attend exclusive Reed College in Portland, Oregon, and later follow his father's footsteps to Harvard to study law. He would later return to Seattle, marry, have two sons of his own, and set up a successful law practice.

Rumors emerge in problematic situations bereft of concrete information.[8] John and Sally Goldmark were "problematic" to their simply educated, provincial rural neighbors. Even though residents advertised northeastern Washington as "God's country," some of them expressed surprise that a couple with the Goldmarks' credentials would deign to live in their midst. Neither of the Goldmarks had known the slightest thing about ranching when they moved from the east, and John, it was said, could have joined any eastern law firm of his choice.[9]

The family name and their place of origin seemed to supply a clue; John's politics provided another. He vigorously advocated repeal of the McCarran Act, which required registration of all Communist Party members. Furthermore, he had voted against an American Heritage Bill, and was a member of the American Civil Liberties Union. The latter, it was rumored, was "an instrument of the Communist apparatus." John and his wife, their neighbors agreed, were "soft on communism."[10]

Rural Americans abide by the adage of live and let live. And after all, it was said, John was serving his district effectively, bringing patronage and even notoriety to an otherwise economically depressed area lacking excitement. But sometimes feelings were hurt. John could be "prickly and impatient," with "no time for small talk," the medium of consensus and feedback in rural towns.[11]

Of course, few were willing to openly debate either Sally or John when they spoke on issues of public concern: at the Methow Grange, for instance, when John denounced a proposed bill outlawing the Communist Party, or when Sally advocated establishment of a regional library, or when both attacked *Communism on the Map* and *Operation Abolition*, documentaries shown by the county Anti-Communist League in their neighbors' homes.[12] But resentment grew against them all the same: John does not salute the flag; perhaps he and Sally are not legally married. And more questions: Why didn't they send their son Charles to a good, local school like Washington State University – an agricultural school to boot – instead of to notoriously liberal Reed College, "the only school in the Northwest," it was incorrectly believed, "where Gus Hall, secretary of the Communist Party, was invited to speak."[13]

Like a compound suspended in liquid, the gestalt insidiously forming around the Goldmarks precipitated during the 1962 primary election.

There were several catalysts: the distribution of 15,000 copies (one for every household in the district) of Albert F. Canwell's *American Intelligence Service* report (see note 15) insinuatingly linking "a local state legislator" to the international Communist conspiracy, and concluding: "These people are professionals. They are dangerous. They are out to kill us"; a speech by Communist Party turncoat Herbert Philbrick of the popular television series "I Led Three Lives" in Omak (March 1962); an article in a newsletter called *The Vigilante* claiming that "Irma Mae Ringe," wife of an "unnamed legislator," was a member of the "Victor Perlo [Communist Party] study group"; and finally, a July 1962 *Tonasket Tribune* front page editorial identifying Irma Ringe as Sally, wife of John Goldmark. The implication to many was obvious: John Goldmark was "a tool of a monstrous conspiracy to remake America into a totalitarian state."[14]

And now the most damning allegation. John and Sally had failed to apprise their neighbors and even closest friends of her youthful association with Victor Perlo. It is not important for present purposes how this oversight was discovered.[15] What is crucial is that its being kept secret seemed to confirm in neighbors' eyes the diabolical character of the Goldmark family. Nor was the fact that in 1962 Sally had no card identifying her as a current member of the Communist Party seen as any less condemnatory. For legend had it that the Communist underground, which is to say the truly dangerous operatives, carried no cards. And even assuming that John had publicly announced his anti-Communism, legend also had it that Communists are taught to lie whenever it serves party interests.[16]

Legitimation

In August 1962 the legislative primary was held. A record 66 percent of the district voters turned out. John Goldmark finished fourth in a field of four, with only one-third the votes garnered by the winner. His political career had been summarily brought to an end. *The Vigilante* congratulated itself in terms that a quarter century later would smack of bitter irony. What happened at an American Legion meeting held just days prior to the election, it said, was "the bullet that got Goldmark." Taped for radio broadcast throughout the district, the meeting had been a staged attack on the ACLU as a Communist front. When John Goldmark and a supporter rose to defend the organization, they received catcalls, and the supporter himself was physically pushed from the podium.[17]

Within a month following his election debacle, Goldmark filed a libel complaint alleging that several parties had conspired to defame him.[18] Civil proceedings were initiated in the Okanogan County courthouse on November 3, 1963. Heading the plaintiff's legal team was a thirty-three-year-old lawyer named William Dwyer. After a two-month trial followed by five days of deliberation, on January 22, 1964, the jury returned a decision completely vindicating John Goldmark on all counts. The award of $40,000 total damages was the second largest at that time in Washington State history. Such are the *materia de jure* of *Goldmark v. Canwell et al.* Beneath the surface, however, a contrary conclusion was forming in the minds of Okanogan County's rightist community.

Recall the discussion in chapter 2 about the conditions necessary for the ceremonial imposition of degrading labels on victims: (1) The ceremony must be staged in sacred precincts and conducted appropriately. (2) The actors, including the victim, must have a solemn attitude toward the proceedings. (3) The accusers must demonstrate that they are motivated exclusively by "tribal values." (4) These values must be made explicit. (5) The accusers must demonstrate that nothing in the accused's life is accidental, but is part of the type "evil." (6) This type must be rhetorically counterposed against its opposite, "good."

All of these preconditions apply to the Goldmark trial. There was the procedurally correct struggle for "proper" definition of the plaintiff in circumstances removed from everyday life; the public denunciation of the plaintiff by a series of credible witnesses presumably acting not for private gain but out of patriotic duty; the claims that John's and Sally's lives were of a general type, "dirty red," or the embodiment of Satan, counterposed against a virtuous opposite, Christian patriot (of which the witnesses displayed themselves as examples).

True, the jury formally exonerated the Goldmarks on all counts. But simultaneously the proceedings proved to extremists in Okanogan County what the defense had insisted all along, that the Goldmarks were under Communist Party discipline. How is it that public consensus can contradict a verdict legally rendered by its own courts? Consider the following observations.

First, in field experiments on the unanticipated consequences of criminal trials, Richard Schwartz and Jerome Skolnick found that job applicants who have been formally acquitted of wrongdoing are three times *less* likely to receive positive job recommendations than those with no court record.[19] Regardless of one's innocence, in other words, criminal court appearances by themselves have stigmatizing consequences for defendants. Schwartz and Skolnick discovered, however, that this does not apply to doctors involved in malpractice suits. Indeed, the practices of some physicians seem to improve upon adjudication of suits against them. The authors speculate that unlike criminal suspects, doctors reside within a "protective institutional environment" of high occupational status, invisibility, and collegial support which neutralizes potentially negative post-trial impacts on themselves. But the most important difference is that criminal accusations imply evil intention on the part of the accused whereas malpractice suits imply, at worst, negligence.[20]

Political libel trials occupy a legal purgatory halfway between outright criminal prosecutions and neutral tort cases. The issue in Okanogan County was never John Goldmark's negligence or incompetence; it was a question of disloyalty to the political cultus of the folk. Thus, as in the innocent-acquittals in the Schwartz-Skolnick study, that Goldmark answered his accusers under courtroom auspices cast an aura of criminality around him. Although, like physicians, Goldmark enjoyed the benefits of high status as an elected official and lawyer, this evidently was not sufficient to protect him from contamination by evil.

Second, when Nicola Sacco and Bartolomeo Vanzetti (1921) and Ethel and Julius Rosenberg (1951) were found guilty of murder and espionage, respectively, these decisions had the unanticipated effect in liberal circles of delegitimizing "right-wing" American jurisprudence and of paradoxically vindicating the defendants. Again, when in 1984 Idaho Congressman George Hansen was sentenced to prison for congressional ethics violations, this "proved" his innocence to many of the state's ultraconservatives and the involvement of "liberal" American courts in the "one-world conspiracy."

While sociologists have been sensitive to trial outcomes as self-fulfilling prophecies, far less attention has been paid to the possibility of their being self-*defeating* enterprises.[21] A condition ignored by Garfinkel in his discussion of public degradation ceremonies,[22] and taken for granted by most reification theorists, is the public perception of tribunals as legitimate. If a court proceeding is popularly viewed as incompetent or subversive, its declaration may be self-condemnatory. This was precisely what happened for right-wing Okanogans witnessing the Gold-mark trial.

Third, in some countries the falsity of libels is actionable at law (as, for example, in suits brought against anti-Semites in Canadian courts in the 1980s for publicly denying the historicity of the Holocaust). In America, however, because of its First Amendment tradition, punitive damages in libel suits may be awarded only if the plaintiff can demonstrate "actual malice" on the defendant's part.[23] One effect of this is that in American courts the defendant in a libel case is permitted hearsay testimony. If the defendant can show that he read or heard something that reasonably led him to make the libelous charge, this is evidence of no malice. While in their instructions to juries, judges distinguish between the *truth* of a libel and its *impression* on the defendant, hearsay testimony can and sometimes does profoundly influence juries and courtroom audiences.

In the Goldmark trial the defendants paraded before the jury a host of one-time Communist Party activists, some of whom had previously gained fame in widely publicized legislative investigations of internal subversion.[24] It is enough to say that they presented well-rehearsed, frightening accounts that must have confirmed to many courtroom observers what local legend had already supposed: They claimed that having no party card (as neither John nor Sally did) was no proof of one's innocence, for truly dangerous operatives worked without formal party acknowledgment; that members (allegedly like Sally) could not marry without party approval (hence Sally could not have married John unless he was acceptable to party heads); that individuals could leave the party only by confessing their sins and becoming FBI informants (which Sally had not done); that the ACLU (of which John was a member) was "not just red, but dirty red"; that Sally once had dinner with convicted spy Alger Hiss (which Sally denied); that Communists would lie whenever it served party interests; that HUAC, the McCarran Act, a popular local anti-Communist newspaper column, and the anti-Communist films shown to Okanogans (the very things so vigorously rebuked by the Goldmarks) were the "most effective tools" in the fight against communism.

All of this is to say that the lawsuit permitted the defense to exhibit hearsay testimony by experts, under oath, lending increased plausibility to suspicions concerning the Goldmarks. Politicized moral crusades have backfired in the past to the detriment of the crusaders themselves.[25] Perhaps the Goldmarks' crusade to clear their name in the political arena did the same.[26]

Fourth, following the verdict, the defendants filed a motion for dismissal. Normally this is a pro forma matter of little consequence. In the Goldmark case, it had profound and ironic results. Before the arguments could be heard by the judge, the U.S. Supreme Court in March 1964 (in its decision in *Sullivan v. New York Times*) restricted the interpretation of "actual malice" in political libel suits, affirming that for all practical purposes libels against public persons are legally inactionable. Virtually no statement, regardless of its distastefulness or patent falsity, could be considered libelous. Within days the judge in the Goldmark case ruled that since Goldmark was a public official when the libels were published, the recent Supreme Court decision must apply. This denied the $40,000 damage award to the Goldmarks, without changing the jury's decision in the case. The Goldmarks chose not to appeal the judge's ruling.

It is impossible to measure what impact this had on the Okanogan rightist community. But what it meant for some is that the defendants' accusations against the Goldmarks came to be seen as fair and true. This is confirmed in an interview with one of the defendants, Ashley Holden, at this writing a ninety-three-year-old Republican, active in Ronald Reagan's Presidential Task Force, and a recent state director of the Conservative Caucus. When asked for his interpretation of the Superior Court reversal of the damage award, he replied that it "proved" the accuracy of the defendants' claims against the Goldmarks.[27]

Mythmaking and Sedimentation

Since the 1920s and 1930s, an imposing underground literature has circulated in America alleging complicity of the Ashkenazim (Yiddish-speaking Jewry) in an international Communist conspiracy. This literature has found a receptive audience in the Pacific Northwest. Chapter 5 will examine more deeply the contents of this library of infamy. Here it is enough to say that following the legally ambivalent conclusion of the Goldmark trial, local legend concerning the family's Jewishness and communism was embellished and put in larger fabulistic context. And the stigma originally conferred upon John and Sally now also encompassed their sons. In these respects the mythologizing of the event corresponds to what was described in chapter 2 as typical in rumors: The intricate details of trial testimony were "leveled," and the first names of the defendants forgotten, the Goldmark myth becoming shorter and more concise. Certain aspects, perhaps misremembered, were retained and emphasized beyond their original importance (for instance, now forgotten was the detail that in throwing out the damage award the judge did not invalidate the jury's decision that the Goldmarks had indeed been libeled); and, finally, those details that were recalled, perhaps incorrectly, were "assimilated" into the larger Jewish/Communist ideology promulgated in the literary corpus alluded to above.

There is no evidence that David Rice, the murderer of the Charles Goldmark family, was ever a member of the Aryan Nations Church, the most noteworthy carrier of anti-Jewish demonology in modern America, headquartered on the Washington-Idaho border, several of whose peripheral members were at one time in the Anti-Communist League mentioned earlier. But he is known to have socialized with members of a Washington State chapter of the so-called Duck Club. Now defunct, it was founded in 1980 by a Cocoa, Florida, millionaire named Robert White.[28] Its periodical, *The Duck Book*, was so titled because of its logo: a comical duck in various ridiculous postures, such as defending the Panama Canal or sassing the Russian bear. This whimsical come-on belied the magazine's serious intent: to serve as a mail-order clearinghouse for the American right. It contained articles, reports, and broadsides on the international banking conspiracy; financial and investment advice; constitutionalist, home schooling, and tax resistance information; and anti-Zionist and anti-Jewish commentary. In addition, it provided pedagogy for *pro se* (self-defense) trial litigants, solicitations by various rightist groups for new recruits, and advertisements for belt buckles, natural pharmacopeia, weapons, bumper stickers, coins, and insignia.

Through the Duck Club, Rice accessed this subterranean world and its literature. More important, he came to know a coterie of individuals who confirmed what he read.

It is not necessary here to review research on socialization to political-religious cults (see chapter 8). It is enough to show how Rice's conversion to Jew-hatred and anti-Communism, and to anger at the Goldmarks in particular, corresponds to the process of commitment to deviant groups first observed by John Lofland and Rodney Stark for the Unification Church, and since then established for other organizations.[29] Conversion (resocialization), they found, occurs not through brainwashing of passive victims or through obsessive self-conversion by true believers. It takes place through active efforts by the disciple, sometimes indifferent to ideology or theology as such, to solidify and preserve social ties with his mentors.

Rice's mentor seems to have been Alice Smith,* a naturopathic physician recently divorced from an Iranian expatriate. That Rice was emotionally attached to Smith is clear. He was "convinced," says the court-appointed psychologist, that his "duty" was to marry her and with her set up a camp in Colorado for survivors of an impending nuclear holocaust. There is also evidence that Smith was "trying to push him away at the end," and that Rice may have committed his crime out of a desire "to inflate himself in her eyes."[30]

According to witnesses, Smith "constantly harangued" not only Rice but others in the Duck Club "to be a hater of the government." Says one of these witnesses:

> all of a sudden she's becoming such a bigot and . . . an anti-Semite. . . . I was wondering whether or not she . . . really wasn't in control of her mental faculties, because she was obsessed with hating Jews and the American government to such an extent that when she'd come around to visit . . . we were subjected to an hour-long . . . harangue . . . concerning Zionism, the banking system and all these types of things. . . .[31]

Ms. Smith not only urged Rice to believe that the Constitution was being violated, and that the Internal Revenue Service was oppressive, but also that American Jewry was "bilking" the country. It was from her that Rice obtained a pamphlet by a Col. (ret.) Gordon "Jack" Mohr depicting the presence of several thousand Korean and South American troops on the borders of the United States awaiting word from Jewish bankers heading the Federal Reserve System to occupy the country. (The supposition was that U.S. troops could not be trusted to shoot their own countrymen.) In testimony to the examining psychologist, Rice claimed that Mohr's pamphlet was the immediate spur to act when he did.

Ed Fasel** was head of the local Duck Club chapter. It was from Ed that Rice received the tragic misinformation that Charles and Annie Goldmark were leading Seattle Communists. In the course of discussions

*Fictitious name
**Fictitious name

concerning local subversives and crooks who were presumably frustrating Rice's efforts to secure a job, Fasel, mistaking Charles for his father John, related to Rice that the Goldmarks had been investigated and that Charles was "regional director of the American Communist Party." Rice took this to mean that Charles was "the highest obtainable target I could reach, the greatest value informationally."[32] After handcuffing the Goldmarks, Rice intended to interrogate them about the next person in the conspiratorial hierarchy, possibly to preempt at the last moment the impending invasion of alien troops referred to above.

What occasioned Fasel to dredge up a name associated with an event that had occurred two decades previously in another part of the state? In a Seattle Port Commission election during the summer of 1985, one of the candidates was Jim Wright, a Republican. Wright's campaign manager was none other than Ashley Holden, a defendant in the Goldmark trial. Upon discovering this unusual link, the Seattle media jumped on it, and the name "Goldmark," with its unfortunate connotations, "got out again," to use one informant's phrase.[33]

In my interview with him, Holden convincingly insisted that he knew nothing of the Duck Club nor any of its members. "I deplored the murder," he said. "There is no question," he went on, parroting local wisdom, "Rice was demented."[34]

Ritual

It would be comforting to dismiss David Rice as crazy; but unless this term is carefully specified, such an explanation is in error. True, the consulting psychologist found Rice to have "schizoid and paranoid features," including a "delusional system" with nonverbal "communications" from "friends" in outer space "who give him urges and feelings about what to do."[35] But he also points out that most of Rice's "delusions" were inculcated by his Duck Club associates.

Rice exhibited none of the diagnostic symptoms of schizophrenia, such as actually hearing voices, having "significant ideas of reference," or experiencing a deterioration of his formal reasoning powers. On the contrary, the ritual, as we have called it, was carefully planned and carried out with full awareness of the consequences. Indeed, anticipating arrest, Rice contemplated turning himself in to a fellow activist who would then collect the reward money to further the cause.

Not only could Rice distinguish between right and wrong, the criterion of the insanity defense under the McNaughton rule, he saw his actions as entirely upright. In the psychologist's words:

> He indicates that his actions with the Goldmarks was the first step in this [anti-Communist] war and, thus, he saw himself as a soldier. "Sometimes," he said, "soldiers have to kill." He now expresses remorse about the harm done the children, but "it might have been necessary to sacrifice these lives for the greater good of mankind."[36]

It is important to emphasize that Rice is not unusual in this respect. Before me sits still another psychiatric report, this one concerning a thirty-two-year-old Kentuckian and devoted husband and father who is thought to have murdered the Jewish radio talk show host Alan Berg (June 1984) as part of his role in the escapades of the terrorist group known today as the Order (*Bruders Schweigen*, or Secret Brotherhood). Here, too, the psychiatrist found "ample evidence of dissociative reaction" during the defendant's life "having to do with . . . an hysterical personality structure." This may, he concluded, lead "to transient mini-psychotic events" such as rages about which he has no memory. Nevertheless, "he is not psychotic and there is no evidence that he was . . . under psychotic command during any of the actions having to do with the indictments." On the contrary, like Rice, this defendant knew his violence was illegal, but felt it to be in accordance with a higher morality commanded by God:

> While alone, he experienced the voice of "Yahweh," a strong "electrifying and spine-tingling voice" which said: "You are to move to Aryan Nations [in Idaho], you are to be a warrior, a leader, a man like King David; you are to lead Israel into the kingdom, you will fight and destroy the enemies of Yahweh, you will meet men like yourself. I will lead and show you the way."[37]

Conclusion

Americans habitually typify deviants and deviance in psychological terms. While this is understandable and probably appropriate given the principle of individual responsibility which underlies our system of jurisprudence, as a plausible explanation of these events it is sorely lacking. For psychologizing abstracts the deviant, and his deeds, out of the historical and social contexts that precede them and make them predictable. Sociology recontextualizes deviance, showing that what at first glance appears to be inexplicable, "insane" behavior is actually socially preconditioned and "sensible" given the circumstances. A powerful tool in this effort is the theory of reification. Among other things, it shows how incidents of political murder are not necessarily spur of the moment, isolated, "crazy" individual acts, but the culmination of a series of group activities over a long period. These social activities include but are not limited to the selection and preparation of an enemy (and potential victim) through social labeling, public tribunals, and mythic demonization, and the imbedding of defamatory images in the minds of young people through preaching and teaching.

When viewed sociologically it becomes clear that, ignoring their private quirks and neuroses, what distinguishes David Rice and the Kentuckian from the conventional population is not so much the manner in which they came to their world view, but its contents. Both resided in bizarre, rigidly dualistic worlds in which Charles and Annie Goldmark and Alan Berg were major antagonists. However, as the psychologist who interviewed Rice reported: "Mr. Rice did not cook up this stuff by himself, out of touch with society, developing delusional fantasies of his own to fill the void. Rather, he belonged to a subgroup of individuals who believed in and supported these ideas. In fact, these people validated these ideas as rational and important."[38]

Likewise, the Kentuckian evidently did not concoct his outlook out of psychotic hallucinations, but received them from taped Aryan Nations sermons and from discussions with specific church congregants, using these to "convert his tremendous [aggressive-sexual impulses] into a system where he feels righteousness, adequacy, and self-esteem."[39]

There is evidence that Rice had "weak ego boundaries" which might have aggravated an already natural inclination to other-directedness. But again quoting the psychologist: "I believe that he felt these people would probably approve of his actions, and support him. Clearly, he is a man who wants to be liked and is capable of trying to do things to build himself in the eyes of significant others."[40] By the same token, while the Kentuckian is said to have suffered "nocturnal dissociative episodes," his psychologist declares that his personal life, with its substance abuse and other problems, "has been massively improved under his submittance [sic] to religious authority."[41]

It can be disheartening to learn that political murder is not just a psychological problem amenable to individual counseling. Were it so, it could be handled without having to address the structural and cultural realities of our life together. And these seem so complex and overwhelming, to say nothing of how costly they might be to change. Where, after all, do we begin?

Although it goes beyond my ability to answer this question definitively, it seems reasonable to think that we could intervene to mollify political violence at any step in the process of enemy reification. I propose to begin by disassembling the library of infamy that sustained Rice's and the Kentuckian's reality of Jews as the evil ones. Before doing this, however, it is important to add a further complication to our analysis. In the Goldmark case we have a family unfairly vilified by neighbors; it is easy to identify the innocent victim and point to the persecutors. In most violent conflicts, however, both sides are victims and executioners alike. Both sides picture the other as the enemy. Breaking through the dialogue of mutual defamation thus requires more than simply critiquing the viewpoint of one of the opponents. Both sides must somehow be brought to account for their actions. This brings us to what I call "the standoff on Ruby Ridge," an encounter that took place in 1992, again in the Pacific Northwest.

4

Standoff on Ruby Ridge
*A Study in the Mutual
Construction of Enemies*

War is upon the land. The tyrants' blood will flow.[1]

In August 1992 an eleven-day armed encounter took place on a granite outcrop called Ruby Ridge in the Selkirk Mountains of northern Idaho. It resulted in the deaths of a federal law officer, a thirteen-year-old boy named Sammy, Stryker his dog, and the boy's mother, as well as the near fatal wounding of Sammy's closest friend, Kevin, and a flesh wound to his father.

Apart from being an affair of local interest, the events on Ruby Ridge are important for two reasons. First, they illustrate what was described in the first chapter as one of the paradoxes of the enemy, that our willingness to harm others grows from a sense of our being harmed by them. Second, the events display how all parties to conflict employ the same tools to devise their antagonists: labeling, legitimation, mythologizing, sedimentation, and ritual. To accommodate limitations of space and the reader's patience, I will confine my observations to the first, third, and last of these procedures, avoiding where possible theoretical interpretation.

The major protagonists on Ruby Ridge were four: Randall "Pete" Weaver, retired Colonel James "Bo" Gritz (pronounced grYtz), and federal marshals William "Billy" Degan and Jack Cluff. But also present at the scene were weeping family members; thin young men with shaved heads and swastikas on their black sweatshirts, shouting epithets at the police and gesturing with Hitlerite salutes; backcountry townsfolk standing vigil in a chilly autumn drizzle by a yellow-ribboned barricade, carrying placards ("Dead: mother & child," "Yahweh pass judgement now on these murderers") and screaming their outrage ("What happened to America? What happened to the land of the free?" "They . . . are baby killers. . . . I hate them, I hate them"). And there were also over two hundred national guard troops, state patrol officers, federal Alcohol,

50

Tobacco and Firearms agents, FBI cadres and border police – equipped with M-113 armored personnel carriers, heavy trucks, Humvees (thirteen in number), water trailers, field electrical generators, and surveillance helicopters.

Once everything has been said, we are left to come to terms with the fundamental significance of the incident: after eliminating Bo Gritz's inflammatory posturing and homespun rhetoric ("My heart soars like an eagle." "All glory goes to God, Almighty"); after putting in proper place Chicago news commentator Paul Harvey's radioed request for Weaver to surrender; after subtracting from the scene the imposition of martial law by the "federales," the news blackout followed by the grudgingly given, contradictory government press releases; and after laying to rest the surrealistic postsiege party at the Deep Creek Resort, where boisterous skinhead teens and Jewish and black journalists posed arm in arm for photographs.

In other words, after getting rid of all the chaff, what remains is this: The standoff on Ruby Ridge was an attempt by society in the person of the state to choke down a monster of its own making. This chapter tells of the fertilization, gestation, and birth of that monster, and how by its actions the state has perhaps let loose an even more insidious specter.

American Paramilitary Culture

In the late 1960s American black revolutionaries were heard to utter an incendiary request to their brothers fighting in Vietnam: "Bring it on home."[2] Bring home the weapons skills, the technowar tactics, and the organizational discipline acquired overseas and direct them against the "real enemy," so-called white honkies and "pigs." Although this program was never carried out by the intended party, Vietnam was nonetheless brought home to America in several striking ways: in the form of a burgeoning drug problem; in an upsurge of gang-related inner-city violence; and most important, for our purposes, by means of a militarization of domestic law enforcement, manifest in a romanticized military argot, dress, demeanor, and "policy" – a phenomenon I call "paramilitarism."

In response to urban riots, skyrocketing crime rates, and several notable assassinations, Congress in 1968 passed an Omnibus Crime Control and Safe Streets Act.[3] This was the first time in American history that the federal government had attempted to address lawbreaking at the local level. Historians see the act as reflecting an emerging public consensus that America's social problems are best handled by metaphorically declaring "war" on them and then mobilizing massive national resources: hence the war on poverty, the war on illiteracy, the war on drugs, and President Nixon's war on crime.

One measure in the Omnibus Crime Act provided for the establishment of a Law Enforcement Assistance Administration (LEAA) for distributing federal funds to local law enforcement agencies for "research and development" related to organized crime and riot control, equipment purchases, construction, and training programs. Aided by generous LEAA grants, local law enforcement departments nationwide began to arm, train, and deploy jungle-camouflaged special weapons and tactics (SWAT) teams. These efforts were duplicated at a federal level by the establishment of "special operations" units in the Department of Energy, the FBI, the Drug Enforcement Assistance Administration, and the Bureau of Alcohol, Tobacco and Firearms.[4]

With variations in detail, all of these teams were explicitly modeled after elite covert operations commando units such as the Green Berets and Navy SEALS (Sea-Air-Land), first employed on a large scale in the Vietnam War. The Green Berets in turn were introduced by the Kennedy administration for the express purpose of engaging in "irregular" combat against Communist subversion overseas.

Like their military counterparts, law enforcement special operations units are trained in a variety of "weapons systems," as they are called, in electronic surveillance, and in "quick response" to nonroutine "scenarios": hostage-takings, domestic terrorism, hijackings, and "political events" such as mass demonstrations, strikes, and sit-ins. It was the presence of a five-member SWAT team of U.S. marshals on Ruby Ridge that precipitated the deadly shoot-out recounted below. This was after the U.S. Marshals Service had determined the situation on the ridge to be "critical": a politically motivated hostage-taking. Following the death of one of the marshals, another SWAT team – from the FBI this time – assumed authority over the affair. According to one marshal, who spent the entire eleven days standing guard at the barricade, "half the guys up there had served in Special Forces in Vietnam."[5]

America's ignominious defeat and departure from Vietnam in 1975 created a profound cultural crisis in the United States, according to sociologists who have studied the period. Not only did it break a long tradition of military victories, but defeat was at the hands of an impoverished third world Asian folk who, by the technical and economic standards of American war managers – "the best and the brightest" – should have been conquered easily. James William Gibson, author of perhaps the most cogent study of the debacle, *The Perfect War,* details how in an effort to make defeat sensible to their audiences, American cultural elites mythically reinvented the war.[6] Our men were fully capable of winning, it was written, but they were "betrayed" by corrupt and cowardly politicians, "restrained" from using their full might, and thus "not permitted" victory. Hence (following the story line of law-abiding banditti operating outside the system to save the town) in our times only paramilitary heroes, acting either alone or with a tightly bound group of buddies, SWAT armed and trained, and working "covertly" (outside regular bureaucratic channels), can achieve success over the enemy, whether garbed as an Asian Communist, an Arab terrorist, or a homegrown American – Hispanic or black – drug pusher. Thus was born *Rambo: First Blood Part II* in 1985 and its cinematic brothers *Delta Force* and *Iron Eagle,* its television cousins "The A-Team" and "Magnum PI," their pulp facsimiles, most notably *Soldier of Fortune* magazine, and Tom Clancy's epic Jack Ryan series, *The Sum of All Fears* and *Patriot Games,* among others.

Paramilitary romance would penetrate not only official circles in postwar America but the civilian population as well – inspiring, at least partly, an explosion of right-wing extremist vigilante groups and people's "militia" in the decade after 1975: the Christian Patriots Defense League, the Posse Comitatus, the Aryan Nations Church (the political-military arm of the Church of Jesus Christ Christian), the White Aryan Resistance (WAR), and the now defunct *Bruders Schweigen,* or Order. Several of these units were founded and staffed by Vietnam veterans themselves, bitter over their alleged betrayal by the government in Southeast Asia.

A typical case in point is Louis Beam, who would become manager of paramilitary training camps for Klansmen in east Texas, the self-appointed prison ambassador for the Aryan Nations Church, and head of KKK military recruitment at Fort Hood, Texas, during the 1970s and 1980s.[7] In 1967 and 1968 in Vietnam, Beam flew missions as a door gunner on a UHID "Slick." He was awarded the Distinguished Flying Cross, an Air Medal with V Device for Heroism, and a record of 1,000 hours of combat flying time: "12 confirmed, 39 probable kills." In a striking document of how the war in Vietnam was literally "brought home" to America, Beam writes about the so-called joke that slowly dawned on one-time idealistic "men on a mission," like himself, while serving overseas. Virtually paraphrasing sociologist James Gibson's argument, Beam insists that "our government never intended to win in Vietnam." This being so, he warns, "we are an army of men who demand these criminals [that is, the politicians] be brought to justice – the same justice they gave us. They sprayed us with Agent Orange, now we're going to spray them with our wrath. . . . Now it is time for them to face their Victor Charlie. Ranger." He closes by asking: "if you are a Vietnam Vet and would like to join with other Nam Vets who have a mission, if you have had enough of these bastards who call themselves our leaders, then let us hear from you. Write: 'Bringing It On Home,' Hayden Lake, Idaho. . . ."[8]

Weaver, Gritz, Degan, Cluff

The four protagonists in our story – Weaver, Gritz, Degan, and Cluff – all accessed American paramilitarism through their association with the Special Forces. Like Beam, each in his own way brought Vietnam home – in a sense refighting the war, this time on Ruby Ridge, with Weaver and Gritz on one side and Degan and Cluff on the other. Not until the siege was well under way did they come to recognize their shared paternity. By that time they had become deadly enemies.

Weaver

Randall Weaver dropped out of community college in Iowa to join the army in 1968. Based on qualities demonstrated in boot camp at Fort Bragg, North Carolina, he was assigned to the Green Berets as part of a training squad for elite troops heading for Vietnam. Included among Weaver's virtues were good work habits and, above all, athleticism and grit. As a close friend once said, although Weaver was physically slight, "He don't back down from nobody, no matter how big they are."[9] And Weaver *would* challenge authority. His father recalls how Randall once confronted a farmer who was paying him less money than older boys to weed a field. He demanded and got equal pay. "I've always been proud of Randall; he was always a guy who stood up for his rights. It just came natural to him."[10]

Contrary to rumors spread mainly by Bo Gritz during the siege, Weaver himself never went to Vietnam. But he did serve in the armed forces until 1971, attaining the rank of sergeant E-5 before being honorably discharged. By then he had become an expert in the use of the M-14 rifle and had earned marksmanship awards for both the M-16 rifle and the .45 caliber pistol. As is customary for Green Berets, Weaver qualified as a paratrooper, but his combat specialty was field engineering. This gave him full knowledge of explosive devices and munitions. At one point during the siege authorities expressed concern that Weaver had used his expertise to wire his property with antipersonnel mines and had built bunkers and escape tunnels. Like other rumors, these too were later proven false.

After his release from the army, Randall Weaver returned home, married his high school sweetheart, Vicki Jordison, and moved to Cedar Falls, Iowa. Randall, dreaming of becoming an FBI agent, enrolled in the criminal justice program at Northern Iowa University but later dropped out because of expenses. He found work as a machine tender for the John Deere tractor company; and Vicki supplemented the family income as a secretary for Sears. After about eleven unremarkable years, mortgaging a ranch-style suburban bungalow and marketing Amway products on the side, they sold everything and moved to Idaho. When I interviewed him at the Aryan World Congress at Hayden Lake, Idaho, in 1986, Randall was contracting with the Forest Service to plant trees. He and Vicki were already assembling their two-story wood-beam plywood-walled cabin on twenty acres of forest high above Ruby Creek, near a year-round spring.

In migrating to the "tops of the mountains," Randall and Vicki were enacting a vision they had shared earlier with family and acquaintances in Iowa: "living off the land" and "preserving family values," the latter of which they had seen threatened by the Iowa public schools "spending too much time on things like Hallowe'en and not enough on studying." These same acquaintances recall an unsettling premonition of Vicki's on the day of their departure: "You might hear of us being accused of being criminals and arrested or even killed."[11]

Randall and Vicki headed for northern Idaho. The area was sparsely populated, with cheap land (going for an average of $200 to $300 an acre at $50 down), no zoning regulations or building inspections, lax school board regulations, and beautiful: snow-covered rounded crags, endless white pine forests, glacier-sculpted lakes, crystalline trout-filled streams, solitude. Getting back to basics, they believed, would involve not just teaching their three kids at home and constructing a root cellar for an anticipated large garden but, as Randall fantasized, "eating wild game." He had begun gathering knives and guns for hunting purposes while still in Iowa. After the shoot-out, probably to prove their claim that the Weavers were indeed dangerous fugitives, law enforcement officials publicly displayed the Weaver arsenal: fifteen firearms, including nine bolt action rifles, semiautomatic rifles, shotguns, and pistols, plus boxes of ammunition and various hand weapons.[12]

Randall made it a point to teach the kids how to use the guns and encouraged them to carry them around the homestead on routine business. Newspaper reporters and the police would later use photographs of the holstered Weaver youngsters as evidence for the claim of their potential violence. In one case the girls were seen wearing side arms while tending the garden. The eldest of the girls, Sara, gives these widely publicized images a more benign interpretation, pointing out that the woods around the cabin contain cougars, black bears, and even grizzlies. "My dad taught safety first," she would later tell reporters. "He never taught us to point a gun at anyone."[13]

The Weavers were known to the Boundary County sheriff long before the siege, having filed an affidavit with the county clerk in 1985 claiming their lives were in danger from unnamed neighbors.[14] Interviews with friends years later indicate there had been a long-simmering feud between the Weavers and a nearby property owner over land and buildings seized by the IRS and then auctioned off by the sheriff to cover delinquent taxes. The yard of the person who made the highest bid on the confiscated property would be used by the marshals as the staging point for the assault on the Weavers' cabin.[15] Disputes such as this are not uncommon in northern Idaho. In the summer of 1991, wire services carried the story of a McCoy-Hatfield-like encounter between the Tracy clan and their neighbors the Randolphs, on Hoodoo Mountain in neighboring Bonner County, over road access and property lines.[16]

In addition to this, Randall had run in the Republican primary for sheriff in 1988 on a platform promising to enforce only those laws the citizens so wished. His campaign flyers had the phrase "get out of jail free" on the back. He received about 20 percent of the vote.

In January 1991, Randall was arrested in Kootenai County for selling two sawed-off shotguns – according to reports, each about one quarter of an inch shorter than allowed by law – to an undercover informant. He was, he claimed, stripped, thrown into jail, and warned, "If this was bad, federal prison was going to be worse."[17] The next morning he was arraigned in federal court and posted a $10,000 note on his property as bond. The trial would be scheduled for sometime the following year.

After being released on his own recognizance, Randall returned to Ruby Ridge and publicly announced his intention never to surrender. Vicki supported his decision, saying her husband's case "would have been railroaded through the court and once he was gone they would have come in, kicked us off the property and torn this place apart." Randall agreed: "If they admitted this whole thing was a set-up, I'd come down off this mountain and blast my mouth off. . . . Right now, the only thing they can take away from us is our life. Even if they did we win. We'll die believing in Yahweh."[18]

Federal officials now admit that given Randall's clean record he probably would have received just a small fine and probation. What happened was that his refusal to cooperate with the court took on exaggerated symbolic importance both nationally and locally. Neighbors gossiped that the family conducted military-like marches, flaunted their weapons, and chanted white power slogans. In April 1992 a video crew from the TV show "Now It Can Be Told" tried to approach the cabin by helicopter. They fled after hearing what they took to be gunshot fire. Randall and a friend who was visiting at the time denied any shots were fired. "No one even waved a gun at them," says the neighbor. For his part, Randall admitted that he gave them the finger. "Yeah, I shot 'em. . . . I shot 'em the bird."[19]

What is important about these incidents, true or not, is that together with the various rumors and misinterpretations mentioned earlier they reveal how the Weavers were becoming demonized in the public mind. And as often happens, the family was complicitous in its own victimization; in this case by emphasizing the religious significance of their stance. "Our situation is not about shotguns," insisted Vicki, "it's about our beliefs. They want to shut our mouths. . . . We moved up here to remove our children from the trash being taught in public schools and to practice our beliefs."[20]

The Weavers called themselves Yahweh believers. Included in their religion were the doctrines of white separatism and Jews as "Christ killers," the ritual avoidance of pork and shellfish, a prohibition against "images" in the house (including toys, paintings, or furniture etched with flowers), Vicki's practice of isolating herself in an outbuilding during menstruation, and patient waiting for the Last Days.[21] Virtually any place else in white, fundamentalist Christian America such views and practices would be considered hardly noteworthy. But in northern Idaho under these particular circumstances, it was almost inevitable that the Weavers' neighbors and local authorities would categorize the family with groups like the *Bruders Schweigen* – which is to say, as neo-Nazi terrorists – and deal with them "appropriately." But terrorism, as we have seen, is the paradigmatic "scenario" for SWAT-team intervention.

Furthermore, at least according to Bo Gritz, "somewhere" a "psychological profile" was done on the Weaver family, determining that Vicki was its "head." Allegedly, it "specifically targeted" her; for what, Gritz does not say.[22] An anonymous contact in the U.S. Marshals Service confirms that the FBI Hostage Rescue Team (HRT) routinely uses staff psychologists to profile the instigators of "hostage situations" to find out who is in control. Allegedly, in its profile of the Weaver clan it was determined that one party was held "hostage" (the ten-month-old girl Elisheba), and that "it was a matriarchal thing." This was "confirmed," the contact told me, when after Vicki's death, Randall turned into a "blithering idiot" and the two older daughters "took over" negotiations.[23]

Disclaimers like Vicki's that "we're not Aryans, we're not Nazis" were lost to outsiders unfamiliar with the arcana of contemporary rightist extremism. Instead, officials began speaking of the children as being held by their father as "prisoners of war" and of being "brain-washed," "indoctrinated," and rendered "into anti-ZOG robots" trained to follow their father's orders "on command."[24] Anti-hate-group pundits also entered the fray, dismissing Vicki's distinctions between racial separatism and racial supremacy as "phony." Vicki insisted that her argument against miscegenation was based solely on biblical injunctions against "mixing the seed"; it had nothing to do with racial supremacy.[25] Irwin Suall of the Anti-Defamation League of B'nai B'rith called this nonsense: "Their very reason for separatism is precisely that they have negative views toward non-whites; otherwise separatism wouldn't make sense."[26]

Close acquaintances and even neutral reporters who were granted access to the Weaver cabin prior to the shoot-out take issue with the image of the family as militant neo-Nazis.[27] The so-called "shack" that authorities spoke of "is actually cozy and comfortable," according to one journalist who spent five hours investigating it.[28]

As for the children, they were described as "beautiful," "always clean," "well-versed," "intelligent," "articulate," and, most significant for our purposes, laughingly "playful" and "content": romping with their dogs, doing chores, tending the crooning baby. The cabin was described as having a "well-read" library along one entire wall – the kids were said to have "loved history books" and scripture study – and a black and white TV and radio fueled by an electric generator. The Weavers were said to have played Risk, Monopoly, and Clue in the evenings, enjoyed cards, read *National Geographic,* and frequently treated themselves to root beer and ice-cream parties. Indeed, it was reported, "aside from the pistols on the hips of Randy, Kevin, and Sam, there is no indication that their isolation is anything out of the ordinary."[29]

The politically oriented material in the Weaver library ranged from Missoula, Montana, antitax activist Red Beckman's *The Law That Never Was,* a conspiratorial account of the Federal Reserve System reiterating standard John Birch dogma (which is widespread in rural Idaho), to tapes issued by now deceased Rev. Sheldon Emry's America's Promise. This group peddles soft-core Identity Christianity and is headquartered just down the highway from Ruby Creek in Sandpoint, Idaho. On a darker note were papers published by Tom Metzger's White Aryan Resistance, which extoll the virtues of racist skinheads and deny the historicity of the Jewish Holocaust, and copies of the comic book "Doublecross," filled with anti-Jewish vitriol.[30]

Despite this corpus of rather ambivalent if not entirely contrary information, it was reported that the police ranked the Weavers "along with a long string of dangerous Christian Identity groups."[31] Thus began a historically unprecedented eighteen-month surveillance of the family using both round-the-clock, movement-activated video cameras and "numerous" photo reconnaissance flyovers of their cabin by Air Force F-4 jets.[32] When the family found and destroyed one of the cameras, theft of government property was cited by authorities as still another reason for proceeding with the arrest when they did.

To repeat sociologist W. I. Thomas's dictum quoted in chapter 1: situations defined as real are real in their effects. Human beings act only on the basis of how things are perceived, on what meanings are attributed to them. The Weavers were defined as neo-Nazis by the authorities, and were thereby transformed into alien objects they themselves could not recognize. All their behavior thenceforth was interpreted in the context of the mold into which they had been cast.

Degan and Cluff

Federal marshals William Degan and Jack Cluff were charged with the job of executing the subpoena on Randall Weaver. Like the man they were about to confront, they too had acquired skills from their military backgrounds including combat involvement in the Vietnam War, Degan as an army infantryman.

Cluff was an army helicopter gun crew chief in Vietnam in 1968 and 1969, providing air support for a Green Beret unit that was training Cambodian soldiers.[33] He earned twenty-six air medals, each requiring fifty hours of flying time, and by the time he was honorably discharged he had achieved the rank of specialist E-5. Following the war Cluff joined the U.S. Marshals Service. Eventually he found himself stationed in Moscow, Idaho. As division supervisor for an area encompassing Ruby Ridge, it was he who organized the effort to bring Randall Weaver to justice. He ended up on what he calls the "shit detail," keeping charge of the dead bodies. One of these was the body of his long-time colleague, Degan.

As a resident of Quincy, Massachusetts, and forty-two at the time of his death, Billy Degan, as his close friends called him, lived with his wife and children just down the street from his parents, in the neighborhood of his youth.[34] Estimates are that over 2,000 mourners attended his funeral, which was televised live from Sacred Heart Church, where he had once served as an altar boy. Law enforcement officials from seven states in a cortege of sixty squad cars and a phalanx of motorcycles witnessed Billy's burial. It was conducted to the notes of "Amazing Grace."

Degan had been an all-star athlete in high school and had attended the University of New Hampshire. By 1992 he had attained the rank of lieutenant colonel in the Marine Reserves. A fifteen-year veteran of the U.S. Marshals Service, Degan was also a member of the Special Operations Group, a national SWAT team trained to resolve situations precisely like the one presented by Randall Weaver. The choice of Degan to head the recon mission was also no accident. He was known throughout the service for his courage, care, and competence. At the time of his final assignment he was its most decorated officer. Said one of his colleagues, "He's the last one you'd think would get killed." He was "the greatest man I've ever met," agreed another at the funeral. "The bravest man . . . he gave his life for all of us."[35]

The Weavers had a far less flattering picture of Degan and his fellows. In written and oral comments they were likened variously to agents of Ba'al (the ancient Canaanite god of cannibalism and sexuality), to the Edomites (descendants of Jacob's "unpleasing" brother Esau), to stand-ins for the "One World Beastly Government," and as servants of the Queen of Babylon – which is to say, as evil incarnate. An Evil to whom, according to Vicki Weaver, "the decree has gone out to destroy Israel, our people."[36]

Both Randall and Vicki were products of border states Bible religion. According to acquaintances, both were "deeply" infused at an early age with its millennial fantasies and apocalyptic prophecy. Randall's parents, as is typical for fundamentalist Protestants, were perpetually in the market for inspired preaching, migrating first from the Evangelical United Brethren to the Presbyterians, and from there to a local Baptist sect. The father still recalls the day Randall was "born again" in Christ: "He was 11 or 12. I cried with joy."[37]

Evidently, as a girl Vicki was less religious than her future spouse. She occasionally accompanied her father when he worshipped at a local branch of the Reorganized Church of Jesus Christ of Latter Day Saints. Her mother remained a lifelong Congregationalist. Once Vicki and Randall were married, however, her religious enthusiasm began to exceed his. While in Cedar Falls, the young couple experimented with a mainstream Baptist church. They watched Jerry Falwell and Jim Bakker on television, and an intimate Bible study group met in the basement of their home. There "miracles" were seen: emotional seizures, speaking in tongues, healing by the laying on of hands. Mostly there was the interpretation of biblical passages and the attempt to apply them to everyday life. Secondary sources helped. One of these was *Satan's Angels Exposed,* a diatribe on the Jewish-Masonic "conspiracy." Another was evangelist Hal Lindsey's *The Late Great Planet Earth.*[38] In this, the number one bestseller of the entire decade of the 1970s ("10,000,000 copies in print"), Lindsey uses the Book of Revelation along with anecdotal observations to forecast in vivid terms the imminent end of the world.

Randall and Vicki were profoundly influenced by Lindsey's book.[39] Here could be found frightening discussions of the evil empire ("Russia Is a Gog") and its allies ("The Yellow Peril"), the emerging new world order ("The Future Fuehrer"), and its cultic arm ("The Harlot") organized by the World Council of Churches, which, according to Lindsey, preaches astrology, advocates hallucinogenic drug use, and practices witchcraft. Above all, Randall and Vicki could read in its pages predictions of how in the End Times believers in Christ (like themselves) would be "ruthlessly exposed," unable "to buy, sell, or hold a job," and "executed en masse" for hindering the "brotherhood of man" program sponsored by the new world order.[40] No wonder, as friends now recount, the Weavers "thought there were going to be problems, [that Randall] thought something bad was going to happen and he wanted to get away." No wonder "he thought the world was full of satans."[41] Numbered among these satans were agents of what the Weavers would later learn to call ZOG (Zionist Occupation Government). The representatives of ZOG included tax collectors (with whom the Weavers refused to deal) and federal marshals like Cluff and Degan. Finally, no wonder the Weavers saw in Randall's apparent entrapment on gun violations confirmation of what they had already long known: This was merely one more tactic in the "war against the white sons of Isaac."[42]

Both the government and the Weavers were now prepared cognitively to violate each other, having diabolized each other as enemies. Furthermore, through their participation in American paramilitary culture, both sides had absorbed the normative rule that guns solve problems. Lastly, both sides were trained and equipped with armories sufficient to execute their intentions. All that was needed to carry the situation to its inevitable and tragic conclusion was a precipitating event.

Knowing that his arrest was going to be difficult, the marshal's office in Boise initiated a yearlong correspondence with Weaver. "In so many words," says Cluff, "he told us to go to hell." Marshal Cluff himself made two attempts to break the stalemate, once with the help of Randall's lawyer in Coeur d'Alene, another time with Weaver's closest friend: "I told his friend we would do whatever it takes (including dropping charges on failure to appear). We would drop in a satellite telephone, and he could talk with us over the phone. I said I'd come up there unarmed. I'd bring up a six-pack of beer or pop or whatever he wanted, and we'd sit down and talk and get it resolved."[43] According to the friend who witnessed the event, Randall was at the point of surrendering when Vicki stepped in and dissuaded him. Says Cluff, "she definitely wore the pants in that family." (It is possible that Cluff's observation was the basis for the so-called psychological profile on the Weavers, cited above, that "targeted" Vicki.)

In March 1992, Cluff reconnoitered the Weaver property, passing himself off as a realtor. When confronted by two of the armed Weaver children, their friend Kevin Harris, and an angry dog, he retreated. On August 21, the Special Operations SWAT team of marshals, led by William Degan, surreptitiously, with neither search warrant nor arrest warrant, returned to Ruby Ridge to collect more information, and presumably to relocate one of the video cameras used to monitor the family. Appropriate to the "scenario," they were outfitted in jungle "camo" and carried automatic rifles. The family hunting dogs caught the intruders' scent and created an uproar. Thinking it was caused by a deer, the Weavers' thirteen-year-old son, Sammy, together with Harris and Randall, all armed, followed the family dog's barking down the trail from the cabin. Sammy and Harris were just rounding a corner as the dog was being dispatched by one of the marshals. In the subsequent shoot-out Sammy was wounded in the arm and fatally shot in the back while fleeing. Degan took a bullet in the thorax and died instantly.[44]

At this point the FBI assumed command of the siege. During the next thirty-eight hours, Randall received a shoulder wound and Vicki was shot through the head from fifty feet by a sniper as she held the baby in one arm and the cabin door open with the other. Bone chips from her exploding skull broke several of Harris's ribs, collapsing a lung, nearly killing him. Vicki's rancid corpse lay under the kitchen table for ten days in full view of the two terrorized daughters.

Critics of the shoot-out believe that the state fully intended to murder the entire Weaver clan. Certainly, the daughters were of that opinion.[45] That this did not happen is due largely to the efforts of James "Bo" Gritz. At first only reluctantly granted permission to intercede, Gritz would spend four days with the family, first using a bullhorn from a distance, later quietly talking to them inside the cabin, trying to secure their peaceful surrender. His position was that being a Christian patriot himself and having served as a Green Beret commander, he alone could sympathize with and win the trust of one of his own.

After one of Gritz's negotiating sessions, an interchange occurred underscoring the irony of the standoff. Marshal Cluff was driving Gritz down the ridge, the two swapping Vietnam stories, when they realized that they had served together in the same unit in Vietnam, Special Forces B-36. Gritz had been Cluff's faceless but heralded "Commander Bo." Cluff had worked as a helicopter gunship crewman providing cover for Bo's ground maneuvers. "I'll be a son of a bitch," exhorted Gritz, who reached over to hug Cluff. "I always do that when I meet somebody who was over there," he later explained. "So many didn't come back."[46]

Cluff later described the encounter as "really weird." Gritz had been, he admits, "a hell of a leader." And yet "it dawned on me, 'God, you radical bastard. What happened to you?' "[47] Gritz had somehow transmogrified himself into one of the enemy. In the intervening years, he, too, had become an exponent of government conspiracies and millennialism, an advocate of armed survivalism.

Gritz

Bo Gritz served as an intelligence officer and reconnaissance chief for Delta Force, a Green Beret unit, in Vietnam from 1964 to 1969.[48] Following hostilities he became commander of U.S. Army Special Forces in Latin America, and later chief of "special activities" for the U.S. Army General Staff at the Pentagon. Burly and slope-shouldered, with a strong chin, dark glasses, and an impish smile, he can talk simultaneously tough and sentimentally. His presidential campaign bumper sticker (he ran for president in 1992 on the Populist Party ticket) says it all: "God, Guns, and Gritz."

Despite accusations of Gritz being a white supremacist,[49] apart from his peripheral association with a Christian Identity church in Laporte, Colorado, there is little evidence to support this. While apparently he does frown on "race mixing" as contrary to biblical injunction, he denies that this implies support for white domination. "Skin color means nothing," he once said. "A bullet in combat doesn't have any prejudice."[50]

Gritz was the most decorated Green Beret commander of the Vietnam War. One photograph pictures his chest covered with sixty-two combat medals, citations, and ribbons. In his memoirs, *A Soldier Reports*, commander-in-chief of Vietnam operations General Westmoreland calls Gritz "The" American soldier. During the course of his Vietnam tours Gritz took part in over one hundred "special operations," including four into Burma's Golden Triangle. There he allegedly met with Khun Sa, the opium warlord of the area, and was shocked to learn that high level American officials were named by Khun Sa as his "best customers."[51] Later in Latin America in 1975–77, Gritz claims to have discovered that the CIA was involved in cocaine trafficking in order to underwrite its covert counterinsurgency efforts.[52] Thus began his estrangement from the government, his turn to conspiracy mongering, and his subsequent emergence in the public eye as the ultimate paramilitary hero.

Commander Bo had always displayed a sincere concern for his men, including those who were missing in action. His name became prominent in civilian circles when in 1983 he led the first of four failed missions to Laos to rescue United States servicemen presumably still held captive by the Communists. He remains convinced that the government conspired to block the rescue of American POWs to cover up its own heroin dealings. As it turned out, he was convicted in Thailand of importing illegal radio equipment and deported. Punished by American authorities for passport violations, he was accused of trying to be a "Rambo."[53] In fact the causal influence here is exactly the reverse. It was Gritz himself who served as role model for the bluff and swagger man-of-action who in the face of government corruption and indifference seizes the day in the movie thrillers *Uncommon Valor, Missing in Action,* and *Rambo: First Blood Part II.* Bo Gritz is not merely a product of American paramilitary culture; he is its archetype.

Conclusion

While the three Weaver daughters stayed with their maternal grandparents in Iowa, and while the two older ones attended public school, Randall and Kevin Harris went to prison awaiting trial on conspiracy to subvert the U.S. government "for the purpose of advancing their views of 'white' or 'aryan' supremacy or separatism." The sixteen-page indictment accused both men of "provoking and sustaining a violent confrontation with federal, and state and/or local law enforcement agents or officers." Another section of the indictment charged the entire family, including Vicki, Sammy, both the elder daughters, and the ten-month-old girl, with "unlawfully, willfully, deliberately . . . kill[ing] and murder-[ing] one William F. Degan."[54] Had the men been convicted on all counts, Weaver would have faced up to life in prison plus forty-five years and a $1.75 million fine, Harris life plus twenty-five years and $1.25 million in fines.

At the urging of Bo Gritz, local supporters of the Weavers, together with Tom Metzger of the White Aryan Resistance and spokesmen for the Aryan Nations Church, have responded in kind, requesting the Boundary County prosecutor to convene a grand jury to return indictments against the federal government for criminal wrongdoing. According to the Christian patriot community, the standoff on Ruby Ridge was an "abuse of power," a "selective prosecution of a citizen [Weaver] because of his race and religious beliefs," and, as Weaver himself describes it, "a horrid, premeditated murder." The prosecutor did not honor this request.[55]

In October, two months after the standoff, 150 self-proclaimed radical patriots from thirty states convened in Estes Park, Colorado. The group issued several reports on the standoff, one from a so-called SWAT Committee (Sacred Warfare Action Tactics). In it Louis Beam (see above) proposed that given the state's capacity to infiltrate and crush centrally directed resistance movements, right-wing militants should borrow a page from Communist guerrilla warfare manuals and deploy "leaderless" combat units nationwide, each acting flexibly according to local circumstances.[56] What this seems to suggest is that far from deterring violence, the state's clumsy, perhaps arrogant, manhandling of the Weaver case may have made it more likely.

In Boise Idaho Federal District Court beginning in April 1993 Randall Weaver and Kevin Harris were tried on the charges described above. The defense team claimed that the government was out to get the Weaver clan for refusing to inform on other Idaho white separatists. The jury heard testimony from fifty-six government witnesses and was shown hundreds of exhibits. The defense did not call any witnesses, claiming prosecutors had failed to prove their case. After twenty days of deliberations, a record for Idaho, the jury acquitted Harris on all counts; Weaver was convicted on two minor charges of failure to appear for the original trial and of committing an offense while on release from a federal magistrate pending that trial. At this writing no charges have been filed for the deaths of Samuel or Vicki Weaver.

The tragedy of armed conflict is not just that one side (ours) is unfairly vilified, true as this is, but that both sides victimize and in turn are victimized. Both sides fit their opponents into defamatory categories ignoring their actual human complexity; both attempt to justify these categorizations through legal tribunals and the generation of legends, "documenting" their claims by citing tactically selected writings and behaviors; both pass these embellished legends on to children, sedimenting the reality of the evildoer in the minds of the next generation; both sides act toward the constructed enemy "appropriately" and, in witnessing its predictable response, have their preconceptions confirmed. In these ways, parties to armed conflict are invariably "confused." They are not just mistaken about each other or bewildered, but fused with them, inseparable from them. And yet as tempted as we are to conclude from this that opponents are therefore equivalent ethically – that is, as one observer said, "this [the Weavers'] was a case with no good guys"[57] – intellectual honesty does not permit us this indulgence. True, both the Weavers and the state were in part figments of each other's imagination; both, furthermore, were deluded about their own righteousness and victimization at one another's hands. But *their* moral blindness does not absolve the rest of us who claim citizenship in the community from having to be partisans ourselves, and thus being subject to the same temptations to illusion. It is not enough to blurt proudly "a plague on both your houses" and then pretend that we are somehow innocent because we are above the battles that define our life together.

5

A Library of Infamy

By all these means we shall so wear down the goyim *[Christian people]
that they will be compelled to offer us international power of a nature that
by its position will enable us without any violence gradually to absorb all
the State forces of the world and to form a Super-Government.*[1]

It would be easy to dismiss racism and religious bigotry as products of
craziness or stupidity. It would be easy, but incorrect. Evidence from
field research on Pacific Northwest neo-Nazis shows that in the main
they are indistinguishable intellectually and educationally from their
more conventional peers.[2] Furthermore, if the cases of David Rice and
the Kentucky terrorist cited in chapter 3 are typical, then the handful of
politically motivated murderers during the 1980s, if psychologically extreme in a statistical sense, at least are not certifiably insane.[3] Nor is
there much support for the popular legend that right-wing extremists
are less integrated into ordinary community life than their more toler-
ant neighbors. Research shows their marriages and church attendance to
be above average in stability and frequency, their political involvement
to be normal, and their rates of geographic mobility comparable to
nearby residents. Furthermore, anecdotal observations reveal many of
them to be friendly and helpful. Randall Weaver, for example, had a
reputation for aiding local residents in need. One winter a single woman
living on Ruby Creek was running short of wood. She relates that
"Randy cut me a load and wouldn't let me pay him for it. You know
what he wanted for cutting that wood and hauling and delivering it? A
cup of hot coffee, because it was cold that day."[4]

The way in which some people become racists and bigots is analogous
to how others become pacifists, civil rights workers, vegetarians, or
Moonies. They find themselves enmeshed in social networks comprising racist and bigoted coworkers, lovers, parents, friends, preachers, and
teachers. It is through these relationships that they are recruited into
activism themselves.

An essential component of the hate community is its "literature." There exists in America a vast underground rightist media, consisting of radio broadcasts, cassette tapes, technically accomplished videotapes, and what concerns us in this chapter: newspapers, journals, pamphlets, and books, all vilifying Jews directly or using abstract categories such as the Hidden Hand, Force X, the Insiders, the Bilderbergers, and so on.

A seminal step in the social construction of enemies is their mythic representation. We can understand neither the Goldmark nor the Weaver incidents sociologically without a detailed grasp of the defamatory literary corpus dealing with Jews and Judaism.

What immediately strikes the objective reader about this body of mythology is its style: the occasional citation of Jewish "scholars" to buttress claims against the Jews themselves; the use of the accoutrements of scholarship, such as footnote references, bibliographies, and indexes; the professional quality of the printing and binding, and the use of eye-catching book covers; the recounting on those covers of the authors' academic credentials; the efforts by the authors to ingratiate themselves with their readers by "exposing," at some alleged risk to themselves, heretofore hidden "truths" – truths that invariably justify the readers' own envy, sloth, lust, and hostility; the display of "reasonableness" by the authors, who dutifully note exceptions to general rules (e.g., All Jews are evil) only to reveal a more sinister reality (e.g., The only way Jews can be moral is by denying their faith). These rhetorical devices together partly explain the impact this literature has on its audience of otherwise intelligent, rational people. The object of this chapter is to undermine this impact by exposing the historiographically questionable roots from which this material has received nourishment.

Like all persons, right-wing extremists learn who the proper objects of love and hate are from what they read. The contents of what I call their library of infamy can be catalogued along the same Manichaean dimensions as the extremist world generally: literature identifying the good guys and literature expounding upon the bad.[5] Although it would be a mistake to consider these two types of texts as absolutely differentiated, here we address only those that are explicitly defamatory: notably *The Protocols of the Learned Elders of Zion* and Elizabeth Dilling's *The Plot Against Christianity* (also known as *The Jewish Religion: Its Influence Today*).[6] If the *Protocols* exemplifies the lowest form of secularistic anti-Semitism, the *Plot* represents its religious variation; although strictly speaking, as mythic texts both fall within the area of "religion" in the broadest sense. With few exceptions all contemporary American neo-Nazi doctrine either unabashedly plagiarizes these sourcebooks, cites them as "scholarly" references in its philosophy of history, or amplifies and updates their motifs in light of modern circumstances.

With no attempt to be exhaustive, included in the corpus of derivative material are the following books: *Know Your Enemy* is by Korean War hero and Christian Patriots Defense League founder Col. (ret.) Gordon "Jack" Mohr. The book is an attack on "Satan's kids," the Jews, for being "Christ killers" who commit "terrible pollutions at their secret gatherings" and for "cursing the followers of Christ on a daily basis as bastards" (the information contained in one of Mohr's reports was the immediate spur for David Rice's breaking into the Goldmark home and murdering them). Wesley Swift is the author of *The Mystery of [Jewish] Iniquity.* Swift was founder of the Church of Jesus Christ Christian (Aryan Nations). Following his death its headquarters was moved to northern Idaho. Gary Allen's *None Dare Call It Conspiracy* is a John Birch Society classic whose cover celebrates it as a "runaway bestseller! Over 5 milion in print." Frank Britton wrote [The Jewish Plot] *Behind Communism* and Rev. Sheldon Emry (deceased) produced *Billion$ for the Banker$, Debts for the People.* The group Emry founded, America's Promise, is now also located in northern Idaho. An organization calling itself The National Emancipation of Our White Seed published *Communism Is Jewish.* The book *The International Jew* has been attributed, probably fatuously, to Henry Ford. In any case, the automaker was awarded an iron cross from Adolf Hitler. As Hitler allegedly said during the presentation ceremony, "We look to Heinrich Ford as the leader of the fascist movement in America."[7] Rev. Jarah Crawford wrote *Last Battle Cry,* an exegesis of the Bible from a racist viewpoint, showing the Aryan race to have descended from Abel, and the Jews, "who are of the evil one," from Cain. This book was recommended to me by a prominent figure in the *Bruders Schweigen.* And, finally, the British fascist Arnold Leese produced *Jewish Ritual Murder,* which "explains" the Lindbergh baby kidnapping as Jewish vengeance for the famed pilot's advocacy of neutrality toward Nazi Germany.

More scurrilous works include Andrew MacDonald's *The Turner Diaries* (the so-called bible of neo-Nazi terrorism, a book to which the Kentuckian mentioned in Chapter 3 had access); the Covenant, Sword and the Arm of the Lord's *Prepare War!* (which advocates taking up arms against "sodomite homosexuals waiting in their lusts to rape," "negro beasts who eat the flesh of men," and "seed of Satan Jews sacrificing people in darkness"); and Louis Beam's *Essays of a Klansman*. Beam's book details a point system for earning the status of Aryan warrior. Liberal sociologists, for example, are worth but ⅟₅₀₀ a point each; the president of the United States rates a whole point.

Deconstructing the Texts

As mentioned above, the object of this chapter is to illuminate the origins of the *Protocols* and the *Plot* with an eye to destroying whatever credibility they may have with naive readers. This kind of procedure today is known technically as textual "deconstruction." Without going into details, the idea is that since social reality is constituted by how it is spoken and written, the "destruction" of that reality entails the deconstruction of the texts sustaining it. It therefore follows that if we wish to accomplish the nonviolent "destruction" of neo-Nazism, we must dismantle the library upon which it is built. The most effective way to do this is by displaying how its texts, which have the outward appearance of objectivity and hence authoritativeness, are either entirely fabricated (as in the case of the *Protocols*) or, if not (as for the *Plot*), grounded on illogic and error.

Textual deconstruction is an important weapon in the arsenal of the so-called postmodernist program that has recently enjoyed an enthusiastic reception in humanities departments in universities throughout Europe and America.[8] Therefore, it will be helpful in locating our discussion to distinguish the way in which I use the word "deconstruction" from the typical postmodernist pattern.

Radical postmodernists agree with Jacques Derrida that "there is nothing outside the text." That is, all we have is discourse; texts have no ultimate reference, no primordial ground. Many implications follow from this, among them that "reality [or what passes for reality] is nothing but words." There is no object world of concrete events, persons, or institutions independent of the observer: no actual trees, people, or groups. Instead there are only written and oral accounts of such things. And even these have no facticity independent of the readers and auditors attending to them. Therefore, there is no single necessarily accurate reading or hearing of such narratives. "The reader looks everywhere and finds only texts, and within the texts only himself."[9]

Although there is a subtlety in postmodernism that cannot be conveyed fairly in a few sentences, I take issue with several of its most extreme positions on both metaphysical and ethical grounds. Regarding ethics, if there is no objective reality, there is no objective truth – "the secret . . . is, indeed, that truth doesn't exist" – and if no truth, then no falsity, and no difference between confirmed propositions and "even the most obvious, distorted forms of propaganda."[10] Elie Weisel's moving first person account of his childhood in the death camps in *Night,* for example, would be equivalent in epistemological stature to A. R. Butz's *Hoax of the 20th Century,* which denies the historicity of the Holocaust. Both stories, radical postmodernists might say, are equally "interesting." As for metaphysics, if social reality is merely the words that write it, then social reconstruction too is reduced to the relatively sweat-free task of linguistic reform. As for the problematic of the enemy: To achieve perpetual peace it is sufficient to deconstruct texts of war. But as we observed in the last two chapters, while the production of enemy texts is certainly pivotal in the social constitution of enemies themselves, it is not the only and not always the most important step. Hence, while deconstructing neo-Nazi literature may be essential in shattering the neo-Nazi world, it can never be enough. As the ghosts of Alan Berg and the Goldmarks remind us, neo-Nazism is infinitely more than how it is written. What might be involved additionally in socially deconstructing the enemy will be treated in the concluding chapters.

The Plot Against Christianity

The author of *The Plot Against Christianity,* Elizabeth Dilling, was one of thirty anti-Communists indicted for sedition in 1942 for their opposition to America's involvement in World War II. Dilling explained that for her this opposition grew from the realization that the actual, if veiled, purpose of the war was to spread communism across the earth, following a plan orchestrated by "Jewish anti-Christ power," whose financial and industrial hub she claimed to be made up of the American Jewish Committee, B'nai B'rith, and its "secret police arm," the Anti-Defamation League.[11]

Using entirely Jewish literary sources, *The Plot* presumes to demonstrate how this strategy of satanic world rule was already spelled out in Jewish holy books centuries ago. The sources presented are photocopies of excerpts primarily from the 1934–48 Soncino English translation of the Talmud, together with Dilling's own interpretation of their significance.

To readers untrained in contextual hermeneutics, *The Plot* is dynamite. So impressed was Henry Ford by Dilling's Jewish "scholarship" (as displayed in her earlier works, *The Red Network* [1934], *The Roosevelt Red Record and Its Background* [1936], and *The Octopus* [1940]) that he agreed to subsidize the work of Dilling's Christian research institute in Chicago. She boasts of having been "entertained at the executive's table at the Ford plant in Detroit" during this period.[12]

"In brief," she writes, "*The Plot* pictures Judaism as: Pomp, silliness, obscenity and more obscenity, a setting up of laws seemingly for the purpose of inventing circumventions, and evasions; delight[ing] in sadistic cruelty; revers[ing] all biblical moral teachings on theft, murder, sodomy, perjury, treatment of children and parents; insane[ly] hat[ing] Christ, Christians, and every phase of Christianity."[13]

Judaism is blasphemous, claims Dilling. "Blasphemy," she says, quoting Jewish scripture, "is an indictable offense only if it is mentally directed against God. If, however, one reviles the Divine Name, whilst mentally employing it to denote some other object, he is not punished."[14] It is immoral (the Talmud appears to condone incest with children as young as three, bestiality, necrophilia, adultery, the murder of non-Jews, theft from strangers, and lying in the courtroom).[15] It is foolish (for hip disease, says the Talmud, let him take a pot of fish brine and rub the wound sixty times; for bladder pain take a purple thread spun by a prostitute and hang it on the man's membrum). It promotes sorcery, necromancy, the casting of lots, and the mystical lore of numbers and letters.[16] Above all, insists Dilling, it is anti-Christian. Under the name "Baalam" (a cult associated with temple prostitution) the most lewd passages concerning Jesus and his followers appear. He was, it is said, mothered by a whore and committed bestiality and adultery himself.[17] Hence religious services in his name frequently devolve into sexual orgies.[18] Just as common criminals in ancient times were executed by the four legal methods – stoning, burning, decapitation, and strangling – then so was Jesus, in addition to being crucified.[19]

Pretenses aside, Dilling is not a scholar. *The Plot Against Christianity* is inspired by, if not completely borrowed from, *The Talmud Unmasked*, produced by Justin Bonaventura Pranaitis (d. 1917), a Russian Catholic priest, and translated from Latin into English in 1939. The Pranaitis

Talmud was introduced to America by Col. E. N. Sanctuary, a cohort of fundamentalist Kansas minister Gerald Winrod, the so-called Jayhawk Nazi.[20] It is based on *Der Talmudjude* (1839–41), by German professor Augustus Rohling, and this in turn on perhaps the most seminal anti-Semitic text of modern times: Johann Eisenmenger's *Entdecktes Juden-thum* (1711) or *Judaism Unmasked: A Thorough and True Account of the Way in Which the Stubborn Jews Frightfully Blaspheme and Dishonor the Holy Trinity, Revile the Holy Mother of Christ, Mockingly Criticize the New Testament, the Evangelists, and the Christian Religion, and Despise and Curse, to the Uttermost Extent, the Whole of Christianity.* Eisenmenger's *Entdecktes* is a two-volume, 2,000-page encyclopedia, allegedly detailing everyday Jewish life, relying exclusively on accurate, unforged quotations from over 180 Jewish lawbooks, the cabala, and homiletic and devotional texts.[21]

Of course, long before Eisenmenger appeared on the scene, Christian civilization had a tradition of Judeophobia.[22] What made his attack different is that he was the preeminent European orientalist of his day. Although a Lutheran, he was conversant in Hebrew, Aramaic, and Arabic, and had studied at the yeshiva under rabbis (according to some legends, passing as a Jew). He therefore seemed equipped to commentate on Judaism with intellectual authority. In addition, the stated motive for his undertaking seemed benevolent to Christians: to aid Jews to discover the "error" of their ways by publicly displaying to them the scandal of their faith. This was after several of Eisenmenger's colleagues embarrassed the Christian community by having themselves circumcised and converting to Judaism.[23]

For all his presumption and credentials, Eisenmenger committed errors typical of Christian interpreters of his time. These errors, fraught with tragic implications, are now blithely repeated by his modern protégés, Dilling and her ilk.

First, although nominally valid, the Talmud does not now and has not for over 1,500 years (if that recently) been a practical guide for living, except within very broad limits. Rather, it is intended primarily for study – study that provides insights into the ancient Jewish world view or, if we prefer, the mind of the ancient Jewish sage. As Rabbi Adin Steinsaltz, the foremost student of the Talmud in our times, says, "The ultimate purpose of the Talmud is not in any sense utilitarian. . . ." It is contrary to its intended spirit to scrutinize it for practical lessons.[24]

Furthermore, the Talmud is not "user friendly."[25] Compiled over a period of more than one thousand years from different sources, it includes commentaries on commentaries. During this time, the political conditions of the Jewish community varied widely. Thus "one has the sense of eavesdropping on snatches of conversation among scholars separated from one another in time and space." The word "snatches" is fitting, for the commentaries are compressed, not elaborated, and they allude implicitly to bodies of related knowledge unavailable to modern readers, even to contemporary Orthodox Jews, but particularly to those outside the community of faith.

To illustrate the difficulties involved in interpreting the Talmud, I cite a single example. It concerns an issue that has scandalized Christians for centuries, and on which Dilling spends pages spewing vituperation, and which is routinely used by contemporary neo-Nazis to justify anti-Jewish violence: the ritual killing of (Christian) children by offering them to the fire god Molech. I present this example in the spirit of the homeopathic physician who fights disease by inoculating the patient with a toxin similar to the one that caused the disease: by ingesting a small dose of talmudic misinterpretation the reader may be rendered immune to any later anti-Semitic plague.

I begin with a relevant talmudic *mishnah* (a written summary of oral law): "He who gives of his seed to Molech incurs no punishment unless he delivers it to Molech and causes it to pass through the fire. If he gave it to Molech but did not cause it to pass through the fire, or the reverse, he incurs no penalty, unless he does both."[26]

Now for the *gemara,* or rabbinic commentary, on this teaching. To begin with, there is an assumption of faith in the reading of the Talmud that the entire body of Jewish jurisprudence (including the Pentateuch and the Talmud) contains no contradictions. But the *mishnah* just cited seems to contravene the biblical prohibition against delivering one's children to Molech (e.g., Deut. 18:10, Lev. 20:2–4). A central inquiry in the talmudic *gemara,* therefore, is to resolve this and other apparent contradictions, sustaining faith in the integrity of Jewish law.

With this in mind, let us fancifully reconstruct the debate between scholars concerning Molech as reported in the *gemara.* We imagine bearded sages amid eager students sitting on mats arrayed in rank order, in an oil-lamped, cool, mud-walled Babylonian academy 2,500 years ago. The discussion opens with one rabbi asking what Molech is in distinction to other idols. Since their names are not explicitly mentioned in the teaching, does that mean the *mishnah* does not apply to them? Another rabbi then asks whether, since the ruling evidently condemns only passage through the fire, one may offer his seed to Molech if this final step is not taken? Or, if one's children are passed through the flames, what if in just one direction, is this permitted? Still another rabbi inquires whether, since the *mishnah* uses the words "of his seed," instead of "all his seed," does this suggest that one can give *all* his children to Molech, not just some? And if, furthermore, one is forbidden to deliver his own seed into the fire, does that imply permission to offer the seed of others, such as one's niece's children? Or non-Jewish children? Or one's own self? And doesn't the proper act of "delivery" to an idol in the first place, asks another, involve the offering to its acolytes, so that if one does it himself in private it is permitted?[27]

If taken literally by an outsider to the faith, like Dilling, who in the manner of a Victorian moralist is searching for black and white answers to legal questions, this kind of discourse can be confusing if not maddening. Dilling's frustrated rage at being unable to untangle the web of argumentation is plainly visible in her handwritten glosses: "Mere hairsplitting!" " 'Mercy' killing!" "How to kill explained!"

If read properly (that is, within the faith), the *gemara* offers glimpses into the mind-set, and hence world view, of the teachers whose arguments make up the Talmud – a world view which Steinsaltz likens to high mathematics: it is a painstaking search for the most precise solution to the question of the Torah's meaning and significance in this particular case. In glimpsing this mind-set the devotee is reconnected to his own roots in the past. To use Steinsaltz's term, he remembers and repossesses the truth of Judaism.

Besides misunderstanding the significance of talmudic argumentation, Dilling commits a more egregious mistake. In the example before us, she willfully leaves out the most crucial section of the *gemara*, that dealing with the meaning of the phrase "pass through the fire." Dilling's gloss reads "burning children to demon Molech allowed." The *gemara*, however, says that the most likely meaning of the word "pass" is "jump," as in to jump over the coals. This brings to mind the folk custom of walking or jumping over coals for good luck or as a test of faith – practices widely known throughout the world. With this section of the *gemara* now added, the entire rabbinic discussion takes on a lighter, possibly even humorous, flavor – entirely missed by Dilling.

This brings us to a third hermeneutic error committed by Eisenmenger and Dilling: their reading of the Judaic literary corpus out of historical and cultural context. Although the sanctity of the entire Talmud is maintained for the purposes noted above, whole sections of its books have come to be regarded as practically irrelevant and no longer binding. What this means, of course, is that mere citation of the sacred writings of the Jews can no more reveal to Christians what Jewish life is now, or has been for millennia, than study of the *Laws of Manu*, for example, can reveal everyday contemporary Hindu affairs.

During the period when the oral opinions contained in the Talmud were first argued (ca. 500 B.C.), the Jewish community was economically self-sufficient. It was granted autonomy to legally regulate its internal – including criminal – affairs, and in some regions it comprised a majority of the population. Not until late in the Christian era would it become ghettoized, occupationally restricted, and dependent for its physical safety on the good will of princes with alien faiths. In pre-Christian times, loyalty to secular officials and the idea of nonperjurious submission to their courts was still novel enough to occasion the suspicion of religious persons; "gentile" paganism was rampant – including, we can imagine, "passing" through Molech's fire; and it was permissible if not to kill *minim* (infidels), at least not to come to their aid; nor was the property of outsiders to clan and tribe considered absolutely inviolable. Regarding sexual matters, the puritanism that many Christians take for granted as "natural" and God-pleasing simply did not exist: marriage was a civil contract, not a sacrament; children conceived in non-incestuous relations outside of marriage were considered legitimate, polygamy (but not polyandry) was legal, and the marriage of a man to his deceased brother's widow was encouraged.

To transpose talmudic regulations generated to meet these conditions to medieval Europe, much less to modern times, is to display the highest degree of historical insensitivity. The "infidels," for example, who the Talmud directs should be "lowered down but not raised up" (that is, destroyed), when interpreted in context refers exclusively to the Canaanites of the legendary Promised Land, whose extermination Yahweh orders in Deuteronomy (25:19). It does not, as claimed by Eisenmenger and Dilling, signify "Christians." So too, the talmudic admonition of which Dilling makes so much: "A gentile who observes the Sabbath deserves death." Not only does this not refer to Christians, who, after all, will not appear for several centuries; it is intended as no more than a severe condemnation, equivalent to the warning "whosoever [including Jews] violates the words of the sages deserves death."[28]

As Jacob Katz has said, while Eisenmenger, Pranaitis, Rohling, and Dilling can indeed draw horrifying portraits of Judaism by quoting selected passages from its sacred books directly, a similar *Entdecktes* (unveiling) could be made of Christianity, using its own ancient texts.[29] In fact, contrary to Katz's belief that "no such book was ever produced," the young Hegelian Bruno Bauer wrote *Das Entdeckte Christentum* in 1843. It so scandalized Swiss authorities that they ordered it destroyed. Excerpts from it were later published by one Wilhelm Marr and would eventually find a place in Karl Marx's pamphlet "On the Jewish Question."[30]

This is not to say that Jewish and Christian sacred law are identical, either in style or in substance. Given Christianity's traditional eschatological indifference to politics and economics, canon law has infinitely less to say about practical daily affairs than the Talmud. Furthermore, given the bureaucratic structure of the Roman Church, which became the model for most Christian denominations, Christian legal rescripts and decretals are typically formulated rationally and systematically. This is totally unlike the seeming arbitrariness which marks the ancient rabbinic rulings. But these formal differences, so abhorrent to Christian students of the Talmud, are due to the different sociological circumstances that have occasioned these two bodies of sacred jurisprudence.[31]

Unaware of the differing social contexts producing Christian canon law on the one hand and talmudic law on the other; unused to seeing sacred law make pronouncements on everything from harvesting to health and hygiene, and invoking popular folklore and humor to do this; and, above all, sensing a "dangerously" good-natured, conciliatory attitude toward the body and its functions, the Christian right-winger must dismiss these differences as due to the influence of Satan.

The Protocols of the Learned Elders of Zion

Herman Goedsche was an obscure, part-time novelist and petty German clerk. In his book *Biarritz* (1868) he spins a fantasy, "In a Cemetery," that would eventually evolve into what Norman Cohn has called a "warrant for genocide" of the Jewish people.[32] This warrant is the *Protocols,* which passes in extremist circles not as fable, but as fact.

Its essentials: One dreary night thirteen bent, white-bearded men in black cassocks kneel in a circle around a grave. At the stroke of midnight a blue flame appears above the grave and a disembodied voice speaks, "I greet you, heads of the thirteen tribes of Israel." It is the devil. The thirteen elders return the greeting, and then each in turn solemnly reports his progress in the last century regarding Satan's goal of world conquest. Reuben: Stock manipulation and banking are now controlled by us and all governments are in our debt. Simeon: We have released all peasants from serfdom so they can now slave for us in factories. And so forth. The narrative then digresses to an indictment of modernization – from the enfranchisement of the propertyless to secularism and civil service examinations – showing each to have resulted from a Jewish conspiracy. At the conclusion of the audit, a golden calf emerges from the grave, and the thirteen elders prostrate themselves before it.

How is it that the Jews, a newly enfranchised, mostly poor minority group, could assume such cosmic powers in Goedsche's opus? And more to the point, how could it be taken not as fantasy but fact? To answer these questions requires a brief excursus into nineteenth-century European political history, particularly into the atmosphere surrounding the democratic reforms introduced in France in 1789 and spread by Napoleon Bonaparte's liberation army.

Two facts stand out about this period: first, democracy and the establishment of a secular state were resisted by the landed aristocracy and the Roman Catholic and Russian Orthodox hierarchies; second, Jews, who were among the supposed beneficiaries of these reforms, were, to use Léon Poliakov's terms, "indifferent" and "passive," if not outright hostile, to their implementation – to the idea, in other words, of dejudaization in the name of liberty and equality.[33] (As Jean-Paul Sartre has shown, European Jewry traditionally has had two foes: conservatives who revile Jews for *being* different, and liberals who attack Jews for willfully *considering* themselves different.)[34] It was for these reasons, then, that the conservative parties originally attributed the fervor of the French Revolution not to Jews but to a Protestant conspiracy, presumably organized in Freemason lodges, the practitioners of whose arcane rites had already been excommunicated in 1738.[35] This notion was given just enough credibility by the machinations of one Adam Weishaupt and his secret society known as the Illuminati to make it plausible to the general population. We will return to Weishaupt in the next chapter.

However this may be, in 1807 Napoleon called a Great Sanhedrin of Jewish leaders from across the world and convened them in Paris, the goal being to co-opt them into legitimizing and eventually implementing his policies. The result of this convention was panic in the Christian community, not only in France, but in Austria, Germany, Russia, and even America.[36] Until this moment Jews had been written off as pawns in Protestant hands; now they came to be seen as the chief instigators of democratic reform themselves, in some renditions the very cabal behind the Reformation. Furthermore, since in the Book of Revelation it is prophesied that the Jews shall return to Palestine and there rebuild Herod's temple, it was feared as well that these were the Last Days – the end of the world. Thus it was, on the eve of the Great Council, that Abbé Augustin Barruel, the canon of the cathedral of Notre Dame, related to Cardinal Fesch that a mysterious Italian soldier, Simonini, had revealed to him, and Pope Pius VII had confirmed its truth, that the Sanhedrin was the final step in Israel's age-old dream of world conquest. Having presumably already infiltrated the church and the Jesuit Order, Judaism was now poised to enslave Christians and use their "seed" as victims in bloody offerings to its gods Ba'al and Molech.

Cardinal Fesch demanded and received a private audience with Emperor Napoleon; and the Sanhedrin was "dismissed without having obtained any positive result."[37] Through the heroic actions of the Abbé Barruel and his father confessor, so we are told, the world was saved, at least for the moment.

This is the cultural and political environment out of which Goedsche's tale, absent now of a long-deceased Napoleon, emerged; and it allows us to understand why it was so readily translated and enthusiastically received in continental Europe. By 1872 it was being published in Russian as an authentic historical document, and a decade later in French as a pamphlet entitled *The Rabbi's Speech* – the addresses of the thirteen elders condensed into the recitation of a single person to a secret Jewish council presumably held in Leipzig three years earlier. In 1905 an analogous tale with the title *The Protocols of the Learned Elders of Zion*, by Sergei Nilus, a tsarist court favorite and Orthodox monk, was published under the imprint of the Russian secret police. In this version the speech, with variations taking into consideration social developments in the three prior decades, is to a secret session of the first Zionist Congress held in Basel, Switzerland, in 1897.

Historiographic research is able to show that the Nilus account is in fact a plagiarism of still another address, fabricated in 1864 by a conservative French lawyer trying to link the reforms of Bonaparte's nephew Emperor Napoleon III (reigned 1852–71) with Zionism. The plagiarism was the work of an aide to the assistant head of the tsarist secret police in Paris named Cyon (pronounced Zion, hence the probable origin of its title: a capricious play on words). Authorship was attributed to Nilus probably to shield the version's seedy origins. Evidently, the Nilus *Protocols* were intended by imperial court luminaries as an attempt to satirize Sergei Witte, a leader in the effort to modernize Russia by removing some of the traditional rights of the nobility and industrializing the economy.

Legend has it that in 1918 a copy of the *Protocols* was secreted to the deposed Romanov empress just days after the Russian revolution. When the imperial family was murdered by the Bolsheviks, loyalist White Guard troops supposedly found it among her belongings, together with a Bible. Also found were swastika-like inscriptions on a window in the room she had shared with Tsar Nicholas. Henceforth the *Protocols* would be issued to each officer in the White army.

When Germany evacuated the Ukraine following the end of World War I, a train was made available to White officers seeking safe passage to the West. One of these officers eventually contacted a German publisher, who issued the *Protocols* in 1920 as *The Jewish Peril*. By 1933 when Adolf Hitler assumed the chancellorship of the Reich, the book had gone through thirty-three printings and had been translated into English.

Gerald Winrod's Defenders of the Christian Faith published a version in 1943 under the title *The Hidden Hand*. "Henry Ford's" commentary on it, *The International Jew*, ran through six English editions and was translated into sixteen languages. In an interview with the New York *World* on February 17, 1921, Ford is alleged to have said, "the only statement I care to make about the *Protocols* is that they fit in with what is going on. They are sixteen years old, and they have fitted the world situation up to this time. They fit it now."

The anti-Semitic Detroit priest Father Coughlin read excerpts from the *Protocols* during his nationwide radio broadcasts. His group, the National Union for Social Justice, reprinted it in 1938. Still another disseminator was Coughlin's colleague and confidant, Rev. Gerald L. K. Smith and his Christian Nationalist Crusade.[38]

From all these sources the *Protocols* has come down to the racists and bigots inhabiting the western United States, the older leaders of whom were in their impressionable early teens and twenties when Winrod, Ford, Coughlin, and Smith were flourishing. My first copy, already frayed and tattered, was surreptitiously slipped to me in blue unmarked covers in the back room of an abandoned warehouse near the railroad tracks in Pocatello, Idaho. "It's all here," I was told, after asking an informant who was behind the one-world conspiracy. My second copy, marked to facilitate memorization of catchphrases, was sent me by the granddaughter of one of the original members of the Church of Jesus Christ Christian (Aryan Nations). The added denotation "Christian" to the title indicates that the Jesus of this church is an Aryan, not a Jew. The grandmother had moved from Los Angeles to Hayden Lake, Idaho, along with the entire congregation after the death of its founder Wesley Swift. Swift had earlier served as a bodyguard for Rev. Gerald L. K. Smith.

Conclusion

Today's library of infamy is based in part on the inappropriate and misleading exegetical methodology of a one-time celebrated Christian orientalist, and in part on the entirely fictional concoctions and cynical plagiarisms by European church officials and a landed nobility resentful of the threats of modernization and democracy to a status quo until recently overseen by themselves. From these two ingredients has come a witches' brew, rich in heritage, vivid in imagery, alluring in mystery, tasting of forbidden knowledge. Through their contacts in the extremist community, David Rice, Randall and Vicki Weaver, and the Kentucky terrorist described in chapter 3 drank deeply of this brew and nourished their hatreds. Let us hope that by the aid of its unveiling and deconstruction, others of like inclination will by immunized against its poison.

6

Who Shall Be the Enemy?
American Political Culture
in a Post-Communist Era

We are going to deprive you of the enemy and then what will you do?[1]

"The End of History?"

Disintegration of the Communist monolith has occasioned consider-able soul-searching in the West, particularly in elite circles. Is the cold war truly over? Are the elections, divestments of Communist Party mo-nopolies, and free market rhetoric mere window dressing intended to undermine the will of the NATO bloc, or worse, to buy time until, economically bolstered, Russia once again entertains imperial dreams?

Assuming the transformations are as authentic as they are dramatic, then what can be credited for "this glorious victory," the "noblest achieve-ment of democracy," "the victory of freedom over tyranny" (to quote the self-congratulations of one of America's leading conservatives, Allan Bloom)?[2] Was it President Reagan "standing tall" to Communist aggres-sion like a cowboy gunslinger? Was it his conciliatory shift toward the onetime "evil empire" due to the advice of his wife's astrologer? Was *perestroika* an internally generated response to the bankruptcy of centrally commanded economics? Did the European peace movement, revivified during the Euromissile crisis, finally succeed in bridging East and West through "détente from below"? Did visitations of the Virgin Mary to East European peasants mobilize them to revolt against their atheistic commis-sars, answering the daily prayers of four decades of American Catholic children for the conversion of Russia? Did the TV series "Dallas," broad-cast behind the iron curtain, instill avarice in the proletarian soul, induc-ing it to throw off the chains of Communist tyranny? Or did the Sex Pistols, John Lennon, and their Soviet counterparts, Gorky Park, shatter bureaucratic routine forever with musical cacophony and eroticism?

Beyond those queries are the questions that concern us here: What now? Who shall be America's enemy in a post-Communist era?

Initial State Department wisdom insisted that the reform movement would fail and its sponsor and leading symbol, Mikhail Gorbachev, would be run out of office by party reactionaries. American leftist cynics even claimed an ability to detect in State Department and CIA position papers attempts to "sabotage" the movement: advising the United States to provide only paltry financial aid to Poland, Czechoslovakia, and Hungary, and recommending that the ante at START (Strategic Arms Limitation Talks) be escalated so as to render it impossible for the Soviets to compromise. Once liberalization was seen as irreversible, a surprising mood swept over the capital. American conservatives, normally viscerally antagonistic toward things Soviet, suddenly waxed wistful for the "good old days." "And there will be times," wrote one nostalgically, "when the old certitudes of the cold war will be sorely missed."[3] Undersecretary of State Lawrence Eagleburger agreed. "For all its risks and uncertainties," he mused, "the cold war was characterized by a remarkably stable and predictable set of relations among the great powers."[4]

The most noteworthy example of post-cold war blues is a sixteen-page essay, "The End of History?" by Francis Fukuyama, deputy director of the State Department policy-planning staff and former RAND think-tank analyst.[5] By October 1989, just months after publication, his paper had been translated into Japanese, French, Italian, Icelandic, and Dutch, with plans for its appearance in Russian. Before a year passed, commentary on it had appeared in at least twenty prominent North American periodicals,[6] and three times in the *National Review,* a biweekly conservative journal. Indeed, rumors from Washington, D.C., street vendors were that the issue of *National Interest* in which the Fukuyama piece was printed was selling faster than pornography. The author had obviously struck a sensitive nerve in the American psyche.

Invoking Hegel, Fukuyama argues that history is the protracted struggle between competing ideologies to realize the idea of freedom latent in the human spirit. Just as Hegel believed that the Napoleonic state of his time represented the highest embodiment of the Idea of Right, so Fukuyama claims that today's Western alliance "is the endpoint of mankind's ideological evolution . . . the final form of human government." But while his forebear unabashedly embraced evidence of liberal progress, Fukuyama greets the news cautiously. Now that the West has triumphed, he fears, "the future will be a very sad time" indeed, a time of "neither art nor philosophy," just obsessive consumption, and "the perpetual caretaking of the museum of history." "I can see in myself, and see in others around me," he confesses, "a powerful nostalgia for the time when history existed."[7]

In our age, the major challenges to Western ideals have been fascism and Marxist-Leninism, says Fukuyama. The first was defeated on the field of battle, the second by the so-called classless society of postindustrial capitalism. Gone, therefore, is the possibility of true heroism. Instead what looms before us is the "prospect of centuries of boredom":

> The struggle for recognition, the willingness to risk one's life for a purely abstract goal, the worldwide ideological struggle that called forth daring, courage, imagination and idealism will be replaced by economic calculation, the endless solving of technical problems, environmental concerns and the satisfaction of sophisticated consumer demands.[8]

Fukuyama acknowledges the likelihood of international disputes persisting between the "historical" and "nonhistorical" (third) world, and of the continuation of terrorist spats instigated by ethnic minorities such as the Azeris, Kurds, Sikhs, and Palestinians. But global scale conflict will soon be a dim memory.

Given his predilection for ideology, Fukuyama's evident scotoma to an idea that has long animated political communities – since well before Western liberalism was ever thought of – is shocking. I refer to an idea transcending ethnic and racial mythologies, political and economic doctrines, and even religious confessions: the idea of the Enemy. The Enemy has everywhere and always drawn men into communion and sated their appetite for cosmic significance. There is therefore no good reason, and even less evidence, to expect its disappearance any time soon, especially its disappearance from the West. To see why this is so requires a brief excursus in sociological theory.

Sociological Propositions

Proposition One

Peace in an in-group is correlative with hostility toward an out-group. As individuals develop self-consciousness in strife with others (notably their own parents), so groups of individuals in conflict with other groups achieve unity and group consciousness and become fighting groups – parties, sects, and nations.[9] As Georg Simmel says, "aggression, much more than peaceful enterprises, tends to solicit the cooperation of the largest number of elements which would otherwise remain scattered . . . , for people engaged in peaceful pursuits limit their actions to friends. During conflict, however, one cannot be choosey about allies."[10] In the more picturesque language of nineteenth-century political romantic Heinrich von Treitschke, "nothing unites a nation more closely than war. It makes it worthy of the name *Nation* as nothing else can."[11] For "war, with all its brutality and sternness, weaves a bond of love between man and man, linking them together to face death, and causing all class distinctions to disappear."[12]

This is not to say that conflict is the sole or even the most reliable vehicle of group solidarity. Sociologists (including Simmel) have long appreciated that people can also be integrated by indoctrination into a common culture, by mutual dependencies growing from their differences in the division of labor (a paradoxical truth emphasized by Émile Durkheim), by the legal compulsion of an outside party like the state, or by all of these together. This, however, does not gainsay the importance of enemies for social order, particularly for pluralistic, multinational societies like America or, more pointedly, like the late Yugoslavia or Soviet Union. In the latter cases, the absence of a common foe coupled with loss of centralized command resulted in rapid social disintegration, even though their respective populations were economically interdependent and presumably socialized into Communist values and doctrine. The situation in America is analogous if far from identical.

In America, the legend of the melting pot notwithstanding, the issue of shared culture has always been somewhat problematic; millions remain alienated from the national economy; and the right of the state to compel citizen compliance has been perennially disputed and hence limited since its founding. What this suggests is that if the United States is to maintain its national integrity (the other factors just cited held constant), it *will* generate novel enemies to take the place of those now obsolete. Indeed, according to some authorities, officials have been "scurrying about trying to redefine the enemy threat, as Communism recedes into the horizon."[13] "As old enemies are transformed, new enemies float into view."[14] Again the words of Simmel may be taken as prophetic: "Within certain groups, it may even be a piece of political wisdom to see to it that there be some enemies in order for the unity of the members to remain effective and for the group to remain conscious of this unity as its vital interest."[15]

It was with this in mind that the Pentagon in 1988 set about rethinking its role in the post–cold war era. By the summer of 1990 each military service had published its analysis of the emerging national security risks. Not surprisingly, each drew gloomy predictions about the future. General A. M. Gray, commandant of the Marine Corps, for example, wrote that "the underdeveloped world's growing dissatisfaction over the gap between rich and poor nations . . . could result in instability and conflict," creating even more extensive military requirements than had existed during the cold war. The United States, he insisted, must maintain "a credible military power projection capability with the flexibility to respond to conflict across the spectrum of violence throughout the world." This requires "mobile and versatile forces" in high states of readiness for "raids, security operations, limited-objective operations, mobile-training team employment, show-of-force operations . . . , psychological warfare, deception operations, . . . and in-extremis hostage rescue operations." The reports issued by the U.S. Army, "A Strategic Force for the 1990s and Beyond," and the Air Force, in its "Global Reach – Global Power," concurred with this.[16] We will touch on these assessments later.

Proposition Two

To fully comprehend a people's enemies, one must first grasp how they see themselves. For enemies in effect serve as receptacles of the protagonists' own unassimilated garbage, what they cannot or will not acknowledge about themselves. Scholarly consensus holds that a major strand in the American "cultural carpet," to borrow an image from Arthur M. Schlesinger, Jr., is the idea of manifest destiny. From John Winthrop's address to the Massachusetts Bay Colony that they were going to be "a City upon a Hill," a New Jerusalem, to the words of President Reagan nearly four centuries later – "this anointed land was set apart in an uncommon way. . . . [and] a divine plan placed this great continent here between the oceans to be found by people from every corner of the earth who had a special love of faith and freedom"[17] – the following theme has been reiterated in theological and secular form: America is a "redeemer nation," like Israel an "elect people," specially chosen by the Lord to "illuminate the unregenerate" and "emancipate the slavish," "a guardian of freedom," "a beacon of liberty to all lands," "the great nation of futurity."

As expressed in the Book of Mormon, the New World was settled by a remnant of Judah. America's Founding Fathers who created its sacred compact, the Constitution, have since been "grafted into" and adopted by this holy tribe. Providence has allotted to their descendants an entire hemisphere as their Promised Land. The "floor" of our national temple "shall be a hemisphere – its roof the firmament of the star-studded heavens, and its congregation an Union of many Republics, comprising hundreds of happy millions, . . . governed by God's natural and moral law of equality, the law of brotherhood – of 'peace and good will amongst men.' "[18]

Given this ruling legend, it is natural for America's historical enemies to assume the attributes of the ancient Canaanites, that they be accused of worshipping golden calves and of prostrating themselves before idols, that they scandalize the Sinai Decalogue by participating in nocturnal orgies and by ingesting nonkosher foods and intoxicants, that they constitute an alien people racially, as reflected by the non-Teutonic, non-Anglo Saxon cast of skin and eyes.

To be sure, nationalistic righteousness is not the only motif in American political culture. Schlesinger, for one, points out a countertheme, also evident in biblical prophecy, of a sense of man's fundamental unredeemability and the inevitability of corruption and social decline. Some historians believe that it was this unflattering concept of human nature that induced the writers of the Constitution to build into it the various checks and balances that so far have protected American citizens from their own worst instincts.

Nor am I saying that xenophobia is either an American invention or monopoly. It can be argued with considerable conviction that because of its constitutionally decreed corrective mechanisms, American style nationalism has been one of the more benign species of collective presumption to appear on the world's stage.

Proposition Three

Enemies promote in-group cohesion, but groups locate enemies in different places over time. This is the third sociological proposition. Rational groups pursue policies of external aggression only when, among other things, their own internal divisions are temporarily mollified. (Among the "other things" are the relative weakness and vulnerability of neighbors.) Failure to honor this principle risks aggravating in-group scissures, threatening the group's integrity.[19] Corollary to this is that periods of diplomatic and military expansion are typically associated with domestic reformism, during which potential internal enemies are asssimilated into the national community. Periods of foreign isolation, on the other hand, are generally characterized by the resurrection and excision of domestic enemies.

This corollary merely associates two variables; it does not prioritize them causally. Social reforms inculcating domestic harmony, for example, may precede foreign adventurism, the latter of which may be presented as a missionary effort to extend the joys of liberality to foreigners. Or wars may come before domestic reforms, which are then undertaken post facto to quell internal dissent. Likewise, withdrawal from foreign entanglements may afford an opportunity for people to focus hostility onto fellow citizens; or once having identified fellow citizens as enemies, attention is thereby distracted from foreign affairs.

American political history illustrates this proposition and its corollaries. In doing so it displays an irregular cyclical pattern, alternating between moments of domestic repression coupled with foreign isolation, and moments of liberalization conjoined with foreign aggression.[20]

Enemies in American History

Rightist Resurgences and Domestic Enemies

In the first moment of the American enemy cycle – let us call it rightist resurgence – American social concern focuses on private moral issues: sexuality, hygiene and diet, the family, religion.[21] Social problem solutions are typified in individual terms, as ameliorable by means of adjustive therapies, religious penance, or criminal punishment. Economic and political affairs are privatized, enlightened self-interest is celebrated as the motor of social progress, there are calls to deregulate the manufacture and distribution of goods. Public services, such as they are, come to be seen as vehicles of private advancement, with the inevitable consequence of corruption.

As seen in Table 6.1, there appear to have been six distinct moments of rightist privatization in American history, and one other of rather mixed character. The first lasted from about 1783, during which the Federalist Party composed a Constitution to dampen the "democratic excesses" of

Table 6.1

Left- and Right-Wing Movements in American History

Fifteen-Year Intervals	Major American Wars	Major Domestic Movements
1992		
	Latin America, Middle East	New Christian Right
1977		
	Vietnam War	New Frontier, Great Society
1962		
	Korean War	McCarthyism
1947		
	World War II	New Deal, Fair Deal
1932		
	Nicaraguan police action	Normalcy
1917		
	World War I	New Nationalism, New Freedom
1902		
	Spanish-American War	Nativist Populism
1887		
	Indian Wars	Reconstructionism
1872		
	Civil War	Abolitionism
1857		
	Mexican War	Democratic Expansionism
1842		
	Indian Wars	Nativist Populism
1827		
	War of 1812	
1812		
	War with Tripoli	Jeffersonian Democracy
1797		
	Ohio Indian War	Federalism
1783		
	Revolutionary War	Democratic Confederation
1767		

the propertyless common folk, to 1800, when Jeffersonian Republicans inaugurated a twenty-five-year period of liberal government. The latest has been the ascendancy of the New Christian Right, which in 1980 swept into office the most conservative president in over half a century and a body of congressmen happy to do his bidding. The mixed period consists of the years immediately preceding and during the Civil War (1850–66). More will be said about this below. During these six periods, American civic hostility, with one exception, has been deflected from foreigners onto either its own citizenry, its native aborigines, or its Pan American neighbors. The one exception is the Korean War.

Momentarily ignoring the Native Americans and their Central American cousins, we note that America's internal enemies have gone by different titles: Freemasons, papists, "un-Americans" (meaning darker-skinned immigrants from Eastern Europe, the Mediterranean, the Orient, or the Hispanic Southwest), Mormons, Communists, Jews, liberals, and "niggers." Whatever their names, and these are the least vulgar, they are all associated symbolically with moral dissolution, with compromising the free play of market forces, or with contravening the country's sacred compact, the Constitution. These transgressions are documented in a "library of infamy," one stack of which was described in chapter 5. Included in its titles: *Maria Monk and Her Revelation of Convent Crimes; Communism, Hypnotism and the Beatles: Analysis of Communist Uses of Music; Mormonism: Shadow or Reality; Martin Luther King: His Dream – Our Nightmare; Death Penalty for Homosexuals*, and so forth. The paradigmatic sourcebook for many of these is *Proofs of a Conspiracy Against All the Religions and Governments of Europe, Carried on in the Secret Meetings of Free Masons, Illuminati and Reading Societies* (1797).

Originally cited by the Federalists in their successful battle against democratic reformism, *Proofs of a Conspiracy* identifies the enemy as the Illuminati (Illuminati = bringers of light = Lucifer, the devil). As we noted in chapter 5, there was in fact a semisecret order by this name established by a Bavarian anti-Jesuit Mason named Adam Weishaupt in 1776 to proselytize Enlightenment ideas. However, *Proofs of a Conspiracy* embellishes this reality with an elaborate fantasy: The Illuminati mean to promote sensual pleasure by means of sinister intoxicants and unspeakable sexual crimes, to abjure Christianity, and to sever the bonds of family life. The Illuminati are the satanic consorters behind the French Jacobins, their Declaration of the Rights of Man, and the American and French revolutions.

In subsequent formulations, Weishaupt, "the monster" as he is today called by American right-wingers, has transmogrified into a Jesuit priest and advocate of "popery"; his order is linked variously to the Jewish High Council, the Rothschild banking family, the fourteenth-century

Knights Templars, and the "Jewish sociologist" Karl Marx. The European street riots of 1848 and the Russian Bolsheviks alike are said to have been products of Illuminati machinations.

Over time, the conspiracy has assumed an ever more frightening aspect as indicated by its name changes: the Hidden Hand, the Invisible Empire, Force X, the Insiders, the Order. Virtually omnipotent, its members are said to be sworn to secrecy by self-condemnatory oaths, and to identify one another by code names and ritual handshakes. Allegedly, it includes in its hierarchy not only "sodomite homosexuals," "seed of Satan Jews," and "negro beasts," but also nuns and priests who cavort at night and then murder the fetal products of their diabolic unions. Beyond this, membership in the conspiracy may be suspected of anyone in the community, not just liberals who support the civil rights of "so-called minorities," but the very persons one would least suspect of treason: teachers, businessmen, professionals, even the United States president himself. George Bush is said to be a member of the Order, his connection with the conspiracy proven by his undergraduate Yale membership in the Skull and Bones Club, his public references to the emerging New World Order, and his friendship with one-time Soviet leaders. Franklin D. "Rosenfeld" was a "closet Jew," Dwight D. Eisenhower "a conscious agent of the Communist conspiracy."

Thus, eradicating the conspiracy requires the kinds of drastic actions depicted in chapter 7 (see Table 6.2 for examples). Each period of rightwing resurgence therefore culminates in legal repression of minority viewpoints, investigations of "un-American" activities, prohibitions on "un-American" intoxicants – those associated in popular imagery with minority groups: alcohol (Irish Catholics), marijuana (blacks and Hispanics), peyote (Indians) – censorship of "un-American" dress, hairstyles, and music (rock 'n' roll and jazz), loyalty oaths, and racial immigration quotas. Typically, times of rightist extremism are also accompanied by upsurges of vigilante citizen "justice," lynchings, assassinations, politically motivated assaults, and arson.

Past moments of American rightist extremity have been led by evangelical Protestant ministers (Jedidiah Morse, Rev. Samuel D. Burchard, Billy Sunday, G. L. K. Smith, Fred Schwarz, Pat Robertson). As Catholicism and Mormonism assimilated themselves into the larger culture, Catholic priests and Mormon elders have assumed positions as

Table 6.2

Major Domestic Movements, Representative Groups, and Social Programs*

Major Domestic Movements (Rightist Movements in Boldface)	Representative Groups	Social Programs
New Christian Right	Moral Majority	Drug War, Immigration Control Act
New Frontier, Great Society	Southern Christian Leadership Conference	Civil rights laws
McCarthyism	John Birch Society	McCarran Internal Security Act
New Deal, Fair Deal	AFL-CIO (unions)	Social Security Act, Wagner Act (legalizing unionization)
Normalcy	Ku Klux Klan	Immigration Act, Prohibition Amendment
New Nationalism, New Freedom	Progresssive Movement	Clayton Antitrust Act, regulatory agencies
Nativist Populism	American Protective Association	Local black codes, Asian exclusion laws
Reconstructionism	Republican Radicals	Freedman's Bureau, Homestead Act, and 14th, 15th, 16th Amendments
Abolitionism	Abolitionists	Civil War
Democratic Expansionism	Free Soil Party	Slave trade abolished in Washington, D.C., land purchases
Nativist Populism	Anti-Masonic Party, American Party	Force Bill abolishing Nullification Act
Jeffersonian Democracy	Republican Party	Universal male suffrage, flogging abolished, repeal of Alien and Sedition Acts
Federalism	Anti-Illuminatism	Alien and Sedition Acts, Alien Enemies Act
Democratic Confederation	Correspondence Societies	Articles of Confederation

*For approximate years, see Table 6.1.

movement leaders: Father Charles Coughlin, Bishop Fulton J. Sheen, Cardinal Francis Spellman, Cleon Skousen, Ezra Taft Benson.

Sometimes the resurgences have developed into full-fledged political organizations, sponsoring annual conventions and nominating candidates for elective office: the American Party, the Anti-Masonic Party, the People's Party, the Prohibition Party. More commonly and ironically, their organizational structures come to mimic those of their foes. They become secret societies in their own right – the Know Nothings, the Ku Klux Klan, the Order of the Star Spangled Banner, the Minutemen, or most recently, the *Bruders Schweigen* (Secret Brotherhood) – with their own cryptic handshakes, initiation rites, hooded raiment, passwords, and oaths. Although these groups rage furiously for a decade or so, when their programs are not accepted into the platforms of established political parties they invariably retreat into the recesses of the American psyche amid rumors of financial and sexual shenanigans and accusations of violence. They reappear some time later with new names, cleansed images and leadership, and a new domestic enemy.

Leftist Reformism and the Foreign Foe

American political history is hardly all domestic scapegoating. Interspersed with moments of rightist extremity are outbursts of sincere democratic enthusiasm, when social concern shifts from privatism to the public domain. In the oft-quoted words of John F. Kennedy, who instinctively sensed a popular renunciation of privatist politics in the early 1960s, it is at such times when Americans ask not what their country can do for them, but what they can do for their country.

During such periods, prying eyes are loosed from bedroom, kitchen, and studio, which become arenas of experimentation and innovation. Cults proliferate, marriages "open," popular imagination is "sociologized," and social problems are attributed to the political-economic structure of society. Instead of dealing with deviation by militarizing the obdurate wills of citizens through therapy, prayer, or imprisonment, thought turns instead to establishing new regulatory agencies, to democratizing government routine, and to ending secrecy and making policy decisions accountable to publics. Indictments for malfeasance decline in number.

Table 6.1 reveals six bona fide periods of liberal reform in American history, beginning with the postrevolutionary Jeffersonian Democracy,

Table 6.3

Major American Wars

War	Battle Deaths	Total Deaths	Total Costs in 1967 Dollars (millions)
Revolutionary War (1775–83)	Unknown	25,300	400–680
Ohio Indian War (1790–94)	895	Unknown	Unknown
War with Tripoli (1801–5)	46	Unknown	Unknown
War of 1812 (1812–15)	Unknown	6,800	170
Indian Wars (1827–33)	44	Unknown	Unknown
Seminole War (1834–42)	Unknown	1,500	76
Mexican War (1846–48)	Unknown	13,300	300
Civil War (1861–65)	140,000[a]	370,000[a]	8,500
Indian Wars (1866–91)	950	2,500[b]	Unknown
Spanish-American War (1898)	385	5,500	Unknown
World War I (1917–18)	53,400	116,500	100,000
World War II (1941–45)	291,000	405,400	816,300
Korean War (1950–53)	33,600	54,200	69,300
Vietnam War (1965–73)	47,000	60,400	148,000
Post-Vietnam police actions (1980–90)	400[c]	Unknown	Unknown
Iraqi War (1991)	141	253	60,000

[a]Union deaths only.
[b]Estimated by multiplying battle deaths by the ratio of Civil War total deaths to battle deaths (i.e., 2.6).
[c]Includes El Salvador, 5; Iran and Lebanon (1988), 244; Grenada (1983), 18; Panama (1989–90), 50.

the first action of which was to revoke Federalism's Alien and Sedition Acts. The latest was the New Frontier and Great Society era of John Kennedy and Lyndon Johnson. These periods have also generally been times when America's public enemies have been foreign.

At first glance there appears to be little correlation between swings in the domestic political cycle and foreign policy postures. The numbers of wars are essentially equal in periods of rightism and liberalization.[22] As Table 6.3 demonstrates, however, two-thirds of America's nine bloodiest engagements, as measured by the total number of deaths and the financial costs, have been fought during times of democratic fervor. (It should also be noted that until the twentieth century, far more war-related casualties were due to disease and starvation than to battle wounds.) The three exceptions are the Spanish-American, Civil, and Korean wars.

The Spanish-American War reflected in part traditional nativist bigotry in the United States against darker-skinned, alien-tongued, Roman Catholic (hence inferior) peoples. In this respect it parallels the antipapist riots and lynchings of Italians taking place in the 1890s. Secretary of the Navy Theodore Roosevelt's contempt for the "backward Latinos," who suffered firsthand the broadsides of his Great White Fleet, has been amply documented.[23] But the war was also viewed popularly as a selfless effort by a freedom-loving folk (us) to rescue the less fortunate from the snares of European despotism. It may therefore be interpreted as an initial phase of a wave of democratic ardor – today called Progressivism – that would sweep across the continent in 1900 and prevail until the end of World War I.

Progressive ideologues like Herbert Croly explicitly equated the fight for federal meat inspection, control of the railroads, and the eight-hour workday with a mission to spread by force the blessings of democracy overseas.[24] Progressive senators, not conservatives, advocated a peacetime draft, voted for ever larger naval appropriations, and vociferously supported increasingly frequent military incursions into Latin America and the Caribbean. The Progressive Party until 1916 hounded President Woodrow Wilson's "weak-kneed wishy-washiness" during the European crisis and then lauded him for finally deploying an expeditionary force to "save the world for democracy." Far from confuting our theory, then, the Spanish-American War, like World War I, seems to support it.

The Civil War, America's most devastating conflict, can be partly understood as still another of our periodic evangelically inspired fixations on internal enemies. Thus it, too, can be accommodated by our cyclical hypothesis. The sectional dispute between North and South, between slavery and emancipation, was also a battle between God and Satan. According to Seymour Martin Lipset, "in a real sense, it may be argued that the fact that evangelical moralism characterized American religion was causally related to the fact that we required a Civil War to eliminate slavery."[25]

Far from being liberal reformers, as they are sentimentally portrayed in modern legend, the abolitionists were strongly opposed to democratic legislation that would have extended political rights to the propertyless. Furthermore, if William Lloyd Garrison and Rev. Charles G.

Finney can be taken as typical, their rectitude was scandalized as much by Catholic rum and Jewish wine as it was by involuntary servitude. Indeed, many Louisiana slaveholders were Roman Catholic, and slavery was considered by some abolitionists a "Romanish" institution. This was further demonstrated by the role played by Catholic clergy in the peace and draft resistance movements in Boston and New York, and by their advocacy of gradual, nonviolent emancipation instead of war. Says Stanley Elkins in his own book on slavery:

> The simple and harsh moral purity of our own antislavery movement . . . gave it a quality which set it apart from the others. . . . Every phase of the movement combined to produce in our abolitionists that peculiar quality of abstraction which was, and has remained, uniquely American. For them, the question was *all* moral.[26]

With the exception of the Korean War, all of America's military involvements during periods of what I have entitled rightist resurgence have either been scuffles in America's traditional zone of imperial interest as enunciated in the Monroe Doctrine (1823) or campaigns against Native Americans. For local affairs, the Indian campaigns can still shock modern sensibilities with their brutality. The casualty lists for the Battle of the Little Bighorn, for example, and St. Clair's massacre comprise entire regiments. Nevertheless, even when summed they do not begin to approach the costs of America's major wars. For this reason they are not customarily counted as wars in government statistical abstracts. Indeed, historians admit that the title "war" more than once was used rhetorically by politicians of the time to further their own ambitions. Like the Blackhawk "War," they were undertaken by ragtag neighborhood militia against an already broken, starving race.[27]

Much the same can be said of America's armed spats in Latin America and the Caribbean. To use the description of the encounter with Spain in Cuba, these have been "splendid little wars." Like Ronald Reagan's weekend foray into Grenada (1983) or George Bush's into Panama (1989), they appear in retrospect as petulant, reactionary, bullying gestures involving little risk to American troops, purposively staged for dramatic effect, and in some cases provoked beforehand by American agents.

Causes

My intention has not been to demonstrate that American political history is a mechanical process. There are too many events that do not quite square with the neat pattern described above. The Korean War is the most telling anomaly, but there are others as well: the electoral popularity of racial segregationist George Wallace and his American Independent Party in 1968 at the very height of the Great Society, the widespread endorsement of anti-Semite Father Coughlin during the New Deal 1930s, the social reforms and utopian communalism of Robert Owen, George Rapp, and Dorothea Dix during the years of anti-Masonic, anti-Irish hysteria. In short, America has never been without proponents of either rightist or leftist politics.[28] Nevertheless, it is unassailable that there have been moments in American history when one or the other of these ideological orientations has prevailed, seizing the public imagination, dominating political discourse, and rendering certain types of enemies available to the collective consciousness. The precession of these moments, furthermore, follows a somewhat irregular thirty-year pattern. Granted this, it may be worthwhile to search for the causes of the cycle in its own dynamics. While foreign events and domestic crises might temper its crests and variously affect its amplitude, the cycle itself can be considered self-generating. What, then, might be its causes?

To begin with, there seems to be no discernible relationship between American business cycles and political moods.[29] Rightist resurgences have occurred during times of recession (for example, the American Protective Association, which grew to at least two million members during the depression of 1893–94) or, more frequently, during times of prosperity (the McCarthy era of the early 1950s). This is equally true for periods of democratization and foreign saber rattling. According to Schlesinger, a major clue to the cycle's "mainspring," as he calls it, can be found in the approximate length of its waves, thirty years. This is the average life span of a modern political generation.

Schlesinger believes that as each political era runs its course, it "breeds" an appetite in those coming to political maturity for fundamental policy change. In other words, political success produces satiation and boredom; fatigue replaces enthusiasm; and the inevitable disappointments of failed programs produce hostility and dissent. The rising generation seizes power, implements its own outlook, only to eventually suffer the same fate as its predecessor.

At any point in American history there are three pivotal generations: the first is currently in power; the second is waiting in the wings; and the third, children of the first, are being inculcated with the political ideals and legends of their forebears. The first generation rules for approximately fifteen years, focusing on the foreign or domestic enemy that provides it, by negation, with that generation's identity as "good Americans": niggers, fags, papists, spics, commies, nips, nazis, huns, satanists, or dope-crazed sex fiends, all drawn from the storehouse of American demonology. But since this enemy is partly (if never entirely) a product of hysterical collective projection, the proposals to defeat it are doomed to fail, disillusioning the younger generation. The rhetoric of the elders comes to be seen by the second generation as banal and hollow; they are rebuked for being, as it is said, "part of the problem." They must, it is agreed, be replaced, and are replaced for a decade and a half by "men of vision," who claim insight into the country's "real" problems. Meanwhile, the offspring of the first generation, coming of age, begin reciting publicly the myths of evildoers first heard at the feet of their now-deposed fathers. They snipe at the willful and irresponsible leaders they now see in power. This political dance produces the modulations in American foreign and domestic policy occurring like rough clockwork every third decade.

Some technical comments on the concept of "generation" as used here should be given. As Karl Mannheim has shown, one's generational identity is theoretically analogous to one's social class identity.[30] That is to say, just as shared income level is never sufficient for class formation, so too "mere chronological contemporaneity" is never decisive in constituting a generation. The crucial generational-forming factor is a common historical experience that "colors" the politics of a very broad age cohort (but not all individuals in that cohort) into adulthood.

While the idea of generational precession has seen little use by American sociologists, Mannheim for one insists that it can fruitfully account for political change in all modern societies. As early as 1924, Arthur M. Schlesinger, Sr., was invoking a thirty-three-year generational standard to successfully forecast that the hooded racism, bigotry, and foreign isolationism of the Roaring Twenties would give way by 1932 to democratic enthusiasm and foreign interventionism. In the same article he correctly predicted that by 1947 a new outbreak of rightist provincialism would again sweep across the country. As predicted, 1947 was the year President Harry Truman introduced to Congress his loyalty program, requiring background investigations of all government employees for potential subversiveness. Looking back on American history four decades later, Schlesinger used the same formula to explain the failure of Barry Goldwater's presidential ambitions in 1964, "since not twenty or thirty years, but only ten had elapsed from the last eruption," the McCarthy witch-hunt of 1954. From his new perch he forecast that the forthcoming heady atmosphere of President Johnson's Great Society would be replaced in the late 1970s by something akin to the grim, gray days of McCarthy.[31]

Schlesinger died before he saw his prediction confirmed. There is no little irony in the fact that the leader of the movement that fulfilled it, Ronald Reagan, was just coming to political age when he gave the speech nominating the ill-fortuned Goldwater for presidential candidacy. Just prior to this Reagan earned his political spurs by denouncing his colleagues for Communist sympathies from his position as head of the Screen Actors Guild in Hollywood. It was Reagan's oration that convinced ten California activists to commit a fortune each to bankroll Reagan's future career as spokesman and spear-carrier for what we now know as the New Christian Right. The rest is history.

Conclusion

Predictive success constitutes presumption in favor of a theory. The generational theory of American enemies thus enjoys some confidence. If so, what does the future hold? To return to the question posed at the beginning of this chapter: who is to be America's enemy in a post-Communist era?

It is important to state at the outset that predictions about human affairs are not assertions of fate or destiny. As Robert Merton once wrote, a sociological forecast is "reflexive" in that it can "enter into the situation as a *new and dynamic* factor changing the very conditions under which the prediction initially held true."[32] This means the prediction can be either self-fulfilling (as when a pessimistic economic forecast precipitates a bank run), or it can be self-defeating (as when a forecast of environmental catastrophe induces behavior intended to avert its fulfillment). Regarding the subject at hand, this author would be content to have his theory disproved.

Second, the following discussion should be read not so much as a set of predictions in the strict scientific sense of that word, but as worst case scenarios, possible eventualities given the most pessimistic assumptions about Americans. It is entirely possible that these assumptions are not justified, but are merely subjective biases.

Assuming the New Christian Right took up the reins of power around 1976–80, then using a fifteen-year generational standard, its demise should be evident at least by the middle 1990s, if not earlier. Already by 1988 cracks in the rightist vanguard were being noted by commentators. Its ideology was being spoken of as "exhausted"; indictments for corruption in the Reagan administration were approaching record numbers; prosecutions of racist terrorist groups and abortion clinic incendiaries were being vigorously pursued. Within a year the Iran-Contra arms trading scandal would be conjuring popular images of bunker fascism, and the evangelical leaders of the movement would be exposed as the very procurers, child abusers, homosexuals, and embezzlers they had accused their enemies of being.[33] At this writing, the anti-Communist banner with which the modern right wing has so effusively wrapped itself is unraveling. In short, the American right wing today is undergoing travails uncannily similar to those of the resurgences of the 1950s, the 1920s, and 1890s.

Taking the middle 1990s as a convenient if not hard and fast date, a program of domestic liberalization may be anticipated, possibly focusing on the environment or on the scandalously inequitable delivery of health care and housing to America's poor minority population. More to the point, in its search for enemies America should begin turning outward. At this writing several candidates to play the role of foil in armed crusades to "illuminate the unregenerate" and "emancipate the slavish" are being auditioned: Japan, the emerging Slavic empire, the Islamic Middle East, and Latin America.

Japan is popularly alleged to have engaged in unfair trading practices, using its capital to "buy up" American real estate, particularly in Hawaii and California, threatening to turn America into a de facto "third world colony." Add to this Japan's racial peculiarity, the fact that it is now a ranking world power, its barely veiled scorn for liberal values and Americanism (expressed in the popular Japanese word *kenbei*, "dislike of the United States"),[34] and the product is potentially explosive. "The current drift in United States-Japanese relations," warns one commentator, "is dangerous."[35] The Japanese reluctance to risk treasure or manpower in behalf of Desert Storm in 1991 inflamed anti-Japanese passions on the

West Coast, the ugliness of which had not been equaled in half a century. The 1992 spectacle of President Bush accompanying American automakers to Japan to demand unsuccessfully that they purchase American goods seems only to have aggravated the situation.

Ethnic and religious irredentist movements, encouraged by a failed military policy in Afghanistan, Gorbachev's subsequent reforms, and the dismemberment of the Warsaw Pact, led to a failed coup by the KGB and Soviet armed forces in August 1991, precipitating the disintegration of the entire Soviet Union. However, if tradition is any basis for prediction, the continued domination of the emerging federation by the military and secret police seems likely. What this means, of course, is a return to a stand-off with the West, perhaps under the guise of anti-Western Slavic mysticism of a type that flourished in Eastern Europe in the late nineteenth century. For American cold warriors this would provide the "comforting security," referred to earlier, of a familiar enemy.[36]

Members of a new political-religious movement in America already see this approaching. Developments in the one-time Soviet Union, they insist, are leading not to an end of the cold war but to the end of the world! The American Study Group – an umbrella organization for the John Birch Society, the Eagle Forum, and the Freemen Institute – bases its belief on apocalyptic warnings in the Bible and Mormon scripture. It was appalled that President Bush contemplated providing economic aid "to an enemy who is about to destroy us," and advocates that members arm themselves against the imminent Russian strike – "small-caliber guns for game . . . and a few high-powered guns for tyrants" – and that they build "places of refuge" in the Rocky Mountains, strong enough to withstand nuclear blasts, supplied with several months' food and water.[37]

Iraq's Saddam Hussein is at this writing being defamed by American opinion leaders as "the most dangerous man of our times" for his bluff and swagger aggressiveness and evident indifference to the niceties of "civilized" (read: European style) warfare. In being so dubbed he replaces Libya's Muammar Qaddafi and Iran's Ayatollah Khomeini as America's archenemy. As it has for centuries, Islamic fanaticism can be expected to hook the projections of equally hysterical Christian and Jewish political plague-mongers, of which America is richly endowed.

Although we are too close to Desert Storm (spring 1991) to analyze its causes with any objectivity, interviews with acknowledged reliable Iraqi sources such as Tariq Aziz (one-time foreign minister) indicate the possibility that while America continued to arm Saddam until shortly before his invasion of Kuwait, Central Intelligence Agency operatives were engaged in a misinformation campaign against Iraq as early as two years before that. When at an Arab summit meeting in Amman in February 1990 Saddam publicly announced that with Moscow in decline the United States was planning to project its power into the Persian Gulf, Washington, according to Aziz, was enraged. Soon after that speech, accusations concerning the Iraqi threat to Middle Eastern security and Saddam's alleged Hitlerian tendencies began to be leaked. Aziz gives the impression of growing Iraqi fatalism regarding war with America. "The Americans," Aziz said, "had decided long before August 2nd 1990 [the day Iraq invaded Kuwait] to crush Iraq, and there was nothing his government could do to stop them."[38]

The Latin American "drug cartel" and "narco-terrorists" such as Peru's Shining Path have already displayed their usefulness to American adventurers. One need only recall the ease with which the American public was mobilized to support the 1989 invasion of Panama. General Manuel Noriega was variously slandered as a pornographer, a sodomite, a voodoo practitioner, an adulterer, a drug pusher, and a murderer. This is not surprising. A 1977 Rand Corporation study, "Military Implications of a Possible World Order Crisis in the 1980s," advocated that American officials begin shifting attention away from the East-West axis to more likely "scenarios" in the Latin-speaking third world. In the event of crises in these poor but strategically located, resource-rich countries, the United States "will be expected to use its military to prevent the total collapse of the world order." To this end Long-Term Strategy (LTS) requires the development of a "low intensity," nonconventional military capability, including electronically armed special forces, amphibious assault troops, covert assassination teams, and native mercenary "freedom fighters."[39]

It is neither possible nor desirable to be more precise than this. However, the following caveat should be kept in mind. As pointed out in the discussion of the paradox of evil in chapter 1, enemies almost always have a dualistic aspect: they are simultaneously "in here" and "out there." In this chapter, I have emphasized the subjective component of America's various past and potential enemies – that is, the fact of their being our own cultural projects. However, we must not forget (as I did before being gently reminded of my oversight by a friendly critic) that if Manuel Noriega, the Shining Path, Saddam Hussein, and the other candidates cited above are in part our own constructs, it is equally true that the depravity of at least some has rendered them available for this purpose. Evil is not just a figment of the American collective imagination; it is also an objective fact to which we have an obligation to respond. The point is to respond to outward evil in a state of what might be called "tension-wisdom," resisting it while constantly acknowledging our own culpability for it.

Part II

The Enemy Socially Deconstructed

7

A Phenomenology of the Enemy

You are a turd,
You are a heap of refuse,
You have come to kill us,
You have come to save us.[1]

One of the most powerful tools of social analysis and criticism developed in this century is known as phenomenology, originated by Edmund Husserl (1859–1938), a longtime professor of philosophy at Freiburg University in Germany. This chapter brings the insights of phenomenology to bear on the problem of enemies.

Simply said, phenomenology assumes at the outset that given human limitations we can never come to know Being itself directly. To use the vocabulary of Martin Heidegger, a onetime student of Husserl's who would later profoundly influence the phenomenological movement himself, Being itself is "unthought," "unseen," "unknown" to man. What alone is knowable is being as typically experienced, being as dispensed to man in different historical epochs. Heidegger's word for the experience of Being is *Dasein*, which literally means "being there" (*da* "there," *sein* "being"). Says Heidegger, we never confront man in the abstract, but only man "there" in a particular frame of time, space, and ideas.

An equivalent, and I believe more straightforward term, coined by Alfred Schutz (another of Husserl's students) and his colleague Thomas Luckmann, which will be employed in these pages, is "life world" (*Lebenswelt*). While renouncing the possibility of ever knowing the absolute truth about Being, phenomenology offers instead the more humble promise of enabling us to become more conscious of our life world (or that of others). It also positions us to grasp why we experience it as we do.[2]

Of the many presences in our everyday life world, one is the enemy. Phenomenology approaches the enemy by asking four questions. In this chapter each will be tackled in turn.

First, what are the experiential features of the enemy? How do enemies typically present themselves to our consciousness? Or, to use Husserl's language, what is the enemy's "eidetic essence"?

Second, how is the enemy "possible"? How are human beings rendered into evil things? We have already anticipated the answer to this in chapter 2. Here we formulate our thoughts more concisely.

Answering the first two queries helps us understand the cognitive preconditions of social violence, the conscious, calculated violation of human life, whether in the form of a single execution or the mass slaughter of millions. Furthermore, seeing how enemies are constructed prepares us theoretically to address the possibility of their *de*construction, the possibility of enemies being transcended. This brings us to questions three and four, our major interest in this chapter.

Question three concerns the possibility of eradicating altogether a sense of otherness from the world. Can our estrangement from others be eliminated? Assuming for the moment that this is unlikely, question four asks whether the other must also be attributed with the characteristics of evil. Need otherness be an enemy?

Question One: The Enemy Perceived

In his masterful volume *Faces of the Enemy,* Sam Keen presents what he calls a "phenomenology of the hostile imagination."[3] His analysis may be taken as preliminary to ours. I emphasize the word "preliminary," because for all his penetrating observations, Keen has not accomplished his goal. He writes of the enemy as criminal, as barbarian, as blasphemer, as faceless, as aggressor, stranger (*hostis*), torturer, rapist, beast, and even alludes briefly to the enemy as a necrological symbol. However, he has not ferreted out the particulars of what he calls these "enemy apparitions" to locate what it is that makes them instances of the concept "enemy" in the first place: the *eidos,* the essence, of enemyhood. In other words, he has not completed the first and foremost task of phenomenology, phenomenological reduction. In the following discussion I draw upon Keen's preliminary labors, together with other sources, including personal self-examination, to locate what I believe to be required for any thing or "apparition" to be an enemy.

Sometimes mere coincidences can be the occasion of illuminating insights. This is true of two words which have no etymological relationship but by chance are juxtaposed in English dictionaries, "enemy" and "enema." For whether embodied in thing or in person, the enemy in essence represents putrefaction and death: either its instrumentality, its location (dirt, filth, garbage, excrement), its carriers (vermin, pests, bacilli), or all of these together.[4] Northrop Frye says it this way:

> Dirt always has some psychological connection with excretion, and is linked to whatever we want to separate ourselves from. . . . People with unusually silly prejudices against social groups different from their own have a strong attachment to the word "dirty."[5]

The enemy typically is experienced as issuing from the "dregs" of society, from its lower parts, the "bowels of the underworld." It is sewage from the gutter, "trash" excreted as poison from society's affairs – church, school, workplace, and family.

The enemy's visitation on our borders is tantamount to impending pestilence. "Alien-Generated Diseases Engulf America" screams the headline of a recent right-wing newspaper, "as swarms of invading aliens occupy" the heartland. Infected with hepatitis B virus, liver parasites, salmonellosis, cholera, and tuberculosis, they seek employment as food handlers for God-fearing, middle-class Aryans.[6]

The enemy's presence in our midst is a pathology of the social organism serious enough to require the most far-reaching remedies: quarantines, political excision, or, to use a particularly revealing expression, liquidation and expulsion. As another American broadsheet says regarding the "cancer" of homosexuality: Already countless young boys have been "infected." What is therefore needed is "immediate and systematic cauterization." The "operation as projected" will not be complete until "the whole sordid situation is cleared up, and the premises thoroughly cleansed and disinfected. This is what we demand, and this is what we expect."[7]

We represent right, *Recht*, law and morality. We are righteous; we are rigid; we are, to use a term familiar to clinical psychologies of anality, "rectal." We comprise the social rectum, as it were. The enemy is what is wrong, what is left, not right, what is left behind, that which remains. What remains is waste material, the refuse of the social body, what it refuses, that which is not permitted. What is not permitted is death.

Moral campaigns purge the social body of its refuse. They represent public enemas of sorts, collective "escapes from evil," and, to borrow another title of Ernest Becker's, joint "denials of death." In the campaign's "liquidation and expulsion" of compacted putrefaction, the social body experiences every bit the relief from tension as does the good little boy for his satisfactory performance at the toilet. The proper discipline for the study of such campaigns is the sociology of colonics, a subfield of thanatology.

Social colonics properly begins in linguistic retrieval, reclaiming the association found in Greek between the communal enemy and excremental imagery. Take the word *katharma,* a variant of *pharmakon,* the designation for the sacrificial victim in the ritual of the scapegoat.[8] *Katharma* is also a foul substance whose extraction from the body purges it, cleanses it, and gives health (from *katharos* "pure"). The result of this action is said to be *katharsis,* the means by which it is produced, *kathairein.* In modern usage, of course, "catharsis" refers to the display of emotions like pity, joy, and inspiration induced by music, poetry, or dance. But anciently it referred also to the movement of the bowels by purging. This resonance still exists in the English "cathartic," a medicinal substance that relieves dyspepsia and constipation.

Another derivative term, *kathairo,* may be understood as the political procedure by which the land is expurgated of its monsters, human garbage, and healed. A clue to what originally might have been involved in this action is contained in the secondary meaning of *kathairo,* "to whip," as in the scourging of the genitals of the *pharmakon* with herbaceous plants, prior to its being paraded through the streets for execution,[9] perhaps to render it symbolically impotent.

A second task in the construction of a social colonics is to indicate how enemy excremental imagery pervades modern consciousness. In this context consider "Studies in Anality," the scandalous appendix to Norman Brown's *Life Against Death.*

Citing passages from the prose and poetry of Jonathan Swift and from Martin Luther, Brown demonstrates that as early as 1700 in European folklore there existed associations between evil, Satan, human enemies, the material world generally, and scatalogical symbols. The evidence is particularly glaring in Luther's case. Even those who righteously anoint themselves with the title "Christian," says Luther in one place, are in truth "the filth of squiredom, merd smeared on the sleeve and veritable ordure."[10] Far worse are Jews (whom Luther berates as *Schweinehunden,* swine-dogs, hence in common usage, "feces-eaters"), papists ("the filth and stench of Satan"), and merchants (who deal in "filthy lucre"). The equation between dung and human affairs in Reformation prophecy, according to Brown, is so intimate as to constitute its "psychological premise" and "central axiom." It is an equation still preached today from many fundamentalist Christian pulpits.[11]

In ancient times, says Luther, those of religious sensibility were permitted escape from the world latrine into the comforting sanctity of monastery and convent (like himself, an Augustinian monk). But now the faithful are required to resign themselves to the world. They must surrender their flesh to the devil, find worldly vocations, engage in commerce (theft), take spouses, wallow in the blood and stench of sexuality and childbirth. In doing so their fidelity to Christ will be tested severely in ways inconceivable to the world-fleeing mendicant.

Luther says little about making the world over after God's image and likeness; however, subsequent commentators like John Calvin do take up this theme directly. Says Calvin: while man can never *earn* eternal salvation by virtue of his petty efforts to cleanse the world of iniquity, the fact that he labors righteously to do so may be taken as a *sign* of his election by the Lord. This is particularly true if his labors are blessed with success. Just how is this holy work to fumigate the world of its vileness to proceed? To answer in the words Luther uses to describe his own struggles with evil: *mit einem Furz,* "with a fart."

Every political realist, including Luther and Calvin, has learned the bitter lesson. The only way to fight the devil is with his own weapons; the only effective remedy for filth is "excremental assault."[12] It is perhaps no mystery, then, why those accustomed to speaking of the Jews in explicit scatalogical terms would see fit to sanitize the fatherland (*Judenreinmachen;* literally, "make clean of the Jews") by means of a perverse anal arsenal: systematic denials of sanitary devices for defecation, regimented once-daily latrine use for all inmates including the predictable sufferers of dysentery, the requirement that one use his eating bowl for evacuation at other times, latrine duty without hand tools, torture by facial immersion in filled receptacles, and so forth.

Nor is this unique to the Germans. The English word "gook" (variant of guck) is defined in dictionaries as "a dirty, sludgy, or slimy substance." It is also used as "a disparaging term for an Asian person." Exactly how this derogatory association came to be is a matter for philological research. What is relevant for our purposes is its application to Vietnamese of *both* sides by American troops during the late war – a label befitting the verb describing the action routinely taken toward them, "to waste," or as applied to whole villages, "to wipe out."

Analogous terminology has recently appeared in American Christian Identity circles in reference to supposedly nonhuman "negroidal" and "mongoloid" species of the genus *hominid*. They are known as "mud people," people whose cast of skin reveals their filthy origin, in contrast to white-skinned Aryan "spirit folk." Policy recommendations concerning the appropriate manner of dealing with mud people – "like the dirt they are" – are found in the library of infamy cited in chapter 5.

Question Two: The Enemy Made

How, according to phenomenology, do we come to "know" other people as garbage fit for waste disposal, as excrement to be flushed into sewers? How, in other words, is the enemy cognitively "possible?" In brief, enemies come into being through what phenomenologists call empathic projection. Let us examine this process and contemplate its significance.

According to phenomenology, in the ordinary life world, knowledge of the mentality of other persons and hence of their characters (such as that knowledge is) is possible only through reflexive empathy, or what Edith Stein, another of Husserl's students, calls *Hineinversetzen*.[13] Empathy in turn is "the objectification of myself in an object distinct from myself." Technically, the knower "takes the role" of the other, imaginatively occupying the other's situation, "feeling into the meanings" the other presumably has toward the world. Again, the knower "projects" (the word is Stein's) his or her own mental life onto the other, reconstructing what the other's response would mean if the knower, similarly situated, were to exhibit it. As such, empathy rests upon the "a priori" assumption that "the mental life of other persons, at least as it is associated with their observable behavior, corresponds to our own."[14] Without this assumption, and granted that one can never literally step into another's head, "the conduct of every other person would remain nothing but a meaningless and incoherent chaos. . . ."[15]

The major implication of the phenomenological characterization of empathy is that knowledge of others is never simply a passive reception of information or an "opening up" to them on the knower's part, although most certainly the knower receives external information. It is also an active attribution, a "superimposition," to use Georg Simmel's language, of the knower's own mental traits onto these others. Hence, "whoever has never loved will never understand love or the lover. Someone with a passionate disposition will never understand someone who is apathetic. The weakling will never understand the hero, nor will the hero ever understand the weakling."[16]

The way I come to know you as an enemy/enema is a special case of reflexive empathy. In short, I objectify my own putrefaction by attributing it to you. This entails two distinct but inseperable actions: first, predicating of you excremental qualities and then responding to you according to the bestowed meaning; and second, "forgetting" my culpability in creating you as my enemy – experiencing your "filth" in a taken-for-granted way as a "natural" attribute.

The significance of the phenomenological theory of empathy for peace studies can hardly be exaggerated. For if there is anything on which all peace students agree, it is on the advisability of empathy for resolving human strife. "We must," urges one, "do everything we can to break down the psychological barrier that prevents us [the Americans and the Russians, for example] from seeing each other and ourselves as we really are."[17] Only in mutual empathy will harmony between us be possible. But what phenomenology suggests is that far from ameliorating enemy images, empathy may be the very device that accomplishes them.

Peace scholars routinely distinguish between empathy and sympathy, the first being a cognitive grasp of another, the second a consonance of feeling with them. Furthermore, it separates what is called "realistic" from "unrealistic" knowledge of others, acknowledging that realistic understandings are not equivalent to good will toward others or a justification for their behavior.[18] Phenomenologists agree that such distinctions are helpful; nevertheless, they beg the issue of how cognitive empathy is itself possible. In doing so these distinctions overlook the profound, perhaps insuperable, difficulty of ever "realistically" comprehending another person, given that such comprehension is (at least according to phenomenologists) a projection of our own mental contents onto them.

While we want to avoid drowning in a morass of technicalities, it is fair to point out that the phenomenological characterization of empathy has fallen under a barrage of criticism because of this rather bleak conclusion. For if, as phenomenologists maintain, society is an aggregate of isolated "monads without windows," to use Alfred Schutz's pithy image, each in "dialogue" with their own projections, then how is true intersubjectivity possible? On what basis can there be real social cohesion, one predicated on a true meeting of minds? Jean-Paul Sartre's answer, of course, is that for all practical purposes, social solidarity of this sort is impossible. "Society" is a nice word disguising the reality of each individual seeking to objectify the other while maintaining his own subjectivity.[19]

Psychological Projection and the Enemy

There are two basic forms of phenomenological theorizing: psychological and sociological. Both posit the working of empathic projection in the accomplishment of the enemy/enema. For example, phenomenological psychology speaks of the objectification of evil as an unconscious "negative transference" by an individual of his own alien substance onto a convenient "snag."[20] This alien substance is what the individual cannot bear to acknowledge about himself – his own carnality, filth, animality. The so-called snag is a "them" distant enough from the individual in skin color, behavior, or belief to be "hooked" by his projective cast. The activation of negative projection is suspected whenever an opponent is indicted with what are called "archetypal" crimes: murder of an authority figure (parricide or regicide) or of children; sexual abominations in nocturnal orgies involving incest, bestiality, or homosexuality; or the ingestion of tabooed food such as human flesh and forbidden intoxicants. It is no coincidence, say psychologists, that the traditional enemies of the Christian Occident – Jews, witches, and Orientals – have been accused periodically of all these depravities.

Sociological Projection and the Enemy

Phenomenological sociology also sees the objectification of evil as a product of negative transference, but mediated by group processes, not simply psychological ones. Furthermore, it is said to involve not one but a series of steps, these recited earlier in chapters 2 and 3: A problematic individual or group is classified as an instance of human refuse; the validity of the label is tested and confirmed in public hearings or tribunals conducted by experts certified in making defamatory pronouncements; legends are then woven by mythmakers to "explain" the necessity for the evil party being as it is; these legends are passed on by pedagogues, priests, and parents as ontological truths, and received by an audience which, not present during the initial steps, is unable to fathom the fabricated nature of the evil; finally, the truth of the myth is recognized (re-known) through its ritual dramatization in armed engagements, domestic and foreign, against the evil object.

Question Three: The Necessity of Otherness

If, as phenomenology supposes, my knowledge of you is predicated in part on knowledge of my own mental contents (for it is these that are heaped upon you), it is equally true that my knowledge of myself presupposes my knowledge of you.

To be sure, there is a sense in which I comprehend myself more accurately than I do you. But in the ordinary life world I know myself only inferentially, not directly – primarily through your response to me. In other words, my musings about myself are occasioned by the attitude I imagine you to have toward me.[21] This is the basis of the celebrated sociologist Charles Horton Cooley's theory of the "looking glass self," that others serve as mirrors of sorts in whose reflections we experience either self-mortification or pride.[22] It is also expressed in Sartre's independently developed notion that "Hell is the others." Because, he says, my self-concept is utterly dependent on your capricious reply to me, then you are positioned to torture me more exquisitely than any pincher-armed devil. And yet if I remove myself from your presence, I begin to doubt my own substantiality.[23]

The upshot of this is that a sense of otherness is definitely required for self-identity, according to phenomenology. Just as one cannot know what "large" means without a standard of smallness, or blackness without white, one cannot comprehend himself in his individuality if he does not know simultaneously who and what he is not. In particular, one cannot experience himself as righteous in all the significance of this word, without an unrighteous alter ego against whom to compare himself. And this is exactly the wondrous, if unconscious, outcome of the objectification of evil. The casting out of evil onto you not only renders you my enemy; it also accomplishes my own innocence. To paraphrase the quotation from Nietzsche at the beginning of chapter 2: In manufacturing an evil one against whom to battle heroically, I fabricate a good one, myself.

It is for this reason that René Girard can say of the rite of the scapegoat, whether enacted in the privacy of the household or in the public square, that it constitutes the nominizing gesture par excellence, the very basis of both psychological and social order. Just as one cannot mature psychologically into a functional adult without disengaging from and then fighting against the parent, there can be no cultural themes, no cultural values, without *ana-thema,* or countervalues. In forcibly "liquidating and expulsing" the enemy/enema from their midst, the group which recruits it and prepares it for sacrifice undergoes catharsis. It is reintegrated in its purity. The enemy is the universal Athenian *pharmakon,* the deadly poison whose destruction serves as antidote to society's ills.[24]

Question Four: The Enemy Unmade

As pivotal as alterity is for my sense of self, must alter also be my enemy? As necessary as projection is to my coming to understand you, must these projections invariably be negative? These two questions bring us to the heart of phenomenology's treatment of the enemy.

Regarding the first, I cite Schutz and Luckmann's phenomenological description of the ordinary life world: Our life world presents itself to consciousness, they say, as "a coherency of objects with definite characteristics." The operative word here is "object," a derivation from the Latin *objectum* – that thrown in the way of (hence available to the senses), an obstacle, a hindrance. By definition a world constituted of objects, including alter as one among them, is in "opposition" to me, the knowing subject. It therefore follows that the orientation proper in such a world is militancy, combatancy, or to use Schutz's softer term, "pragmatism." I relate to the objective life world, Schutz tells us, as I would to an opponent in a zero-sum game; either I defeat it, or it me. The life world "is something to be mastered according to my particular interests. I project my own plans into the life world, and it resists the realization of my goals."[25] More emphatically, "in order to realize our goals, we must master and transform the life world . . . , for these objects offer to our actions a resistance which we must either subdue or to which we must yield."[26]

If this is true – and given the full meaning of "object" it *must* be true – then the possibility of complete and final reconciliation between subject and object, between me and you, must, according to phenomenology, be dismissed as a utopian dream. This is the source of Sartre's pessimism regarding the possibility of authentic social solidarity alluded to under question two above. It is also the starting point for the post-phenomenological revolt against phenomenology's supposed ethical futility. Instead of addressing this critique, however, here we consider how phenomenology argues its way out of this quandary.

We begin by asking if it follows that because you, alter, are my object and opponent, you must also be my enemy. Must you be garbage fit only for the sewer? That it does not, should be clear from the following comments.

As stated above, from the standpoint of phenomenology the enemy is a product of negative transference. The enemy is the repository for that which I refuse, my "refuse." This being so, the theoretical possibility exists that persons who have fully digested and assimilated their own garbage might inhabit a world without enemies. For having come to acknowledge and embrace their own filth, they have no need to transfer it to some external thing. This is the position adopted by Sam Keen in *Faces of the Enemy*, his "philosophical-theological-attitudinal breakthrough": "how we may reclaim the shadow we have projected onto the enemy."[27]

These hypothetical enlightened ones, of course, would continue to reside in a world of objects. This, according to phenomenology, is unavoidable. As such, strife is the inevitable price of our life together. However, alter need not devolve into a fully constituted enemy/enema, resonating excrement. This is no small gain: while *opponents* in disputes can be rationally and temperately engaged, the enemy/enema is best flushed into oblivion.

But is enlightenment realistically possible? Is consciousness of the fearsome mystery of our own putrefaction, and what it amounts to – our own mortality – really achievable? More immediately, can the project of self-reconciliation be reasonably recommended? Or does confrontation with the ultimate enemy, death, risk its glorification?

Nazism ostensibly affirmed death, believing it the source of greater, richer life. Indeed, Ernest Becker once called Nazism a "death potlatch,"[28] a perverse cult overseen by SS "death-head units" (*Totenkopfformationen*). It is therefore with considerable unease that we contemplate Heidegger's assertion that death is man's fundamental essence, and that "authentic being in the world" requires an "impassioned" embrace of death, what he calls "freedom towards death."[29] Careful scholarship now confirms what has long been suspected, that Heidegger was an unrepentent intellectual leader of the Nazi SA (*Sturmabteilung*).[30] He evidently saw in Nazism the "heroic" sublimation of pleasure-seeking – natural to ordinary men – to duty toward Being (*Sein*), which for him was nothingness. This example illustrates the risks of making policy recommendations on the basis of phenomenological psychology. Those who "resolutely" face death, or write of so doing, may be more dangerous to our welfare than those who energetically repress it.[31]

This aside, is full consciousness even humanly possible? The testimony of experts is by no means unequivocal. Again, Ernest Becker provides the cautionary note, ridiculing the pretensions of what he derides as "guru therapies" and "therapeutic religionists" promising reconciliation of man with his own darkness. "Why do brilliant thinkers become so flaccid, dissipate so carelessly their own careful arguments?" he asks, when it comes to the issue of death?[32] "There is simply no way to transcend the limits of the human condition or to change the psychological structural conditions that make humanity possible."[33] Just what are these psychological conditions? They are, he says, the orientation to always be beyond our bodies, the urge not to acquiesce mystically to our creatureliness but to overcome it, which is to say, to repress our finitude and project death onto alien people and things.

Thanatologist Elisabeth Kübler-Ross would disagree with Becker.[34] Citing her own work with terminally ill patients, she claims to have discovered a natural psychological history of dying. The denial of death, she says, is merely the first stage through which the patient goes. After next angrily admitting his demise, then trying to bargain with fate for more life, and then mourning the inevitability of the end of existence, the patient finally surrenders, peacefully, to his mortality.

This is not the place to determine which, if either, of these positions is empirically accurate. But it is hard to disagree with Becker when he says that the promises of some Western therapists – for example, "You shall be as gods"[35] – are at best mere fancy; at worst, they represent "the undiluted infantile unconscious speaking." To demand a life of complete nonrepression is "boundless megalomania," says Becker. We can never be "whole men," even if we could define the term. "Repression is not falsification of the world, it is 'truth' – the only truth that man can know, because he cannot experience everything."[36]

This conclusion, however, should be tempered. After all, individuals differ greatly in their capacity to swallow their own shadows. Some pacifists, for example, have undertaken arduous campaigns of self-examination as an essential, ongoing component of their vocation. One such group calls itself Ground Zero. Until recently it was head-quartered on property adjoining a Trident submarine base on Hood Canal, Washington. Its members speak of conducting "experiments with truth," modeled after the analogous labors of Mahatma Gandhi.[37] These are excrutiating efforts at recognizing that they are somehow complicitous in the evil of the Bomb against which they struggle.

Ground Zero responds to each step on the exterminist escalator not by striking against the enemy "out there," but by absorbing it as its own partial responsibility. Through their mutual confessions its members are rediscovering what the Greeks called hubris: evil larger than a matter of individual choice, seemingly built into human nature, exhibiting itself as overweening arrogance and presumption.

The realization of hubris has not completely paralyzed Ground Zero politically; but it has clothed its resistance in tragic garb, dampening any hopes its members might once have entertained of instituting a world without murder. From his prison cell, James Douglass, its founder, writes that the "deeper question" of politics is not how to become "more effective" against state violence in the conventional sense, but of "reaching that inner point out of which one could respond more fully, more deeply, more unitedly, to . . . evil."[38] Accompanying any political refor-mation, he says, there must be "metanoia." The compulsion to act politi-cally prior to such conversion explains the impasse of militarization in which we of the Occident seem to find ourselves.

Ground Zero displays the promise of a phenomenologically in-formed, unsentimental, yet still optimistic politics. What does this mean concretely?

Negatively, it means a politics without scapegoats. Repeatedly, Ground Zero corrects itself against every temptation to find a "them" at fault for the arms race. They themselves are the "them" with whom they fight. Positively, it means a politics of invisibility – that is, of becoming indistinguishable from one's neighbors. Just as Ground Zero beseeches workers at the Trident base to end their employment in war work, it reaches out to them in small ways – offering employment, shelter, child care, food, medical support – so as to overcome their ap-prehensions at taking such a radical step. In this way Ground Zero remains in the community while gently urging it to change.

Conclusion: The Problem with Phenomenology

That we are in some way causally responsible for the enemies against whom we fight is both the great boon and, unfortunately, the danger of phenomenological thinking about politics. This danger is starkly revealed in Husserl's words: "The objective world, the world that exists for me, that always has and always will exist for me, the only world that ever can exist for me – this world, with *all* its objects . . . derives its whole sense and its existential status . . . from me myself."[39] (The only difference phenomenological sociologists have with this statement is a preference for the term "we ourselves" over "me myself.") If enemies are included under the category of objects, then the implication is obvious: the enemy is entirely my own project, receiving its whole sense and existential status from me alone (or from us together).

Prior to Husserlian thinking, we perceived ourselves as entirely righteous and "them" as diabolical: but this was "false consciousness." Now we see ourselves "correctly" as authors of the world's darkness; "they" are absolved of guilt. Moral theologians have long recognized that both stances spring from the same source, ego inflation, or to use the ancient term, vanity. The price of vanity is imprudence. By failing to recognize that evil is infinitely larger than ourselves, we are put at risk of becoming its victims. It should hardly require mentioning, but even if we ourselves could completely absorb our own shadows, others might still wish to destroy us. To dismiss this possibility as being a symptom of a "persecution complex" is the height of sophistry.[40]

To underscore this let us conduct a brief phenomenology of evil doing. Husserl calls for a return to "things themselves." In regard to evil doing, this requires what he calls "bracketing" our "natural attitude" (that is, our falsely conscious attitude) toward evil, temporarily suspending our naive belief that morality is given in the nature of actions themselves. At this point a difficulty arises: when we disconnect the natural attitude toward morality, goodness and evil cease to be anything more than fashionable conventions. This may be invaluable in the comparative study of cultural patterns by anthropologists, but if it is taken as the last word on morality, it is, to use Berger's phrase, "woefully inadequate." For it can lead to an intellectualistic denial of one of mankind's most indubitable experiences: outrage at a fundamental violation of life. By this I mean evil so monstrous that it "compels even people normally or professionally given to [phenomenology] to suspend relativizations."[41]

My shame and disgust at a blurry black and white photograph of a mutilated, starving teenage girl being stood as a specimen naked in front of a coterie of leering Nazi physicians is, at one level, an "appropriate response" to a scene that violates my liberal moral standards. But this is true only superficially. It is more faithful to the passion of my rage – passions being passively suffered rather than deliberately chosen – to say that this scene *in itself* is terrifyingly hateful. Our natural human response-ability to it must be absolute condemnation.

Again, the problem with phenomenology and its reduction of the object world to the status of my (or our) project is that it disallows speaking of Evil (and therefore of Good) that is "already" there prior to our constitution of it as such. It is no small irony that both the introspective Jewish professor Husserl (who concluded his last work with these words from Saint Augustine: "Do not wish to go out. Truth dwells in the inner man.")[42] and Edith Stein, the student who so sensitively composed her Ph.D. dissertation on empathy under his tutelage, were victimized by the Nazis. Stein died in Auschwitz in 1943.

8

Out of Hate
*A Sociology of Defection
from Neo-Nazism*

*You know, I've learned from this: Nobody's hopeless. Just because someone
has an attitude at some point, it doesn't mean that they can't change. You
should never throw somebody away.[1]*

In a short period, peace studies have produced an impressive bibliography relating to the causes, nature, and consequences of collective violence. But ironically the portion of this literature devoted to its namesake, "peace," is relatively small. One comprehensive review of peace studies research conducted in Finland from 1979 through 1985 finds that only about 15 percent concerns peace education, or the altering of perceptions of youth toward violence and the enemy.[2] The bulk of peace studies during this period (76 percent) deals with problems of European security, foreign affairs, the arms race, state-initiated disarmament proposals, international law, the emerging world system, descriptions of wars and local conflicts, and histories of the field itself. The remaining articles involve the mitigation of disputes that have already broken out (i.e., conflict management and the resolution of misunderstandings). These proportions are probably typical for peace studies elsewhere. Nor is this surprising given the disciplines from which the average peace studies researcher writes: international politics, political science, international jurisprudence, and political history. Less than one-fifth of the scholars cited in the review were trained in sociology or psychology, the fields best suited to conduct close, experimental studies of peace.[3] This chapter intends to partly close that gap.

It almost goes without saying that a psychological mind-set associated with acts of violence toward the enemy is hatred. Whether it is true, as Georg Simmel once claimed, that hatred is a practical reinforcement of specific conflicts – "It is expedient to hate the adversary with whom one fights"[4] – or whether hatred is a necessary precondition of conflict (or both), it would be hard to argue convincingly that peace in any profound sense is achievable without coming to grips with its contradiction, hatred.[5]

Antagonistic societies may for reasons of enlightened self-interest establish systems of mutual deterrence, may hook up direct-access emergency telephones, may fund institutions to study one another's cultures; they may agree in writing to fight within the rules of civilized war, may sponsor cultural and sports exchanges, and may even engage in gestures of arms reduction. But if the issue of mutual hatred, the root of their antagonism, is not effectively addressed, such institutions invariably rest on a flimsy foundation.

It is in this context, then, that I place before the reader a modest study of individuals, once devoted to hatred, who have come to peace with their onetime antagonists. The object is to analyze sociologically the conditions of their conversions and so to add a proposition to the general theory of peace.

Background

Beginning in about 1980 the United States experienced a resurgence of right-wing extremism. At one level it culminated in the election of President Ronald Reagan and a slate of senators anxious to turn back various civil rights programs, to restrict rights of sexual and religious privacy, and to "modernize" America's allegedly faltering military defenses. Domestically and in foreign policy these efforts were seen as parts of a larger struggle against "atheistic communism." This story is familiar and nothing more need be said here. What is less commonly acknowledged is that this rightist resurgence had a more chilling, sinister face: first, the establishment of what some have called a "secret government" in the White House whose operations (later exposed as the Iran-Contra scandal) were coordinated with the World Anti-Communist League and, second, the proliferation of paramilitary political-religious cults throughout the American West. Included among them are the Church of Jesus Christ Christian (Aryan Nations), the Covenant, Sword and the Arm of the Lord, the Posse Comitatus, the *Bruders Schweigen* (or Order), the Order Strike Force II, the Aryan Youth Movement ("skinheads"), and the Christian Patriots Defense League.

Associated at the time with a university in the state of Idaho, one of the centers of rightist paramilitarism and the provisionally named "capital" of a five-state "Aryan Nation," this author was situated to research directly the most extreme manifestations of these developments.[6] Starting in January 1985 and continuing for about two and one-half years, I conducted field research on the movement, including participant observation of Christian patriot gatherings, lectures, workshops, annual conventions, and church services. In the course of this work, I collected biographical data on several hundred radical patriots by means of goal-directed but unstructured conversational interviews, as well as by using secondary publications.

The stated goal of this research was to compare these data against standard sociological theories of causality of right-wing extremism. However, while this goal was being accomplished, an issue of salience to peace studies inadvertently revealed itself. I went into the field to learn what causes people to hate. But while pursuing this goal I came across several individuals who had voluntarily disaffiliated themselves from these same groups; that is, people who had ceased to hate and had begun, at least provisionally, to express love for their enemies. This chapter discusses the social conditions of their conversions.

Making inferences from a sample of seven hardly constitutes scientific proof of a proposition. Therefore, the following pages should be read in a heuristic vein as pointing the direction for further research. Some more words on the sample are appropriate.

As a rule, political-religious groups are more interested in recruiting members than they are in grousing about, or indeed even admitting, membership losses. As a consequence, there exist technical difficulties in analyzing their disaffected members. These difficulties are multiplied in the case of extremist groups with violent aims. First, for purposes of protecting their associates from police surveillance, few extremist groups will open their membership rolls to inquisitive outsiders. Second, those who have dropped their affiliations are typically anxious to hide the darker side of their pasts from neighbors (and from sociologists who might compromise them). It is not unheard of for those who have quit hate groups to change their names and move some distance from their original domiciles. Another reason for this is to protect themselves from their old associates who may feel betrayed by their apostasies. In three cases brought to my attention, apostates from hate groups were assaulted verbally and physically by their onetime colleagues for being "spies," "race traitors," "Communists," or "Jew sympathizers." One was found stumbling near his house, his hands nailed crucifixion style to a six-foot plank, and his chest slashed with a razor.[7] The second died of heart failure, which his wife, at least, claims to have been precipitated by months of threatening telephone calls, being assaulted with a pistol, and having his property bombed and arsoned.[8] A third, a disenchanted female member of the Chicago Area Skinheads (CASH), had her home broken into, her face maced, her body beaten limp, and a swastika painted on the wall with her own blood.[9]

The implication is that the cases of hate-group apostasy about which there is concrete information may not be representative of such defections generally, but stories of exceptionally courageous individuals. To reiterate: the observations reported here should be read as suggestions for further research, not as definitive confirmation of a theory.

Arrivals and Departures

Compared with the vast literature on why people join political-religious cults, there is a shortage of data concerning apostasy.[10] Recent research, however, has begun to correct this oversight. A summary of its more salient conclusions provides background for my own findings.

First, in analyzing cult defections it is important to distinguish between three kinds of leave-taking: *expulsion* from the group at the behest of its leaders, forcible *extraction* from the group by outsiders (known as deprograming, this often involves kidnapping the individual in question), and voluntary *exiting* by the member.[11] While each type of disaffiliation takes place from neo-Nazi groups, our concern here is exclusively with the latter. What interests us, in other words, are occasions wherein dedicated haters evidently take it upon themselves to renounce their past.

Second, political-religious defection takes place at two distinguishable but not entirely separable dimensions: a belief dimension and a social-communal dimension. A complete account of voluntary exiting from neo-Nazism, then, involves an explanation both of how hate creeds are renounced and how ties to specific hate groups are severed.[12]

Third, of these two dimensions, the most important causally seems to be the social-communal. The prototypical cult apostate first severs his bonds to the cult, and as this happens the plausibility structure supporting and validating his belief system crumbles. In a study of defection from a doomsday cult, for example, it was found that those having the strongest social connections with the group were least likely to lose faith when its apocalyptic forecasts were disproven.[13] This finding is consistent with the sociology of knowledge: Human beings do not adhere to beliefs in a void. Rather, for knowledge claims to be credible, they must be borne up by structured social activities like rituals. When such structures disappear, individuals are thrown into what is technically known as anomie, cognitive chaos.[14] As applied to hate-group apostasy, it is therefore reasonable to expect most defectors first to become disillusioned with their social relations with the group and only later to begin questioning its doctrines.

Fourth, to this extent and in this way cult defections are, to use the phrase of Rodney Stark and William Bainbridge, "a mirror image" of cult recruitment. How does recruitment to cults take place? In a now classic piece on affiliation with Rev. Sun Myung Moon's Unification Church (the Moonies) in America, Stark and John Lofland found that effective cult recruitment rarely proceeds through mass solicitations or door-to-door proselytizing. Instead the recruiter forms intimate ties with the candidate. Those who were not in some way deeply linked to their Moonie recruiters failed to convert to the faith. The most effective recruiting agent has one foot in and one foot out of the movement, and thus is positioned to speak to outsiders in their terms while also initiating them into the inner mysteries of the cult.[15]

This sociological principle has been intuitively grasped by the Unification Church and implemented in a three-step recruitment strategy: (1) isolate candidates from their usual environment during long weekends at rustic retreats; (2) "hook" them by displaying an obsequious interest in their lives; and (3) "love bomb" them with affection and affirmation. Analogous tactics, developed independently, have been employed with equal success by the Church of Jesus Christ of Latter-day Saints (Mormons) and by the Children of God (its so-called flirty fishing, or use of sexual allurement).[16]

This investigator has found similar processes operative for growing neo-Nazi groups. The prototypical candidate for neo-Nazism first "joins with" an agent and then begins subtly altering his beliefs so as to maintain this relationship: in some cases a love bond, in others a valued friendship, and in still others a work partnership, a school tie, a marriage, or a family relationship.[17] It is not uncommon to meet dedicated neo-Nazis who when they first read or heard their group's doctrines were shocked, morally revolted, incredulous, or simply amused by what they took to be patent absurdities.

Fifth, when speaking of the seminal importance of social bonding in joining cults or in leave-taking, one must consider both the social forces that "push" the candidate in a particular direction and those that "pull" him there. That is to say, recruitment and defection alike must be understood as instances of social migration generally (although here we speak of psychic rather than geographic mobility). The probability of an individual defecting from a hate group is a function of the net balance of these social pulls and pushes. A person who finds the group highly rewarding and life outside bleak is likely to be strongly committed to the group. One who finds membership excruciatingly painful socially but perceives no alternative outside the group is also not likely to defect, and indeed may fortify his faith in hate doctrine so as to decrease the psychological dissonance of being trapped in a painful situation.[18] Still another person may find hate-group affiliation pleasurable, but may also enjoy beneficial ties outside the group. He may retain membership if for no other reason than inertia, but his continued affiliation may be unstable. Table 8.1 summarizes these speculations.

Sixth, notwithstanding these points, it is inaccurate to picture the typical leaver (or joiner) as a passive victim of group forces that compel him willy-nilly to disaffiliate (or affiliate) regardless of his understanding of his own best interests.[19] As implied in the use of the word "reward" under point five, the average defector (or recruit) plays an active role in his apostasy from (or commitment to) the cause. Only if he sees the act of defection as enhancing his private and public interests is he likely to act on his inclination to leave the group.[20]

Seventh, by public interests I mean the importance (the utility) of the political success of the movement to the candidate. By private interests are meant two things: one, the utility to the candidate of "material" pleasures contingent on membership in a hate group (sex, money, sociability, and power), and two, the utility to him of "ideal" satisfactions (a sense of personal life direction, esteem, or what I called in chapter 2 experiencing oneself as "heroic"). It is recognized that these interests are not entirely separable; however, evidence from my own field research indicates that for right-wing extremists they are ranked in the following approximate order of declining importance:

Table 8.1

Types of Social Relationships and Their Impacts on Retaining Hate-Group
Membership and on Hatred toward Outgroups

Social Relations in Hate Group	Social Relations outside Hate Group	Likely Career Trajectory	Impact on Hatred
Nonrewarding	Rewarding	Leave group	Hatred diminishes
Nonrewarding	Nonrewarding	Stay in group	Hatred increases
Rewarding	Rewarding	Unstable membership	Unstable attitude
Rewarding	Nonrewarding	Stay in group	Hatred unchanged

personal esteem, the public "good" (as they understand it), and personal material benefits.

In summary, then, disaffiliation from hate groups and the subsequent renunciation of hate doctrines involves a complex interplay of social forces and personal utility calculations. Seeking to enhance their sense of worth in the world, as well as other private and public goods, hate-group members weigh social relationships both inside and outside hate groups in terms of their reward potential. In this way, even the most vicious haters are indistinguishable from their more conventional peers. Apostates have come to believe that social relationships outside the hate group have more promissary value, at the moment, than do relationships inside the group. Voluntary exiting from hate groups thus entails both a social shove from and a being allured to certain social bonds. Once the social links to hate groups have been cut, the plausibility structures undergirding hate dogma disappear, making reconversions to new, less hostile belief patterns possible.

Evidence

Of the seven cases in the sample (Table 8.2),[21] the biographies of six clearly illustrate the theory just described.[22] Information on the Rollins case is vague enough to raise some questions. Data concerning Rollins were gathered from a television transcription of Rev. Pat Robertson's "700 Club" in the spring of 1987. The object of Rollins's appearance was to display to the audience the saving power of Jesus Christ; hence his story is posed in religious language. Attempts to contact Rollins personally failed; thus I was unable to determine whether or not there is also a

Table 8.2

The Sample: Gravitation Away from Hate-Group Membership

Name	Hate-Group Role	Location	Social Push from Hate	Social Pull from Hate
Tommy Tarrants	KKK terrorist	Alabama	Imprisonment, isolation from support group	Christian prison ministry
Greg Withrow	Founder, White Student Union	California	Harassment from colleagues, death of father	Love tie with Sylvia*
Clinton Sipes	KKK recruiter and vandal	California	Imprisonment, isolation from support group	Christian pastor
Tommy Rollins	KKK leader	Texas	Anxiety over safety due to KKK activities	Born again experience
Joyce Benedict*	Identity Christian**	Idaho	Physical abuse by husband	Daughter, women's group
John Lufkin*	Aryan Nations Church	Idaho	Physical isolation	Asian girlfriend
David Waughtal	Identity Christian**	Arizona, Oregon	Imprisonment, isolation from support group	Christian pastor, rabbi

*Fictitious name.
**Identity Christianity holds that Aryans are God's chosen people and that Jews and/or Judaism are of Satan.

sociological angle to his account. The following speculations, however, are not unreasonable. A "born again" experience such as Rollins is said to have had presupposes social contact with a specific style of Christianity and probably with specific Christian acquaintances, namely fundamentalist Baptism and Baptists, the very kinds of Christians who dominate the religious scene in and around Rollins's hometown of Irving, Texas. To use the terminology introduced above, this Baptist community can be considered the "social pull" from hate. As for the "push": Just prior to his conversion from hate, Rollins reports that he was beseeching God for salvation because of his increasingly unsatisfactory relationships with the Ku Klux Klan (KKK). His paranoia about impending arrest and the danger to his family from those harboring vengeance grew to the point that he posted armed guards outside his house. If this is true, then Rollins's case also seems to fit the model of hate-group defection laid out above.

For most of the sample, the social push from hate appears to have preceded the pull into conventional life. Greg Withrow's story is typical. Just before Withrow's pivotal meeting with Sylvia* (described below), his father died of cancer and alcoholism. It was his father who originally sponsored Greg's involvement first in the KKK and then the White Aryan Resistance (WAR). "I honored my father," Withrow says. "When he died it hurt. But there was also a sense of relief. . . . I had this thought that, 'gee, maybe I don't have to carry this on any more.' "

This leads to a related point. When individuals in the sample announced their intention to defect from a specific hate group, a common response was for the group to anathemize them. This action may have had the effect of confirming the defector's original intentions, propelling him even more rapidly into conventional life. The result is thus a "mirror image," so to say, of the recruitment process. When recruits tentatively express their interest in a cult, their horrified family and friends often disown them, unwittingly easing their final passage into the cult's waiting arms.

Other observations. First, for all the cases of apostasy about which I have concrete information, the social pull out of hate involves a specific person: a Christian minister, a girlfriend, or a daughter. Second, the pushes from hate, with one exception, are relatively general. In three cases they appear to involve little more than physical separation from the social support of the hate group in question, through either imprisonment or geographic distance. Third, personal violent attacks play a role not only in pushing people out of hate (Withrow and Benedict) but equally often in pushing them into it. Lufkin was tormented by black students and Withrow and Sipes were both physically beaten – Withrow even claiming to have had his throat slashed in one encounter. All three were imagining revenge when invited to join hate groups. In all three cases their victimization was brought on in part by their own social isolation.

*Fictitious name

Lufkin

John Lufkin* was referred to me by his psychologist. An adopted child who recently graduated from high school with a B+ average, Lufkin was raised in a nominally Lutheran household. The father, with whom he was never close, is a staunch believer in Aryan superiority; he also fought in the Pacific in the Second World War and has a visceral animosity toward Asians. The ease of Lufkin's assumption of racial hatred may be due in part to this familial situation where racism is taken for granted.

Lufkin's IQ of 136 places him statistically in the "genius" category of the American population. For an American of any age, he is remarkably well read in history and comparative mythology.

As early as the fifth grade Lufkin's fascination with Nazism was evident. He recalls seeing a film when he was ten in which Adolf Hitler's speaking ability struck him as "overwhelming." The following year he witnessed another film, concerning the Holocaust. The evident willingness of the Jews to participate in their own victimization convinced him of their "cowardice." (The reader will espy in these observations the budding symptoms of the Authoritarian [fascist] personality.) By the second year in high school Lufkin's political transformation was virtually complete. Holocaust films were "shoved down our throats," he said, increasing his hostility towards Jews. And what he read about the hippy movement of the 1960s convinced him that "Hitler had the answer; he would have gassed them [the hippies]."

About this same time two "black chicks" started "calling [him] down," that is, making lewd suggestions and then teasing his response. Already introverted, Lufkin's reaction was to fantasize about revenge; many of the images he conjured were inspired by his reading of German history. It was then that a seminal event occurred. Lufkin had a history teacher who collected Nazi regalia and who noticed Lufkin's peculiar reading habits. It was his custom every Christmas to give his favorite pupils gifts reflecting their presumed interests. That year he gave Lufkin a swastika, a Luftwaffe insignia, and a Nazi memorabilia catalogue. At first Lufkin "stashed" the gifts at home, embarrassed that his secrets were so evident to strangers. But the teasing by the girls persisted and his

*Fictitious name

shame soon turned to antiblack rage. In time he proudly posted the swastika on his bedroom wall. "This is when I really became a neo-Nazi. I was fifteen at the time." He dreamed of ruling an all-white, heterosexual, drug-free, Christian society, and wrote out a subscription to the periodical published by the Aryan Nations Church. Given the two-day drive to Aryan Nations headquarters, however, and his own agoraphobic inhibitions, Lufkin never became a member of a neo-Nazi support community.

After graduating from high school, Lufkin got an eight-week summer job with the city parks department. There he chanced to meet an intelligent, sensitive Japanese girl who, it turns out, was using drugs. Another coworker, a friendly Caucasian female, was also a "druggie." Faced with glaring inconsistencies between his racially pure, morally puritanical fantasy society and two real human beings who displayed a fondness for him, "I realized I would have to make exceptions. . . ." In a perverse kind of inductive logic he concluded that in his future society Japanese people would be preserved, although they would be sexually segregated from their white masters. Indeed, he began contemplating the possibility that Asian culture might be superior to his own, seeing in Buddhism a doctrine more sophisticated than any form of Christianity. But alas he then discovered, "much to my horror," that Gautama Siddhartha (Buddha) was not Asian after all, but Aryan. Slowly Lufkin's racial cosmology was collapsing.

Through the influence of the two young women, Lufkin began experimenting with alcohol and marijuana. Later that winter he was arrested for public drunkenness and fighting. When his parents were humiliatingly marched into the police department, he felt that he had betrayed not only them but himself: "*I* was now everything I was opposed to." The implication was obvious: "now I must be exterminated." Fortunately, given the choice between suicide and renunciation of his social theory, Lufkin made still another "exception" to his exclusionary rule. Having already admitted Asians into his fantasy world, now "I played with the idea of Aryan hippies." He claimed to discover the Asiatic roots of the American counterculture, and developed a taste for the rock 'n' roll of the Grateful Dead and the Rolling Stones. His father, never much of a role model, evolved into "the great Satan."

At this writing Lufkin has completely given up Nazism. In the 1988 presidential primary he expressed a preference for liberal candidate Gary

Hart: "I felt they made too much of his adultery; Thomas Jefferson did the same." His favorite candidate after Hart was none other than the charismatic black radical activist Jesse Jackson.

In the spring of 1989, as a curious observer, Lufkin attended a three-day racist skinhead conference held at the Aryan Nations compound in Idaho. He found most of the conferees "stupid," "violent," and not worth his while.

Withrow

At the July 1986 Aryan World Congress in Idaho, Greg Withrow demanded in his keynote address that non-Aryan men, women, and children "be expelled" from America "or be terminated." The utter seriousness of his attitude, the anger in his voice, and the collective "Hail victory" answering each of his exhortations led me to believe that here was a truly dangerous man, one best placed under hourly police surveillance.

Before the year was over, Withrow was publicly renouncing his words, stepping down from his leadership of the White Student Union (now known as the Aryan Youth Movement, a front for the White Aryan Resistance), and declaring himself converted through "love" to acceptance of his onetime enemies: "I've said a lot of terrible things and I've spread a lot of harm; I don't want to hate anymore. I don't want to hurt anymore," he told reporters. What we have here is either an incredible effort at dissimulation or one of the most noteworthy spiritual transformations in recent record.

Outwardly, Withrow's background is like Lufkin's, only more extreme in its instability. Raised in an emotionally cold family setting, Withrow had a father who he claims "had a plan for me to be like Hitler." Following his parents' divorce, Withrow became in his words a stray, living in the streets, eating out of garbage cans, sleeping in brush near libraries, and being tormented by prowling black teens. Winter days found him in reading rooms in the company of Mussolini, Nietzsche, and *Mein Kampf*. By the age of thirteen Withrow was a self-acknowledged racist with delusions of grandeur and fantasies of racist revenge. Unlike Lufkin, however, Withrow set about translating his dreams into action. Starting at American River Junior College in Sacramento, California, by the early 1980s he had founded chapters of the

WSU on thirty campuses: "We had science fiction, cartoons, skinhead rock 'n' roll tapes, slam dancing, T-shirts – all programmed for your minds, all oriented toward violent behavior."

In November 1986, Withrow chanced upon a cocktail waitress at the gambling club he frequented. As it had been for Lufkin, Withrow's experience with the opposite sex was to be decisive for his development. Sylvia* had already read about Withrow's activities in the news, but evidently refused to believe he was not underneath the bluff and swagger a "nice guy." Following their first date, viewing the sadomasochistic movie romance *9½ Weeks*, Sylvia uttered the words that "just blew my [Withrow's] mind: 'I love you.' " Within a month Sylvia had moved into Withrow's apartment. "For the first time in my life," he said, "I was just having fun. . . . For the first time in my life, I loved someone."

Possibly sensing weakness in his composure, Withrow's followers began testing his authority. By the spring of 1987 he had been replaced as head of the WSU by Tom Metzger's son (see below). Withrow responded by publicly announcing his intention to resign from the group altogether and ridiculing its pretensions. It was then that the assaults began. In one incident three bat-wielding gang members threatened to kill him if he spoke out again. To lend credibility to their threat they broke his nose and jaw.

Withrow has since split up with the woman who led him from the labyrinth of racial hatred and has made two halfhearted attempts to poison himself. Again, we are reminded of Lufkin's solemn announcement that in light of the fact that he had become the very thing he most loathed, he must now be eliminated. It is not easy to leave behind everything one once proclaimed and forge a new destiny. Nevertheless, Withrow insists that his conversion is final: "Some people might regret what's happened to me, but they should rejoice at what's happened to my soul. . . . I know one thing – if I live, I'm going to find peace." Greg Withrow now works with the Anti-Defamation League of B'nai B'rith, helping others to negotiate themselves out of lives of hate.

Sipes

"I guess it runs in the family," says Clinton Sipes of his enthrallment with the Klan. His first exposure occurred when he was about ten,

*Fictitious name

visiting his grandfather in Galveston, Texas. Sipes remembers watching his grandfather pull white KKK robes from a closet after viewing a Klan rally.

Sipes's biography reiterates the Lufkin and Withrow scenes: a family history of racism, domestic hostilities culminating in divorce, placement in a public child care institution in a futile effort to keep him off the streets, and repeated assaults by black youths. "I despised the blacks who beat me as a kid and I just grew up hating them all. I was filled with anger." Run-ins with the police followed, gang involvement with a loosely organized racist group called the Dublin Rangers, and an invitation at sixteen to join the Klan. Within two years Sipes was a Ku Klux Klan "Kleagle" or recruiter, and brags (probably with exaggeration) of bringing two hundred new believers into the fold. Already by fourteen Sipes had shot a black man in the head with a pellet gun ("He . . . said something back and that was the wrong time. . . . I got him right in the forehead"). Now in the Klan, Sipes participated in cross burnings, wore a hood, and took part in "night rides": "We used to drive through the ghetto of Oakland and shoot people. . . . It was happening once a week for two or three months maybe. We figured the cops would think it was drug-related drive-by shootings. They did."

Sipes's conversion from hate was mediated, like those of Tarrants and Rollins, not by a female friend but by a Christian minister, Rev. Paul Travis, pastor of the California Community Church. Travis had clashed with Sipes in the past. In November 1988, Sipes arranged a meeting with him to bury the hatchet. Why? In his own words: "I was tired of hating, tired of hurting innocent people." While it is not clear what he means by this, it can be inferred that Sipes was finding Klan life something less than entirely rewarding. At the time of this call to Travis he had just been released the second time from the California Youth Authority, convicted of carrying a loaded weapon into a shopping center. His first sentence, six and one-half years, was for armed robbery and assault with a machete. Perhaps more to the point, Sipes says: "I have a two-year-old daughter and I didn't want her to grow up thinking bad of her father."

At their first meeting Travis found Sipes a man "whose spiritual dimension was zero." "He was spiritually dead. . . . If one word could sum up Clinton it was 'hate.' He just hated and hated and hated." With all the sincerity of a man of faith, Travis pleaded with Sipes to ask God for help and forgiveness. What happened next the pastor interprets as a miracle: "I couldn't believe my eyes. It just seemed to me that no one had ever talked to this kid before. I know it is hard for many people to understand, but he was reborn."

Other meetings followed; Sipes began memorizing Bible passages and joining group prayer sessions. At first Travis was skeptical; now he is convinced of the authenticity of Sipes's transformation. As for Sipes, there was never any doubt about what happened that afternoon in the restaurant. ". . . I'm out, definitely out," he says. "There's no future in hating. I was either going to kill somebody or be killed." "I'd like to set an example," he told reporters. "I changed, others can change. God says that we are all created equal. I can accept whatever happens because I am finally at peace."

Conclusion

It is a mistake to view involvement in neo-Nazism as necessarily enduring. Like cultism generally, hate-group affiliations and their associated faiths are in constant flux. The act of joining a hate group is like disembarking at a railroad way station: the passengers depart when they sense their interests are better served elsewhere. Assuming society has a bona fide concern in encouraging early departures from the way station of hate, there appear to be two major points of intervention: Society can make hate-group membership increasingly uncomfortable, or it can increase the perceived rewards of conventional social bonds. The data reviewed above suggest that *both* ploys are required if defection is to occur. Consider the cases of Joyce Benedict* and Tom Metzger. Both have found hate group affiliation costly, but only Joyce has seen a way out.

After she married "a good Christian man," an ex-Nazarene preacher, and converted to Identity Christianity and its Judeophobic ideology, Joyce discovered that her mate had betrayed her trust. He was an alcoholic, an adulterer, and even sexually abused her daughter. "I hated him," she says, and was fully prepared to leave him and his organization. Sensing no alternative to her role as docile "Christian wife," however, she sought escape through suicide. Only with the aid of her daughter, now come of age, was she able to leave her destructive situation. Mother and daughter got their own apartment and part-time jobs. With the

*Fictitious name

counseling and guidance of a local woman's support group, she entered Boise State University. Upon graduating with a degree in social work she will deal with the very people – poor, uneducated racial minorities – she was reviling months earlier.

Tom Metzger's story has a different ending. Founder of the White Aryan Resistance, in October 1990 he was found liable for $12.5 million in civil damages to a black Portland, Oregon, family, one of whose members was brutally slain by three skinheads allegedly acting as Metzger's agents. (Metzger was not implicated criminally in the case.) After the judgment, the plaintiff's lawyer confidently predicted that now "there will be a new season of justice in the Northwest. . . . This is a major setback to organized bigotry. . . ."[23] But this happy forecast is doubtful. Metzger himself insists that far from deterring him from hate, the verdict has actually "freed" him to preach it more vehemently than before. "People who have very little," he says without elaborating, "have very little to lose. . . ."[24] Even the plaintiff's attorney has had reason to reconsider his first prediction, admitting that the sheer size of the lawsuit may have trapped Metzger into a corner from which the only escape is violence:

> What bothers me about Tom Metzger is that in the last year he has become more violent. He is training with AK-47s and he's passing out military manuals on how to make explosives. . . . I think . . . Tom Metzger is ready to snap. I believe that you are going to hear some pretty drastic things out of him because he's gotten frustrated and driven back and I don't think he sees any way out.[25]

While the $12.5 million damage suit may have been intended to inhibit racial violence in Portland, it may have the opposite effect. As the murder victim's father clearly saw, the lawsuit "has avenged my son's death for me."[26] True, retaliation may be a natural and satisfying response to wrongs, but it hardly suffices to solve the problem of violence. Retaliation must be accompanied with conciliatory gestures advertising the attractiveness of life without hate.

Nor, it should be obvious from the previous discussion, are such advertisements by themselves sufficient to propel people out of hate groups. While they may momentarily destabilize hate-group affiliations, truly dedicated members may dismiss them as contemptible signs of society's fear and weakness.

In short, then, actions intended to make hate-group involvement costly may in fact render the candidate for defection unavailable to what we have called social "pulls" from hate, the possibility of bonding with outsiders to the hate movement. On the other hand, attempting to "pull" haters from their old support community by unconditional love and forgiveness may be taken by Authoritarian personalities, who admire sternness and discipline, as a sign of weakness and hence one more reason to avoid conventional, liberal social life.

There is an added problem. If the defections from hate reviewed above are typical, then increasing the attraction of conventional social life must involve much more than mass indoctrination such as exhibiting the horrors of the Holocaust and teaching about the dangers of hatred or about the equality of all peoples – as laudable and helpful as these may be for educational purposes. Just as mass appeals are generally ineffective in recruiting individuals into cults, they are probably ineffective in inducing them to leave. What *are* required are specific significant others – pastors, daughters, friends, or lovers – willing to establish ties with candidates for defection and to display to them the rewards, especially the sense of esteem, awaiting those who renounce hate. These must be others standing outside the hate movement, but willing to forgive and to affirm haters with no ulterior motives. How such significant others are to be generated, assuming they can be, is perhaps the most challenging policy question of all.

9

The Cantor and the Klansman
A Love Story

This is a sociological tale of two men: cantor (music and educational director) Michael Weisser of the Congregation B'nai Jeshurun in Lincoln, Nebraska, and his onetime antagonist, ex-Klansman and self-proclaimed Nazi Larry Trapp. It is a study in the deconstruction of enemies, in mutual disarmament, in what Europeans have in mind when they speak of "détente from below" (as in the aphorism that peace is too important to be left in the hands of the state; the people must establish it themselves). In the last months of 1991, Weisser somehow induced Trapp to renounce his past, apologize to those whom he had threatened, and establish a hot line to encourage others in the hate movement to follow suit. The Associated Press picked up the story and I followed it up by conducting three lengthy interviews with Weisser.[1] Weisser related to me that he interpreted what had transpired between himself and Trapp as a "love story." This chapter takes Weisser's intuition as an opportunity to examine the practical significance of love in mollifying deeply antagonistic relations, the sort routinely confronted by everyone in political life.

It was not without considerable unease that I consented to view the Weisser-Trapp encounter as a case of love. As the social phenomenologist and Thomistic scholar Josef Pieper once observed, ". . . we only need leaf through a few magazines at the barber's to want not to let the word 'love' cross our lips for a good long time."[2] Honorific language has a nasty habit of attracting pernicious company, particularly in political discourse. What crimes have not been committed with the blessing of "love"? Still, I thought it might be helpful to go back to this much maligned word, retrieve its original meanings, and then try to apply them to the present situation, with an eye to understanding ourselves more deeply, perhaps even finding a way out of certain impasses.

In saying this, however, it should be kept in mind that the impasse before us, the phenomenon of enemies, is not a "problem" in the sense that liberal reformists and social engineers sometimes express – that is, an undesirable social condition posed for a solution. To use the phrase invoked in the first chapter, the enemy is a paradoxical duality (Jungian psychologists might even say an archetype) residing "out there" as an object but also deeply embedded in our own psyches. Hence it is not something that can be (or, perhaps, that we should even want) eradicated. To express it more pointedly, the following account is not intended to demonstrate that love is causally necessary and sufficient for deconstructing enemies. Our observations are presented instead, if nothing else, to provoke self-examination.

To begin with, there are at least three problems with the word "love" as used in everyday conversation: The first, just alluded to, reduces love to an often cheap sentiment which enraptures and overwhelms one – for example, producing throat lumps and tears at celebrations of the national cultus.

The second problem is to picture love, as is frequently done in popular Christianity, as agape, pure unselfishness. This has the effect, again to quote Pieper, of making "the reality of love [at least for human beings] evaporate."[3] This is because to be human means in some respect to be self-seeking.

The third problem is to psychologize love, lifting the individual act from the social circumstances that make it possible in the first place.

In the pages that follow an effort will be made to circumvent these difficulties. First, the love I report is an *act*, not a feeling – an act possibly unaccompanied by affection, at least initially. Second, it is an act conjoined to mixed motives, as much by fear and possibly even by loathing as by a desire to do good for another. That is to say, love is an entirely human gesture available to the most ordinary folks. Third and most important, love is written here as socially mediated. By this I don't mean simply that it involves a relation between the lover and the beloved. In addition, loving, especially loving one's purported enemy, presupposes a socialized altruistic outlook and a preconditioned habit of responding to danger not by flight or fight, but by increasing one's vulnerability. Nor is this all. For love to "succeed," the beloved must accept the gesture of reconciliation. But a readiness to accept rather than to throw it back in the lover's face also requires favorable social circumstances and preparation. Exactly what these various preconditions and circumstances are and how they might be produced are as yet largely unknown to sociologists.[4]

Love Defined

In chapter 7 we conducted a "phenomenological reduction" of the enemy to its ideal form. In doing this we were led to the reality of death and to death's prefigurement in scat and garbage. The enemy, we concluded, is essentially excrement, and as excrement it is treated. Having said this our attention now shifts to love. What permits us to identify selfless giving to others, erotic attraction, benevolence, and friendship all as species of the same genus love?

Fortunately, there is considerable agreement among students of the subject, beginning with Aristotle's own reflections in the *Nicomachean Ethics*. Josef Pieper summarizes their conclusions. "In every conceivable case," he says, "love signifies much the same as approval."[5] But insofar as "approval" literally stands for a judgment of goodness (from the Latin *ad* "to", *probus* "good"), then whether in the form of word or deed, and whether addressed to a musical score, a scenic vista, or a human being, love announces the goodness of an object. "It testifies to being in agreement, assenting, consenting, applauding, affirming, praising, glorifying, and hailing." All of these, Pieper tells us, mean "I want you (or it) to exist."[6]

The reconciliation between Michael Weisser and his nemesis Larry Trapp began at the lowest level of this series of approbations, grudging toleration of the other; it then progressed first to nondefensive listening to the other, to acknowledging the validity of the other's comments, then to expressions of concern, to displays of trust and words of need and hurt, and from these to apologies, deeds of care, exchanges of gifts, culminating in mutual acclamation and, at this writing, to *philia*, an understanding of what the two men share: their common humanity. How was this possible?

The Reconciliation Analyzed

One who loves another will have already seen in the other something worthy of affirmation, something lovable. What, we begin by asking, did cantor Weisser see in Larry Trapp? How, in other words, did Weisser "know" that Trapp was approvable?

By his own admission the only information available to Weisser at the outset were the comments Trapp had made at open meetings of the Lincoln Coalition Against Racism and Prejudice (CARP) concerning miscegenation and race "mongrelization," a vituperative phone call from Trapp, an envelope stuffed with Nazi and Klan propaganda, and Trapp's own unprepossessing appearance as a wheelchair bound, legally blind, double amputee. Certainly, then, Weisser did not respond to Trapp as he did because of his admiration of the latter's qualities. (Indeed, were one to acclaim another solely on the basis of the other's qualities there would be a serious question of whether love is the basis of this acclamation.)

Rather, Weisser seems to have made his judgment based on what he discerned *behind* Trapp's outrageous behavior, or to use Weisser's own words, "that he has potential to be a nice guy." To use philosophical jargon we might say that Weisser affirmed Trapp not for his *essentia* but for his *existensia,* not for his particular characteristics but for Being itself (to use the term introduced at the outset of chapter 7), for his personhood. If this is true, what kind of insight permits one to penetrate behind the veil of appearances to Being itself? And knowing this, what social conditioning avails one of such insight?

Nor do our difficulties end here. Weisser's first communications to Trapp appear to be far from equivalent to the phrase, "Larry, it is good that you exist." In other words, they don't appear very loving. In the course of ten to twelve telephone messages, Weisser variously reminded Trapp of divine judgment – "Larry, you're going to have to answer to God for all of this someday," that "the Nazis would have exterminated handicapped people like yourself," and in response to a thirty-second flatulent noise left by Trapp on his answering machine, this reply: "Hey, it sounds like the voice of the master race to me." (Trapp later confessed to Weisser that he laughed so much at this that he almost fell off his wheelchair.)[7]

In his original phone messages Weisser shamed Trapp, rebuked him for his foolishness, and called down on him heavenly vengeance. Understandably, then, Trapp's first response, when he was no longer able to ignore the messages, was to angrily inquire why Weisser was "harassing" him. The question posed above can thus be rephrased to read: How did Trapp, to use his own words, "sense something in his [Weisser's] voice that I hadn't heard before . . . something I hadn't experienced. It was love." Again, all Trapp knew of Weisser was the cantor's own "essentia" – that is, Weisser's appearance as an instance of the category "Jew," to Trapp the very embodiment of evil. Must we finally be satisfied with Weisser's own explanation of the event, that Trapp "had a religious experience?" Must we, to cite Pieper's moral theology, be content with the idea that both Weisser and Trapp for some gratuitous reason (that is, because of "grace") were both granted insight into the other which only faith can bestow? Before being forced to accept this conclusion, let us examine the reconciliation more closely in psychological and then sociological terms.

The Event Viewed Psychologically

In answer to Trapp's query concerning the reason for Weisser's "harassment," Weisser countered with the defense that Trapp had misunderstood his intentions. Given his position as a cantor, and his knowledge of Trapp's incapacitation, "I said I'd like to help him. I offered him a ride to the grocery store." Taken aback by the evident generosity of a Jew – that is, to use technical psychological jargon, thrown momentarily into a state of cognitive dissonance (being confronted by information inconsistent with his stereotype of Jews as eminently mercenary and self-serving) – Trapp uttered a brief "Thanks," turned down the offer, and then requested that Weisser no longer call him.

Psychologists tell us that when placed in a state of cognitive dissonance, as recipients of data contrary to their world view, individuals typically make adjustments to reestablish consonance, favoring devices least costly to themselves.[8] The easiest of these is simply to ignore information inconsistent with their viewpoint; a more difficult tactic is to acknowledge the existence of contrary information but invalidate it ad hominem, by attacking the messenger; still another tack, normally undertaken as a last resort, is to begin altering their point of view, initially by granting the existence of "exceptions."

Although it is impossible to reconstruct what went through Trapp's mind at the so-called moment of grace, the following speculations are not implausible. Upon receiving Weisser's initial calls, Trapp's prejudices were confirmed: Jews "really are" aggressive, persistent, and self-righteously "Phariseeic," although not entirely without "Jewish" humor, as evidenced by the flatulence joke. Upon angrily confronting Weisser and demanding an account for his "harassment," Trapp probably could not believe his ears when Weisser replied in a conciliatory, nonjudgmental, helpful manner. This may explain Trapp's abrupt "no thanks," and his request for no further, profoundly disquieting offers of help. Weisser, however, not to be dissuaded, promised (threatened?) to "keep in touch" by phone.

Within days Trapp removed his "Race and Reason" tapes from the local community access channel. This is an anti-Semitic, racist television talk show produced by Tom Metzger and his White Aryan Resistance out of Fallbrook, California.[9] Although again we can only ruminate about the causes of Trapp's actions, it might have been that he had now admitted into his mental framework the existence of "exceptional" Jews – people like Weisser who fail to conform to the defamatory stereotypes "Race and Reason" promulgates. Whatever the reason, sensing a change in heart, Weisser again left a message on Trapp's recorder reminding him that "help is available." This time Trapp did not return the call. Nevertheless, that the relationship between Weisser and Trapp had been profoundly altered already is evidenced by the next incident.

On November 15, 1991, Trapp appeared in court for sentencing on an unrelated charge of trespassing and racial harassment. The hallway to the courtroom was crowded with reporters, two of whom were women, one of them black. To the latter he shouted: "Fuckin' half breed, get out of my face!" To the other he mumbled, "She works for Jews and Kykes, I don't talk to the 'Jews-media.' " That evening Weisser, who witnessed the exchange on the evening news, called Trapp and, "believing that I had the right to do so," demanded that he "explain" his outburst. The "right" that Weisser alludes to had somehow been created, he felt, in the course of Weisser's and Trapp's prior, albeit brief, interaction, and had been confirmed by Trapp's conciliatory handling of the "Race and Reason" show. Evidently Trapp seemed to share this sense of mutuality, for according to Weisser he "was sheepish and admitted 'I was nervous with those people in my face.' " In other words, instead of defensively insisting on the appropriateness of his courtroom outburst, Trapp agreed that it was wrong and asked that it not be excused, but forgiven. Furthermore, understanding that forgiveness is customarily predicated on symbolic compensation to the victim, Trapp promised to "apologize" to the reporters for his behavior.

The next day Trapp called Weisser, saying, "I want to get out [of the hate movement], but don't know how." Everything now rested on Weisser's response to this gesture of helplessness and vulnerability, of Nazi opening himself to Jew. Weisser's answer in retrospect was perfect: He and his wife Julie "grabbed a bucket of fried chicken and took him dinner."

The couple talked with Trapp for hours. Says Trapp, "they showed me so much love that I couldn't help but love them back." Tokens of the evening's communion were passed. Trapp gave Michael and Julie his

swastika rings, Klan robes, and some pamphlets; the Weissers recipro-
cated with a silver ring with a twisted strand design. "I called it my
brotherhood ring. Julie bought it for me several years ago. She said it
could symbolize Trapp's twisted past."

The following Saturday the Weissers invited Trapp to dinner at their
home. The occasion of the engagement was to provide Trapp the opportunity to carry out his promise to formally apologize to those individuals
and groups in Lincoln who had suffered firsthand his demeaning epithets. Included among those present were representatives of the NAACP,
CARP, and the Interfaith Coalition. At first the situation was tense. Once
the apology was offered, however, words of forgiveness were expressed.
Larry Trapp was readmitted into the community, acknowledged as a member in good standing. The enemies on both sides had been deconstructed.

Since that evening, Trapp has also apologized to the Anti-Defamation
League and has returned to the Weisser house frequently to share meals.
The Weissers' teenage children, two daughters and a son, have, to use
their father's term, "adopted" Trapp, hug him when he comes through
the door, and have dubbed him with the endearing title "Uncle Larry."
On the first night of Hanukkah, the Weissers again invited Trapp for
dinner.[10] Their gift to him was a Star of David. He promised to pin it on
the green beret he had donned as a "mercenary soldier in Rhodesia"
(more on this below) and wear it to his new vocation: reaching out to
others like himself who want to get out of the hate movement, but don't
know how. To this end he has already enlisted his telephone service to
broadcast messages like these: "Here's something to think about – Have
you told your minority neighbor that you love him?" "Happy Hanukkah, love for all people." His hope is to take this message nationwide.

A concluding word for this section. Recently, a bowdlerized rendition
of the criterion of love used here – it is good that you exist – became the
title of a pop psychology bestseller, *I'm Ok, You're Ok*.[11] The point of the
book is that love accepts the other unconditionally, "where he is now,"
with all his weaknesses, faults, blemishes, and wrongs: That's okay, because I'm okay. This is not the place to critique a work which has probably
relieved a good many of surplus guilt and preserved their acquaintances
from their condemnation, but the following point should be emphasized
lest Michael Weisser's initial reaction to Trapp be mistaken for something
it was not.

As Josef Pieper has demonstrated, true love in fact discounts, ignores, and excuses nothing. "If you are without chastening," he reminds the reader by quoting an ancient proverb, "then you are bastards and not sons."[12] The significance of this for us is that first impressions notwithstanding, the very fact that Weisser repeatedly admonished Trapp ("in," says Weisser, and this is important, "a friendly voice") indicates that he took seriously Trapp's dignity as a human being capable of choice. He did not simply present the matter to the police (although this was his first inclination, after locking his doors and agonizing about his children's safety), and then ignore it. Nor did he dismiss Trapp as a nut (which, if taken literally, would have implied that Trapp was unable to do other than he did). Instead, Weisser promised himself, "I'm gonna confront this guy if I can" and, at his wife's suggestion, "kill him with kindness," believing that as a human being Trapp could not help but respond in kind.

The contrary of love, Pieper argues, is not really hate; it is indifference. Friends are not indifferent to the actions of companions, but want what is best for them and provision them to attain it. But what is best for those companions is sometimes what is most difficult. Perhaps the most difficult thing of all is to acknowledge that the world view in which they have invested energy, emotion, and treasure is fundamentally mistaken, destructive to themselves and to others, and must therefore be changed. True love not only affirms, it demands and shames. By this measure Weisser was a true friend to Trapp.

The Event Viewed Sociologically

At first glance it appears that the Weisser-Trapp story is little short of miraculous. On closer view it seems to have been socially preconditioned, if not mechanically predetermined and hence inevitable.

The reader will recall our discussion in chapter 8 of the social pulls and pushes, as we called them, that can propel people into hate and cause them to apostatize. This model can be used profitably to account for Larry Trapp's affiliation with the hate movement and his subsequent trajectory away from it.

Larry Trapp's biography as a youth parallels the stories recounted in chapter 8. In brief, he was raised in a working-class household of nonpracticing Roman Catholics. He came to take for granted as common sense the kinds of racial and religiously bigoted stereotypes familiar to white American Christians everywhere.

Trapp's upbringing was "rugged"; at the age of ten his father knocked him unconscious in a rage. Larry dropped out of high school and was unemployed when arrested for auto theft and sentenced to Kearny State Reformatory at the age of fifteen. The reformatory experience was both good and bad. During his sentence, Trapp earned his GED and his certification as a barber. At the same time he had a "bad experience," being brutalized by five black inmates. Everything he had learned about them was "confirmed" by this incident. As for the barber's license, when he proudly displayed it, his father ridiculed it with the words "big deal."

So much for the summed forces pointing Trapp toward a life of hate. What about hate's seductions?

In a state of depression, after a brief marriage during which he acted as a "bum," Trapp, now in his mid-twenties, happened across an advertisement in a men's magazine for a "survival camp" in Florida. In reality the camp was a recruiting station for disgruntled white men being enlisted by Rhodesian landowners as mercenary soldiers in their struggle against the African nationalist movement. Already sated with antiblack hostility and looking for a quick way – death – out of his problems, Trapp contemplated becoming a soldier of fortune. (He had already lain in a street hoping for a car to end his misery.)

As it turned out, however, Trapp failed to make the excursion to Africa, bummed around Florida for a time, and during the course of his stay had a boil on his cheek surgically removed. (When Trapp first shared his past with the Weissers over chicken dinner in November 1991, they asked about the scar. Trapp invented the fantasy that he did go to Rhodesia, where in one battle he received a face full of shrapnel and was sent home. He later tearfully confessed that it was all a lie. As is their habit, the Weissers smilingly forgave him, speculating that the tale merely documented Trapp's need "to be a big shot"; or, to use our terminology, his need for acclamation and love. It is worth mentioning that several months after the Persian Gulf war in the spring of 1991, Trapp, customarily outfitted in camouflage fatigues, and aboard his wheelchair, met an older man who praised him for the heroic "sacrifice" of his legs and eyesight in the Vietnam war. Trapp didn't have the heart to disabuse him of his misimpressions.)

Trapp's intention upon arriving in Nebraska from the Deep South was to sign up with the Ku Klux Klan. Initially this too was frustrated, as the group is virtually nonexistent in the Middle West. As a last resort he went to the public library, found the address of the Invisible Empire of the KKK, and applied for membership. Finding the Empire too tame for his tastes, however, he soon quit and, after certifying his racial and religious (Christian) purity, affiliated with the more radical White Knights of the KKK. Trapp so impressed national headquarters with his skill in passing out hate literature and in soliciting membership inquiries that he was promoted through the ranks to the position of Grand Dragon of the Nebraska White Knights.

Ordinarily, heading an organization increases an individual's commitment to its program. This being the case, it is hard to understand at first why Trapp would have apostatized from the Klan. The following observations should help make his actions a bit more comprehensible.

The stability of one's group affiliations is a product of the net force of the social pulls and pushes playing on him at that time. Among these are forces pulling and pushing the individual into further group engulfment, and forces working in the opposite direction. In retrospect, it is obvious that in Trapp's case, the net weight of these forces would lead him away from hate.

Although nominally Trapp enjoyed an impressive title as regional director of a group with a notable if infamous heritage and considerable size, essentially the Nebraska White Knights is a fiction. By the time Trapp left, it consisted of only two flesh and blood members, about thirty faceless applicants, a handful of telephone acquaintances, some unsigned fax messages, and an occasional teenage skinhead admirer. This is to say that the very things that nourish group commitment – social activities such as meals together, intimate discussions, mutual confession, rituals, acknowledgment, and affirmation – were nonexistent. Trapp had received a poem from one groupie entitled "The Hero of Nebraska," extolling his courage and persistence in the fight for "equal rights" for whites; too, Klan pamphlets, broadsheets, and videos such as "Race and Reason" would have provided Trapp an elaborate world view and a sense of existential mission. Nevertheless, this all seems like thin soup indeed. Even if we add to this a further social push in the form of a sense of being "persecuted" by the police and by anti-Klan groups like CARP, we are not left with much upon which to base an ongoing group commitment.

On the other side were, first of all, the concrete persons of Michael Weisser, his wife Julie, and their three teenagers, showering Trapp with the kinds of attention, affirmation, and succor that every human being craves; the family acting out what they understood to be the heart and fiber of all bona fide religiosity: reverence, prayer, nonharm to others, justice, tolerance, and, above all, love. Add to this later, the acceptance, admittedly proffered skeptically and grudgingly, of the larger community. We may even cite the considerate gesture of an Asian woman who, when Trapp arrived at the courthouse for sentencing on the charges mentioned above, offered to help him onto the elevator. While he proudly refused the offer at the time, it was important enough for Trapp to mention later as still another reason for his renunciation of hate. In short, if it is true as Weisser claims that "if you get hate you give hate back," the opposite is probably equally true.

Apart from this there is the immeasurably important role played by three anonymous nurses in Trapp's conversion. Long before meeting Weisser, the diabetic, wheelchair-bound Trapp was being given house care and insulin by three different day nurses. While each felt under professional obligation to be "nice" to him, "they did not like to go there" to his apartment. Each in turn told him in effect, "You've been in [the hate movement] too long; you have to get out." Again, although it is impossible to estimate the importance of their encouragement, Weisser believes that they "planted the seeds" for Trapp's apostasy – seeds which his family merely tended.

When Trapp publicly announced his intention to disaffiliate permanently from the Klan, two things occurred. Both had the effect of further solidifying his decision – the first by decrying it, the second by applause.

The first incident was the publication of Trapp's excommunication from the movement over various racist hot lines, including that produced by Tom Metzger. To paraphrase Metzger's announcement: "Update: 'Loser.' Jews are free to have the freak loser Larry Trapp. . . . Losers – find 'love' and freak out. . . . Like [Greg] Withrow [see chapter 8] and [Tom] Martinez [a member of the *Bruders Schweigen* who turned state's evidence] losers want someone to hold their hands . . . and tell them they are wonderful human beings. . . . Gimme a break!" While the ostensible purpose of this message was to sanction Trapp's nonconformity and get him to rethink his decision, in fact it has had the opposite effect of proving his intuitions correct.

Soon after the nationwide publication of the Larry Trapp story under a headline that reveals more about the editor's own outlook than anything else – "Friendship Therapy Gets Results" – Michael Weisser received a phone call. It was Trapp's father, now in Omaha, wishing to contact his son after all these years. Weisser took the father's number and promised to give Larry the message. At first the son rejected "violently" any thought of reconciliation with the man who had once beaten him unconscious and belittled his accomplishments. A couple of hours later, evidently reconsidering his response in light of his conversion, Larry phoned Weisser and asked for his father's number. While it is premature to speak of the future of this relationship, it is enough to know that just as the antagonists Trapp and Weisser ended hostilities over chicken dinner, the ancient rivals, father and son, have now done the same.

Conclusion

The social construction of the enemy is a project in public "refusal," in the communal making of refuse, trash, rubbish. By means of defamatory labeling, public degradation, mythic diabolizing, and ritual exorcism, the community spurns, disgards, rejects, casts out. To reverse our now familiar formula: In the constitution of the enemy the community declares that some one or group is evil and thus ought not to exist. Not "We wish they weren't here," and not "We wish they were dead," but "They ought not have been created."[13] The constitution of the enemy, that is to say, denies creation and accomplishes death. In this light it is easy to imagine the Weisser-Trapp case culminating in a manner analogous to that of the Goldmarks. Had Larry Trapp himself not executed the final scene, then perhaps one of his younger followers might have done so. That the tale has thus far taken a happier turn appears to be due to a phenomenon "scientific realists" are reluctant to admit into their vocabulary – love. For insofar as love encompasses the wanting to be, which is to say, the *willing* to be, it accomplishes the very opposite of nonexistence – life.

Being loved by a mother, for example, we now know, is the very precondition for a child's flourishing. In the earliest reported work on this subject, René Spitz studied an orphanage where six nurses cared for forty-five infants less than eighteen months old. Although the children were well clothed and well fed, they had little contact with the nurses. Within one year their scores on developmental tests had fallen by one-half; within two years a third of them had died and the balance were severely retarded. When compared with children raised in prisons in the company of their own mothers under abject conditions, the orphans were far worse off.[14]

In the second chapter we repeated the truism that human beings rarely are satisfied with merely "feeling good." They yearn to "feel good about themselves"; they seek confirmation that their being in the cosmos is somehow worthwhile, significant. It is this urge for significance that lends impetus to the heroic quest, one form of which is the attempt to "save the world" symbolically by "killing death" – by annihilating the enemy who, as excrement, *is* death. Larry Trapp's biography prior to his chance encounter with Michael Weisser clearly illustrates this proposition. Now assuming that love affirms the goodness of another, then its recipient can feel justified in his existence. If this is so, love may be a partial answer to the question of how to overcome violence. The issue remaining before us, then, is how to institutionalize love into the thinking and actions of everyday life. This is our concern in the next chapter.[15]

10

A Community with a Heart
A Sociology of the Kootenai County Human Relations Task Force

Is there a spiritual reality, inconceivable to us today, which corresponds in history to the physical reality which Einstein discovered and which led to the atomic bomb? Einstein discovered a law of physical change: the way to convert a single particle of matter into enormous energy. Might there not also be, as Gandhi suggested, an equally incredible and undiscovered law of spiritual change, whereby a single person or small community of persons could be converted into an enormous spiritual energy capable of transforming a society and a world?[1]

Prologue

In American folklore, racism and bigotry are associated with the states of the old Confederacy. While this is not entirely without justification, it has become less and less accurate since the mid-1970s. The best data available, those collected by Laird Wilcox and his Editorial Research Service, demonstrate that the greatest concentration of right-wing groups is found in the Rocky Mountain and Pacific Coast states, not in the deep South (Table 10.1).[2]

Of these states Montana, Idaho, and Oregon are the three top-ranked extremist locales in the entire country, with Wyoming, Colorado, Arizona, Washington, and Alaska all in the top ten. Montana alone boasts nearly twenty right-wing headquarters per 500,000 inhabitants. Idaho has seventeen. Alabama, Florida, Kentucky, Georgia, Mississippi, and Louisiana all have rates three to four times less than this.

We need not spend inordinate space examining the reasons for the West becoming a haven to American right-wingers. However, two hypotheses are worth mentioning. The first is that relative to the eastern United States, the Democratic and Republican parties are weak in the West; larger proportions of westerners take pride in their political independence. As a result, the political vacuum is filled by a plethora of

Table 10.1

Right-Wing Extremist Headquarters by Region in America (1989)

Region	No. of Right-Wing Headquarters[a]	Population (000)[b]	Right-Wing Headquarters per 1,000	National Rank
Mountain	298	13,166	.023	1
Pacific	731	36,533	.020	2
West North Central[c]	275	17,634	.016	3
South Atlantic[d]	535	41,063	.013	4
Northeast	158	12,844	.012	5
West South Central	308	26,910	.011	6
East North Central	462	41,474	.011	6
Mid Atlantic	376	37,433	.010	8
East South Central	137	15,290	.009	9
National totals	3,496	242,969	.014	–

[a]From Laird Wilcox, *1989 Guide to the American Right* (Olathe, Kans.: Editorial Research Service, 1989).
[b]From U.S. Department of Commerce, *Statistical Abstracts of the United States, 1989* (Washington, D.C.: Government Printing Office, 1989).
[c]Montana placed in Mountain Region. Including Montana, the West North Central regional rate = .017.
[d]Leaves out Washington, D.C. Including D.C., the South Atlantic regional rate = .018.

smaller groups which, because they are not controlled by larger parties, tend to extremism in both ideology and tactics. The second reason is that the West has relatively low rates of conventional church membership, rendering the population more susceptible to appeals by cult movements.

What concerns us in this chapter is the response of local residents to hate groups when they move to town. The following pages describe one such community response that has since earned its citizenry plaudits by national civil rights organizations. It is known as the Kootenai County Human Relations Task Force (KCHRTF).

The name Kootenai honors the Indians that once resided in northern Idaho and southwestern Canada. The seat of Kootenai County is Coeur d'Alene (Heart of the Sharp Leaves), a tourist and light industrial town situated near a large glacier-carved lake, about fifty miles east of Spokane, Washington. In 1973 the Church of Jesus Christ Christian (Aryan Nations) built a headquarters in the woods just north of Coeur d'Alene on Hayden Lake and began proselytizing neighbors with its Judeophobic, white supremacist message. These headquarters have since become the scene of annual summer gatherings of the "great minds," as they call themselves, of the white racist movement from North America and Europe, and more recently of skinhead conventions held on the anniversary of Adolf Hitler's birthday in April. At the 1986 Aryan World Congress, which I attended, Hayden Lake was declared provisional capital of a five-state Pacific Northwest Aryan Nation.

Why the Aryan Nations Church moved to Idaho is a matter of debate which can be largely ignored here. It is enough to note that other radical political-religious groups have followed suit. Among these are America's Promise, a Christian Identity church founded in Phoenix but now located in Sandpoint, Idaho, just up the highway from Hayden Lake; and the Church of the Creator, founded by self-proclaimed "Pontifex Maximus" Ben Klassen, author of the White Man's Bible, "a powerful religious creed and program for the survival, expansion and advancement of the White Race." It boasts two "parishes" in Montana – one in Superior, the other in Missoula, just east of Coeur d'Alene.

Some say that what attracted the Aryans to Idaho was the state's deep-forested alpine splendor, acreage going at giveaway prices at the time, and the promise of relief from the brown-skinned polyglot mobs and polluted congestion of Sun Belt megalopolises. My own belief is that church members found a preexisting support group of sympathizers in eastern Washington and northern Idaho. The Gem State in the 1970s also offered the promise of respite from harassment by police officials then cracking down on paramilitary activities in the desert southwest.[3]

But again, our concern is not with why the Aryan Nations Church chose Idaho as the site of a twenty-acre, barbed-wire-enclosed compound, complete with watchtower, armed guardhouse and gate, chapel, hall of flags, and outbuildings; it is with what nearby residents did when they could no longer ignore the Church's presence.

That there was a menace is now clear. Although never directly associated with the Church, the *Bruders Schweigen* (or Order), the most violent rightist organization in American history since the Black Legion of the 1930s, drew its most dedicated cadres from Church membership rolls. This group was complicitous in at least three murders, a death at the hands of police, and one teenage suicide.[4] When the Order was crushed by the FBI, a successor group calling itself Order Strike Force II, made up exclusively of Aryan Nations congregants, was founded. It was implicated in at least one murder and, more pointedly for our purposes, a bomb attack in 1986, with evident intent to kill the person who was then leading the KCHRTF, Father Bill Wassmuth, whose story is related below. Again, in the spring of 1990, long after most commentators had thought that the remnants of organized hate in Idaho had scurried underground, still another Aryan Nations–based terrorist group was exposed by authorities just as it disembarked to Seattle to bomb a popular homosexual bar in such a way as to ensure "a high body count," together with a synagogue and a tavern frequented by blacks. In February 1992, the FBI exposed another plot, this by a seven-member so-called Bob Mathews Brigade, to murder Wassmuth and a fellow KCHRTF member, Marshall Mend. The alleged plan was scuttled when immigration agents moved to deport two skinhead members of the group who were from Italy and Canada. The group was named in honor of the founder of the *Bruders Schweigen*.[5] As this suggests, combating hate is far from being risk free; nor is it a task accomplished by reading pamphlets, listening to inner peace tapes, and getting "cleared." The individuals whose political biographies are sketched below are all well above average in their sensitivity to prejudice, including their own propensity to malign others. However, this has not armored them against attacks by others not so conscious. At this writing all of them are cognizant that they and their families are in constant danger.

To continue living quasi-normally in the face of gnawing anxiety that unnamed others mean you harm is part of what peace workers mean by "holding the tension." Holding the tension is nothing less than heroic in the best sense of that often misused word, for it counters a natural inclination either to psychically numb ourselves to community peril through the infinite distractions culture makes available for this purpose, to flee altogether from danger, or to strike out violently against the enemy. Below are the stories of six people who could not or did not follow these inclinations. The six, in order of presentation, are Dina Tanners, Larry Broadbent, Glen Walker, Bill Wassmuth, Sandy Emerson, and Marshall Mend (their real names).[6] It should be mentioned that these were not the only individuals who originally took a stand against hate in Kootenai County. Several others are cited by name. Still others, for reasons of practicality, are not mentioned.

For a sociologist, however, specific names are not important as such; what interests us are groups. One kind of social grouping is technically known as a voluntary association, an aggregate of people who perform a set of coordinated actions outside established channels in response to a common concern. The KCHRTF is an example of a politically oriented voluntary association.

For present purposes the various explanations for the rise of voluntary associations can be reduced to two.[7] First and most obviously there must be a natural constituency affected by a particular event in the world. Although we are oversimplifying the situation, it is fair to say that the natural constituency for the KCHRTF was Coeur d'Alene's white, college-educated, hence moderately liberal middle class. Around forty-ish in age at the time the KCHRTF was founded, they were imbued with the slogans and ideals of the civil rights era widely invoked during their political maturation in the late 1960s.

While a natural constituency is always necessary for a voluntary association to flourish, it is never sufficient. If it is to be mobilized, this constituency must also be integrated into the community. As observed in chapter 8, it is through social contacts that people learn of, receive invitations to join, and eventually commit themselves to crusades. People may live in abject misery or crave racial justice, but unless they have solid communal attachments, they will not participate in movements to advance their cause. In regard to the KCHRTF, the reader should attend to how the social networks of the six individuals listed above made them available for recruitment themselves and also positioned them to mobilize others to publicly stand up against hate. In Coeur d'Alene these communal bonds turned out to be stronger than the occupational, gender, confessional, and income differences characteristic of American towns which ordinarily frustrate local efforts at social reform.

Dina's Story

Dear "Abby"

Two years ago our family moved from a large southern city to a new life in north Idaho. The beauty of the area far exceeds that of any place we have known and we thank God for the clean air, wildlife and beautiful scenery the locals take for granted. . . . However, having lived in the South, our family has never known any place so ignorant and full of racism as north Idaho.

A college friend of our son was to have spent two full weeks with us last summer and left after just five days due to comments such as "what's a nigger doin' driving a car like that" or upon entering a local restaurant heard "niggers stay out" from two cowboys seated nearby. Recently, while departing a local college basketball game while in the parking lot we heard "you gotta hand it to those jigs they can sure play ball." . . .

Signed,
Calling It Like It Is in North Idaho[8]

Dina Tanners remembers how Jewish vacationers to her Coeur d'Alene home would ask: How can you live here in the midst of all this racism and anti-Semitism? Her response was always, It isn't so bad, once you get to know the people. Brought up in a liberal Jewish home, Ms. Tanners had learned to live and let live while attending inner-city Franklin High School in Seattle, long noted for the racial and religious balance of its student body.

Lunching one afternoon with a summer visitor at Coeur d'Alene's famed North Shore Inn, Ms. Tanners and her guest had just stepped into the sun when they were handed hate literature bearing the Aryan Nations inscription and addressed from its nearby Hayden Lake compound. It dawned on her that perhaps her ingrained tolerance was sentimental, maybe even dangerous.

Out of her awakening was born what would come to be known as the Kootenai County Human Relations Task Force, an association that would earn Coeur d'Alene the reputation of a "model community" among national law enforcement officials and civil rights workers for its handling of racial and religious strife.

Graduated magna cum laude in Latin American studies from Brandeis University and a world traveler, Tanners is by her own admission a natural teacher and community organizer. Instead of stewing in her newly awakened concern, she directed it at what seemed the perfect audience: the Coeur d'Alene Ecumenical Council, then presided over by the bearded pastor of the First Christian Church, Rev. Rick Morse. During a fall 1980 meeting held to discuss the issue, members of the Council discovered that they had all been receiving unsolicited Aryan Nations pamphlets and that they were not alone in their abhorrence and resentment at what they read in them. It was time to take a stand as leaders of the Christian community.

With the help of Rev. Edgar Hart of the First Presbyterian Church, head of the independent Coeur d'Alene Ministerial Association, and Methodist minister Rev. Al Aosved, Morse composed a six-point denunciation of racism and anti-Semitism as "heretical and apostate." At the September press conference announcing the document, Morse confessed anxiety for his own safety, but expressed greater worry that "if we are going to operate on that premise – 'Don't say anything or they'll do something' – we might as well turn the world over to the bad guys."[9]

Several days later Rev. Richard Butler of the Aryan Nations Church sent a personal letter to Morse seeking to calm his fears for his well-being, while insisting on the doctrinal correctness of "Identity Christianity," and inviting Morse, Hart, and Aosved to "sit down and reason together . . . go over the Scriptures." Receiving no response to the invitation, Butler denounced the group as "modern day Pharisees" and likened himself to John the Baptist and to Jesus Christ who were also "crucified" for preaching truth.

Signed by twenty-eight religious leaders representing at least seventeen denominations, the ministerial association's denunciation asserted that racial bigotry "distorts and corrupts both Scripture and history" and encourages "hate tactics and coercive intimidation" which are contrary to the Gospel. While affirming support for minorities in the city who had suffered harassment, at the same time it acknowledged the right of groups like the Aryan Nations to preach their version of Christianity.

These words had the desired effect of permitting others in Coeur d'Alene to voice their outrage at racial hatred in a civil manner, most notably the *Coeur d'Alene Press* in an editorial entitled "Racism Must Be Combatted":

> As responsible citizens of this great land, we must always . . . combat and denounce those among us who seek to distort the great liberties given us by our democratic form of government. . . . In this respect, nothing is more insidious or heinous than the persecution of a people because of their color or their ethnic heritage. We must never be apathetic on this subject.[10]

Sheriff Broadbent's Story

Aryan Nations activists point to Larry Broadbent's arrival as the county's undersheriff in December 1980, just after publication of the Coeur d'Alene ministers' petition and newspaper editorial, as part of a larger conspiracy to rid the area of its lily-white image so as to promote the introduction of gambling by Las Vegas and Reno interests.[11]

Broadbent's supporters agree that his hiring by the recently elected sheriff "Merf" Stalder was more than coincidental; but they prefer the

Table 10.2

Acts of Racial and Religious Harassment in Northern Idaho (1979–1983)

Coeur d'Alene: Hispanic family living in trailer receives repeated telephone threats to leave the area. Someone attempts to set fire to trailer; family dog's throat slashed; family receives threats of harm to their chldren. Family moves from area (1979).

Post Falls and Spokane, Washington: Targets, consisting of caricatures of black males running, posted in area (1980–82).

Hayden Lake: Jewish restaurateur's seventeen-year-old business defaced with swastikas and anti-Semitic references. Stickers with the message "Do Not Patronize This Place" applied to wall of the restaurant (1981–82).

Coeur d'Alene: First Baptist Church of Idaho defaced with swastika (1982).

Coeur d'Alene: Printing business defaced with swastika (1982).

Coeur d'Alene: Two teenagers, a minority male and a white female, verbally and physically assaulted by young white males associated with the Aryan Nations Church outside roller skating rink (1982).

Coeur d'Alene: Cross burned on lawn of area home which is also defaced with swastikas and "anti-Christ" graffiti (1982).

Kootenai and Bonner counties: Paramilitary target ranges discovered containing Jewish "Star of David" targets riddled with bullet holes (1982).

Coeur d'Alene: Cross burned on property of all-white family. Interracial families live on the same block. Police believe that the "wrong" home was targeted (1983).

Source: U.S. Department of Justice, *Bigotry and Violence in Idaho* (Washington, D.C.: Government Printing Office, 1986), pp. 3–4.

theory that it was something like Divine Providence, which for Its own reasons chose to gift the county with a man who would spearhead the effort to outlaw racial violence in Idaho. For far from putting an end to racial-religious harassment in the area around Coeur d'Alene, the ministers' public petition seemed to occasion its escalation. According to the Community Relations Service of the U.S. Department of Justice, twenty-two instances of racial and religious harassment were reported in Idaho between 1979 and 1983 (Table 10.2), sixteen in the period immediately following the published denunciation cited above.

Already by December of that year the Justice Department had grown so concerned about developments in northern Idaho that it had sent one of its top experts in discrimination, a one-time Protestant minister named Bob Hughes, to investigate the situation and to help organize an effective community response to it. Broadbent, the Reverends Morse and Hart, and Dina Tanners all attended the first meeting.[12]

The state of Washington was then in the process of passing a malicious harassment bill. In May 1981 at a seminar on community relations at Spokane's Gonzaga University, the above four, with others in attendance, formally resolved to work for similar legislation in Idaho. To christen its efforts the group agreed to call itself the Kootenai County Human Relations Task Force, although the intent at first was to function purely on an ad hoc and informal basis.

Malicious harassment had always been a misdemeanor in Idaho. Until the upsurge in racially motivated attacks in the 1980s – not only in Coeur d'Alene, but in Boise, Twin Falls, Pocatello, Jerome, and Idaho Falls as well – the official line was that this was sufficient to deter violence. What has come to be known as the Connie Fort incident proved that notion wrong.[13]

It was July 1982 when Connie Fort's eight-year-old black son, Lamar, came home crying that someone had called him "nigger." Upon confronting the perpetrator, an adult neighbor, Ms. Fort was maligned and her son was again reviled.

A Coeur d'Alene police officer who was subsequently called to investigate the incident told Ms. Fort that while he sympathized with her, because racial slander was only a misdemeanor he was powerless to take action against it.[14] From this conversation, Ms. Fort got the impression that the only way to get legal satisfaction was to make a citizen's arrest. "I told him I didn't feel I was big enough to go in there," she later told authorities, "considering that the man was 100 pounds more than I am, plus he might have had a weapon or something."[15]

Terrified by her assailant's epithets and overcome by feelings of isolation that reminded her of when she was a little girl and the German Army had occupied her hometown of Amsterdam and begun whisking people away at night, Connie Fort sought the aid of Undersheriff Broadbent. In his presence she opened a mailed envelope containing a poster with these words:

> Race traitors, those guilty of fratinizing [sic] socially or sexually with blacks, now stand warned that their identities are being catalogued. . . . Miscegenation is race treason, race treason is a capitol [sic] offense; it will be punished by death. . . . Negroes involved . . . will be shot as they are apprehended.[16]

To lend credibility to the threat, another letter was sent containing a news report of the decomposed body of a black man shot through the head and found floating in nearby Spirit Lake. To Ms. Fort the message implied, "Look what I did, I can do this to you."[17]

The harassment continued, now against Ms. Fort's eighteen-year-old son. In one incident in March 1983, the attacker asked him: "How art thou today? Thou shalt not live very long."[18] Another time, while riding his bicycle at night, he was run off the road by a car.

Ms. Fort later commented on the effects these incidents had on her family:

> A lot of sleepless nights for one. Afraid that the Ku Klux Klan is going to drive up. What this has done to my family and me, the children have been very upset and have dreams and nightmares, and there's nights when I can't sleep and I run through the house afraid that somebody's going to start burning crosses for some reason.[19]

It is hard to say exactly what emotional impact the Connie Fort incident had on Undersheriff Broadbent. There is little doubt that it and the other cases cited in Table 10.2 cemented his determination to rid the county of hate groups. In any case, no event did more to galvanize support for the KCHRTF than the publication of Ms. Fort's frightening tale by the *Coeur d'Alene Press* later that fall, using the fictitious name "Kathy."[20]

Rick Morse immediately understood his responsibility as spokesman for the Christian community, and through his position in the Ecumenical Council, he organized overwhelming public support for Ms. Fort. A petition circulated among Coeur d'Alene's denominations obtained more than 800 signatures, several hundred from St. Pius X Catholic Church alone, where Ms. Fort was a nonpracticing parishioner. With a bouquet of roses, the signed petition was presented to Ms. Fort, followed later by financial contributions, job offers, and personal counseling.

As for the perpetrator, he was later found guilty of misdemeanor assault. More important was the impetus the incident gave to efforts to elevate racially motivated assault to the status of a felony in Idaho. This brings us to Glen Walker.

Prosecutor Walker's Story

Raised a fundamentalist Christian in a racist Florida village, Kootenai County Prosecutor Glen Walker had virtually no contact with nonwhites as a child. His life since that time has been a reluctant odyssey first toward toleration and then active support for minorities and the less fortunate. He now laughs at the following story, which, he says, is just one of many displaying how far he has come since his migration to the Northwest.

Working one summer in Maine when he was eighteen, "Rebel," as he was known to coworkers, was approached by a black man gesturing to him to shake hands. Walker was taken aback. "I didn't know what to do. . . . I didn't want to hurt his feelings, because I didn't dislike him. But would it be proper?" His question was answered when, sensing his disquiet, the man teased: "Come on man it won't rub off."

Walker insists he is still "not a social gooder type." "I'm not a bleeding heart" or an "egghead." A less likely candidate to support the fight for a malicious harassment bill in Idaho's notoriously conservative legislature could therefore hardly be found. And yet for all his self-deprecation, Walker is a man of compassion. "Sometimes," he confesses, "I care too much, and let things affect me too much." Fearing that lobbying efforts in behalf of the senate bill were floundering, "I said shit, if I don't do it, it won't get done."

A malicious harassment bill was introduced to the 1983 session of the Idaho legislature by Senator Norma Dobler of Moscow. In essence it proposed that it be a felony to intimidate another because of that person's race or religion, either by physical attack or by words, the latter if there is reason to believe that physical attack will occur. The draft legislation was composed by the Idaho Human Rights Commission following a panel discussion it helped to conduct in July 1982 on racial and religious harassment. In attendance at that meeting were representatives of the American Civil Liberties Union, the Justice Department, the KCHRTF, and the Kootenai County sheriff's office in the person of Larry Broadbent.

An ad hoc lobby calling itself the Citizen's Coalition Against Malicious Harassment was organized to expedite passage of the bill through what was anticipated to be a legislature reluctant to restrict speech by conservative religious groups. The Coalition claimed knowledge of over one hundred voluntary organizations and churches throughout the state favoring adoption of the bill. In addition to heading an aggressive letter-writing campaign, KCHRTF members Rev. Rick Morse, Dina Tanners, and Undersheriff Broadbent, as well as representatives of the Idaho Human Rights Commission, all testified in favor of its passage.

As feared, the bill indeed faced considerable opposition. Rev. Richard Butler, Montana Aryan Nations chief Larry McCurry, and Louis Beam (mentioned in chapter 4) all witnessed against it. Conservative spokesmen expressed concern that such a bill might infringe on constitutional rights of free speech and freedom of religion. One midwestern fundamentalist minister claimed, for example, that provisions in the bill would inhibit house-to-house proselytizing if it were interpreted by the host as harassment. Still others believed that the bill's adoption would imply ratification of the United Nations genocide convention. Given the reputation of the legislature, it appeared that the malicious harassment bill was doomed to failure.

With his well-honed conservative rhetoric, Glen Walker was called to negotiate an end to the impasse. To religious missionaries he pointed out that preaching by itself is an insufficient basis for charging persons with malicious harassment unless there are grounds for believing a physical assault will follow. To this author, Walker admitted that even the Connie Fort incident might not qualify as a felonious attack under the law. To mollify right-wing constitutionalists, he helped compose an amendment explicitly denying that passage of the bill implied support for the United Nations genocide convention. He also agreed to eliminate the section in the proposed law providing civil cause of action for malicious harassment (although one may seek civil remedies under other laws). This he was happy to do, since it protected victims of harassment from being countersued by their assailants for harassment. The consensus of observers is that Walker's efforts were pivotal in the bill's eventually winning majority support in March 1983.[21]

A less biased view, however, suggests that even with Walker's compromises, the bill probably would not have passed had not Keith Gilbert, leader of the National Socialist Aryan Peoples Party, a splinter group of the Aryan Nations Church, unwittingly helped it along. Under the signature of "Rabbi" Schecter and the letterhead of a fictitious "Anti Defamation League" lobby chartered by himself in February 1983,[22] Gilbert sent a letter to legislators ostensibly supporting the bill. He assumed that upon seeing it lobbied by a "Jewish" organization, Idaho lawmakers would vote against it.

Gilbert's strategy backfired. Somehow the scheme was exposed, Gilbert held up to public ridicule, and lawmakers, resentful of such a blatant attempt at manipulation, voted in favor of the bill.

Father Bill's Story

The KCHRTF was originally established in reaction to provocations by local racists. Seeing its goal of a malicious harassment bill accomplished, the number of reported acts of racial harassment in Kootenai County decline dramatically, and its chairman, Rev. Rick Morse, reassigned to a new congregation near Seattle, the task force was allowed to slip into dormancy. This was only temporary, however, because beginning in late 1983 a series of articles about north Idaho as a so-called neo-Nazi haven began appearing in regional and national media (including *People, Geo, California, Reader's Digest, Time, Newsweek, Harper's,* and not the least, *National Enquirer*).[23] In reaction, the KCHRTF was resurrected as a nonprofit corporation in 1985 under the leadership of Father Bill Wassmuth, pastor of Coeur d'Alene's St. Pius X Catholic Church. Henceforth, it would no longer merely respond to religious bigotry and racial intolerance after the fact, but assume an active stance toward them.

"I need a priest!" pleaded the voice over the phone. Father Bill Wassmuth's finely tuned antennae were immediately alerted. The voice was that of Barbara Strakal, a Coeur d'Alene educator. It seems that the Third Street Cantina, where her husband was assistant manager, was becoming a congregation point for a number of distraught "Fatima Crusade kids" who had recently fled from the religious group of that name. Burdened now with certain knowledge of their eternal condemnation to the fires of Hell for having left the crusade, and disowned by the parents who still remained in it, they had gravitated to the Cantina for mutual support and solace.

The Fatima Crusade (otherwise known as the Blue Army of Mary) is an authoritarian cult devoted to the Virgin Mary, end-time prophesying, and anti-Communism. Its existence in the area is still another indicator of the amenability of the local populace to political extremism. Now located at a former Jesuit seminary in Spokane, it emerged in the 1960s in Coeur d'Alene from disaffection with Vatican II, the changes in sacramental practice introduced during the reign of Pope John XXIII.

Ms. Strakal, her brother then a "Moonie" and herself a self-described refugee "Jesus Freak," had firsthand knowledge of religiously grounded psychological tyranny. This was the evident reason for the attraction of the Third Street Cantina to the "Fatima kids": here could be found a sympathetic adult ear. Nevertheless, the youths seeking harbor at her husband's café needed counseling from an expert in Catholic doctrine. Who better to go to than the local priest, "Father Bill," as he was affectionately known to his parishioners.

Until Strakal's call, Father Bill had dismissed the Fatima Crusade as a harmless if annoying conservative movement. He knew virtually nothing about the inner workings of cults. Strakal and Wassmuth's conversations were mutually enlightening: the Lutheran Strakal was introduced to Roman Catholicism, and Wassmuth to what he now calls "destructive cults." Together in the fall of 1981 they founded the Coeur d'Alene Cult Awareness Center to monitor the activities of such groups in the surrounding area. Soon after its establishment the Center sponsored a weeklong symposium on cults and kids. Aryan Nations members in attendance are said to have publicly agreed with Strakal that their own organization met the criteria of a destructive cult, when these were itemized in a nonthreatening way.

Wassmuth was the natural replacement for Rick Morse to head the KCHRTF when Morse left Coeur d'Alene. (Dina Tanners was unavailable to assume leadership because she had just been hired as a full-time special education teacher for the school district.) Already heavily involved in Alcoholics Anonymous and in Hospice, and an administrator of perhaps the most active parish in the Boise Diocese, Wassmuth already had a reputation as a top-flight community organizer. As for the work of the task force, he had always supported it, but from a distance, signing the 1980 Ministerial Association petition and lending his skill from the pulpit to secure signatures for the Connie Fort support letter. More than this he was acutely aware of the danger that racism constitutes for the integrity of a community.

Wassmuth's father had been the owner and manager of the local roller rink in the small Catholic farming town of Greencreek, Idaho, located on the very edge of the Palouse wheat country. In the middle 1960s a Job Corps Center was built in town. Poor, urban, minority youngsters were introduced into its prosperous, rural, all-white population. The product was fear and antagonism. Certain community elements accused the boys of preying on local girls at the roller rink on weekends (although Father Bill's own experience, he says with a grin, was that the reverse was true). In any case, when his father refused to close the doors of the rink to his Job Corps customers, he lost his white patronage, and with it, eventually, the entire business. Father Bill uses this story to explain why he chose to assume responsibility for a reconstituted antiracist group.

Whatever the reason, once having received his charge, Father Bill set about applying his organizational skills to creating a formal institutional structure with clearly identifiable lines of authority and a division of labor. Decision-making procedures and rules of membership and expulsion were put to paper, and a recording secretary delegated to keep meeting notes. A logo for the group was chosen between two aspirants: a black and white yin-yang figure and a multicolored Indian peace circle; stationery was printed; and fund-raising procedures were developed. In sociological terms, under Father Bill's leadership the KCHRTF came to be fully "institutionalized," its structure resembling a well-oiled machine, its parts all meshing, its moral stance neatly integrated into Coeur d'Alene's everyday life. Institutionalization is the typical fate of most successful voluntary associations in America.

Headed by an executive committee, of which Father Bill was then chair and spokesman, the task force essentially was to be run by subcommittee chairs with agendas set by the executive committee. The prominence of the subcommittee chairs and the diversity of interests they represented display the degree to which the KCHRTF was now part of the larger community: Marshall Mend, Kootenai County's top realtor for 1983 and 1984 (with a total volume of sales and listings each year of close to $4 million), chaired the speaker's bureau; Doug Cresswell, administrative assistant to the superintendent of the school district, headed the educational subcommittee; Peter Vaughan, a furniture distributor and realtor, the public affairs and community response subcommittee; Ann Salisbury-Brown, a prominent volunteer whose husband was then serving on the City Council, the victim support group; Bill Brown, the legal end of things; and Dave Peters, school teacher, the legislative subcommittee.

Undersheriff Broadbent attended executive committee meetings as the law enforcement consultant, and Sandy Emerson, executive director of Coeur d'Alene's Chamber of Commerce, as its business community consultant.

The KCHRTF has both legislative and educational agendas. Regarding the first, it has helped successfully lobby for passage of a paramilitary training bill that outlaws clubs engaged in arms training for purposes of racial or religious harassment. Undersheriff Broadbent believed that one of the main reasons white supremacist groups moved from California to Idaho in the first place was precisely the lack of such a law. Idaho is now one of only eighteen states having such legislation, the only state in the Pacific Northwest.

Regarding its educational agenda, the task force has a library of literature and films on prejudice available to local teachers. Furthermore, it has helped North Idaho Junior College direct its annual Popcorn Forum to the subjects of bigotry, racism, and conflict resolution. A number of nationally known speakers have appeared at these meetings.

Beyond this, the task force has printed and distributed posters ("North Idaho Is for Everyone"), has built and driven its own float in Fourth of July parades, has organized a speaker's bureau available for local groups, and has manned booths at the county fair featuring, among other things, guitarists singing songs advocating tolerance. The KCHRTF also earned national acclaim by sponsoring widely endorsed, hugely attended multiethnic and racial counterassemblies on the July weekends during which the annual Aryan World Congresses are held just down the highway.

While it plays a less visible role given the decline in cases of harassment, the KCHRTF's victim support group has established a telephone and message service for victims, and intends to monitor incidents with pin maps to identify danger areas in the community. At this writing a big brother/sister program is contemplated at the junior college to alert minority students to possible risks and to guide them through the harrowing assignment of living in an alien community. "Coffees" are currently being held for women in biracial relationships to encourage them to share their experiences.

Sandy Emerson's Story

Sir,

It is with deep regret that my family and I will *not* spend our vacation in Coeur d'Alene this summer as we had planned. We have been through your beautiful area before and fell in love with the mountains and lakes. However – the continuing regional and national news reports from Hayden and Coeur d'Alene area disturb us greatly. I would hope that the violent, "white-supremacy," hate-filled group up there is not supported by a majority of the people around there. But they must have a pretty fair amount of support – or they would not choose that area as their base. . . . As much as my family and I love the natural beauty up there we will have to boycott your area for future vacations until this hateful and violent group leaves. We will encourage everyone else we know to do the same. . . .

Thank you,
Salt Lake City Resident[24]

Sandy Emerson, at this writing executive director of the Coeur d'Alene Chamber of Commerce, and a frequent recipient of disheartening messages like the letter above, must have one of the most difficult jobs in town: reconciling potentially explosive differences among friends so that the economic base that sustains them all will not be devastated.[25]

Knowing from his experience with the Fatima Crusade that extremist groups feed off publicity, his first inclination regarding the Aryan Nations Church was simply to ignore it. Hence "silence is eloquent"[26] happily reigned as official Chamber policy until on an afternoon during the height of the Connie Fort incident Emerson was "visited," to use his own term, by an angry Dina Tanners demanding that the business community "do something." Still reticent about taking sides on such an inflammatory issue, Emerson realized that the Chamber was backed into a corner when the articles about Idaho as a so-called neo-Nazi homeland began cropping up.

Educated in business administration at the University of Idaho and having worked ten years as a real estate broker, Emerson makes no apologies for the fact that the subsequent public denunciation of racism by the Chamber in September 1983 began with the phrase, "to promote and protect a positive business climate."[27] While a number of groups such as the Lions Club[28] and the Soroptimists embraced the document without difficulty, others in Coeur d'Alene – including some in the task force itself – did not like the mercenary sound of its emphasis. It may be, as one suggested to this writer, that in the short run at least, racism has been "good" for the economy by bringing in moneyed media. Others express the belief that while "racism is bad for business," it is even worse for people. As one Coeur d'Alene city councilwoman said in justifying her refusal to endorse the Chamber statement: "There's a little too much in it about positive business climates. . . . It's a sweet thing . . . but it's not for us."[29]

True to his nature, Emerson takes a diplomatic view of the matter. It is not important that the City Council or any other organization endorse the specifics of Chamber policy, he says. What is important and truly newsworthy is that virtually the entire community of Kootenai County, each part in its own way, has strongly come out in favor of human rights and against bigotry.

One of the great paradoxes of institutionalization of political associations like the KCHRTF is that their very successes can be their undoing. As a movement successfully integrates itself into the everyday routine of community life it tends to lose its critical edge, accommodating itself to the world view of the dominant sectors of the community.

As the executive director of the KCHRTF, Father Bill worked best not as a dictator but as a delegator of authority. Subcommittee heads were given virtual autonomy to develop their own programs. This explains the vast scope of responsibilities that the task force has taken on. The downside is that two of the six subcommittee chairs under Wassmuth's directorship were energetic and outspoken businessmen, and Emerson of the Chamber of Commerce, one of the task force's two major consultants. The result was that the task force sometimes gave the impression of being a public relations front for Coeur d'Alene's commercial interests.

Wassmuth recognized the danger early, admitting to this author that the task force probably was overly dominated by a business outlook. At the same time he believed that it was "balancing out." If it did not do so, he said, then the task force "is not where I want to place my energy."

For reasons probably unrelated to the assassination attempt mentioned at the outset of this chapter, Wassmuth left the priesthood after 1987, married, and moved to Seattle. There he helped found and now serves as executive director of the Northwest Coalition Against Malicious Harassment. His apprehensions regarding the possible conservative drift of the KCHRTF seem to have been confirmed.

In early 1989, Reverend Butler announced plans for a "Skinhead Weekend" to be held in honor of the centennial of Adolf Hitler's birthday in April of that year. He even threatened a skinhead march down Coeur d'Alene's main street, Sherman Avenue. The executive board of the KCHRTF met to discuss an appropriate response. Lisa Anderson, part Native American, proposed a countermarch for racial equality up Highway 95, which leads to Aryan Nations headquarters. She insisted that failure to vigorously stand up to the skinhead challenge would be interpreted as indifference or cowardice. In either case it would put minorities like herself at risk. Norm Gissel, then director of the group, and a prominent Coeur d'Alene lawyer, disagreed, arguing that a march would merely dignify the skinheads and provide them surplus media attention, while changing nobody's attitude.[30] As a businessman and professional he was reluctant to see Coeur d'Alene once again spotlighted as a "nazi haven" by the press. Evidently agreeing with Gissel, the executive committee voted Anderson's motion down, proposing instead to distribute orange ribbons for the yards of local citizens (orange symbolizing self-confidence, enthusiasm, optimism, and courage), and to organize a weekend of quiet interfaith services, public concerts, picnics, and "friendship dinners." Anderson angrily denounced the decision, resigned her position on the executive committee, and announced the establishment of her own Citizens for Nonviolent Action Against Racism. Schismatic dissent is one more stage frequently observed in American voluntary associations as they become routinized.

With the help of several others, including a local black woman named Inez Anderson (no relation), Lisa went on successfully to orchestrate a six-hour, seven-mile protest march involving over a thousand activists from throughout the Northwest, encompassing eighty peace, gay rights, civil rights, lesbian, and socialist groups (including the Communist Revolutionary Action Group carrying inflammatory signs like "Smash the Fascists"). The marchers were estimated to have outnumbered the skinhead conferees by a ratio of anywhere from twenty or forty to one.

As Gissel feared, the national media were visibly present throughout the weekend; but as he could not have anticipated, they pictured northern Idaho not in negative terms, but as overwhelmingly in support of equality.[31] Perhaps because of its intimate ties to the leading circles of the community – the very fact that occasioned its success in the first place – the KCHRTF had momentarily surrendered leadership of the struggle against hate in Coeur d'Alene. Whether it can once again become the vanguard remains to be seen.

A Sociological Summation

Beginning in 1980 and lasting until about 1988, the city of Coeur d'Alene was deeply shaken by conflict between civil rights supporters and right-wing extremists, the latter hoping to cleanse the surrounding area of its "alien" religious, ethnic, and racial population. The civil rightists won the dispute and the racists lost. To say it more technically, the civil rights advocates succeeded in mobilizing Coeur d'Alene's financial and human resources to advance their cause; the right-wing extremists failed. Why?

By all appearances, both opponents had natural constituencies from which they could draw. There is nothing in the political culture of northern Idaho permitting us to have predicted that its population would favor liberalism over a right-wing racist agenda. On the contrary, northern Idaho and the region of eastern Washington contiguous to Spokane have at least since the 1920s (the heyday of the Ku Klux Klan) been home to a virulent brand of flag-waving intolerance and conspiratorialism. One of the first and largest chapters of the John Birch Society in America was established there in the 1950s. It drew some of its original members from the Anti-Communist League, whose machinations were complicitous in bringing grief to the Goldmark family (see chapter 3). My research indicates that one of this area's main drawing cards for the Aryan Nations Church (and later the National Socialist Aryan Peoples Party and America's Promise) was precisely its reputation for congeniality to rightist causes.

But the existence of a natural constituency, as we said earlier, is never sufficient for the success of a voluntary association. This constituency must in addition be actively recruited. As a rule, effective recruitment takes place not by the posting of broadsheets on telephone poles, by radio messages, mail-order campaigns, or even by door-to-door missionizing. If that were true, the Aryan Nations Church, which regularly employs all these devices to solicit support, would have done far better than it did in Coeur d'Alene. Instead, effective recruitment proceeds indirectly through a multilevel series of communal connections.

Prudent movement activists first of all attempt to win local opinion leaders to their side through ties of friendship and patronage. These opinion leaders, themselves strategically positioned in various local communication networks – churches, schools, business clubs, philanthropic organizations, labor unions, study groups, and sports clubs – will then mobilize their own followers to the cause.

Two related implications follow from these propositions: First, people who are not involved in local community groups are unlikely to participate actively in community conflicts. Or if, as sometimes happens, they do become involved, their activism tends toward extremism because

Table 10.3

Strategic Positions of KCHRTF Members in Coeur d'Alene

Name	Position in the Community
Tanners	Community volunteer
Morse	President, Coeur d'Alene Ecumenical Council
Hart	Pastor, First Presbyterian Church; head of Coeur d'Alene Ministerial Association
Aosved	Pastor, Coeur d'Alene First Methodist Church
Broadbent	Undersheriff of Kootenai County
Walker	Prosecuting Attorney of Kootenai County
Wassmuth	Pastor, St. Pius X Catholic Church of Coeur d'Alene
Mend	Kootenai County's top realtor
Cresswell	Coeur d'Alene public school administrator
Vaughan	Coeur d'Alene furniture dealer
Salisbury-Brown	Community volunteer; wife of Coeur d'Alene city councilman
Brown	Coeur d'Alene lawyer
Peters	School teacher, Coeur d'Alene public schools
Emerson	Executive director, Coeur d'Alene Chamber of Commerce

they are less constrained by institutional norms.[32] Second and more important, associations unable to win the support of opinion leaders will also be powerless to induce the average citizen to join them.

This said, we can now grasp sociologically why the KCHRTF enjoyed the success it did in Coeur d'Alene while the hate groups did not. In short, it was because the KCHRTF was inspired and organized by the institutionally pivotal opinion leaders of the city (see Table 10.3). Most of these individuals were either northern Idaho natives or in some way deeply invested occupationally, religiously, and familially in Coeur d'Alene. By contrast, the Church of Jesus Christ Christian (Aryan Nations) and its loose affiliates such as the National Socialist Aryan Peoples Party, America's Promise, and the Gospel of Christ Kingdom Church, and so forth, were without exception just recently imported from out of state, mostly in the person of retirees from southern California. Having few community connections, their efforts to solicit the support of the local citizenry were repeatedly frustrated. In fact, the perceived clumsiness of their enlistment campaigns had the effect of further isolating them from the very people they wanted to impress.

The racialist groups were able to secure a handful of local residents. But these were individuals themselves alienated from Coeur d'Alene's conventional structure. Consider the five who constituted the Order Strike Force II, the terrorist group mentioned above. One of its couples, both ex-sheriff's deputies, had migrated to northern Idaho from California just a few months before joining the Aryan Nations Church; they were recruited out of a bar near its Hayden Lake headquarters in Garwood by an ex-convict who would later be imprisoned for his association with the Order, an individual himself enlisted by the Aryan Nations prison ministry. Another couple had been long-time Coeur d'Alene residents, indeed had been associated as children with St. Pius X Catholic Church; but like the first two, neither was well integrated into the community. They had long since dropped their affiliations with the church, were unemployed at the time of their recruitment, and both had police records. Their marriage itself was faltering. The fifth recruit had just arrived from New Jersey in Coeur d'Alene following his release from prison.

As could have been predicted, the politics of none of these five persons was constrained by the rules of democratic decision making. All five are as a consequence serving sentences for their roles in the white supremacist movement.

Conclusion

"Turner Ashby" (one of Louis Beam's pseudonyms), a traveling ambassador for the Aryan Nations Church, once publicly challenged the task force "to back their words up with action. . . . Is [its] statement [of human rights] issued to protect everyone, or only those that the [KCHRTF] is philosophically in agreement with?"[33] The task force has satisfactorily answered Ashby's challenge several times.

The first occasion was the so-called Aryan Buster T-shirt fiasco. Ostensibly to raise money for the task force, an enterprising Coeur d'Alene resident in February 1985 began marketing T-shirts inscribed with an encircled red line drawn through a saluting Hitler figure. "I don't agree with (the Aryans) at all," he told the press. "There's no room in this world for racists." To its credit, the task force saw this as bigotry in reverse and publicly disassociated itself from the campaign.[34]

The second incident was the closure of a public meeting of the task force in 1985 to local National Socialist leader Keith Gilbert, who (speaking from experience) "could not but make the comparison in my own mind of the same sort of thing happening at a meeting of the KKK."

Not all task force associates agreed with the expulsion. For one, Sandy Emerson nearly walked out with Gilbert when it was voted that Gilbert be excluded. The executive committee later developed procedures for dealing with similar disturbances in the future. Today, meetings are open to all interested parties, but actual participation requires consent to the principles of the task force. Included among these is advocacy of equal rights for minority groups.

What is important about these examples is not so much their specifics, but that the task force has agonized over questions of political civility instead of self-righteously dismissing them. And in the course of self-examination, its members have been forced to confront *their own hatred.* This is the first and perhaps most crucial step in breaking through the deadly logic of enemies. Ann Salisbury-Brown, one of the executive board members, sees this clearly: "I just believe he [Rev. Richard Butler] has performed an invaluable service for our area, in that he has challenged all of us to root out bigotry *in ourselves!"*

Our initial inclination is to account for Salisbury-Brown's conciliatory words by invoking psychological attributes like liberality. Such explanations, however, are probably circular. After all, how do we know Salisbury-Brown is "liberal" except for her conciliatory gesture? Let us once again examine the issue sociologically.

It is not simply because KCHRTF members categorically eschew violence that they deal with local hate groups moderately. It is also because as fully integrated community leaders – as the members of the hate groups are not – they are subject to the democratic political conventions characteristic of small American cities. KCHRTF members hold each other to the standards of political fair play as the price for their involvement with the group. Take the case of Marshall Mend.

Better than anyone, Marshall Mend represents the personal transformations task force members have undergone in the course of their struggle with hatred. "When I first got in I thought the best solution to the problem was to bring in the machine guns," he confesses. Father Bill "turned me around." Mend now understands, "this is America. We can't throw people out even if we want to."

"The time has come to eliminate bigotry," Mend once told me, with all the enthusiasm of the steak and chicken drummer he once was before becoming Kootenai County's top realtor. Shaken by his evident naiveté, I suggested that there might be some "problems" implementing such an ambitious scheme. "Problems?" he asked incredulously. "There are no problems; there are only opportunities." "You gotta reach for the moon," he blurted, repeating the catechism of one of the motivational tapes he shaves to each morning, "because even if you miss, you're going to come down with a handful of stars."

Kootenai County, the community with a heart, is now in the process of reaching.

11

Apocalypse and the Hero

Man must not disclaim his brotherhood even with the guiltiest.[1]

In the opening chapter we set out on an excursion into enemy territory, briefly inspecting three of its pitfalls. Outfitted now with equipment gleaned from our subsequent studies, let us return to our point of embarkation to examine these paradoxical traps more closely: the sense of crisis that has inspired *This Thing of Darkness* in the first place, the theme of heroic questing to save the world, and, above all, the paradox of evil. Not, as we discussed earlier, how evil grows from good (intentions), but how good seems to emerge from evil.

We are concerned with these themes as they bear on the pivotal political question of our (and every) generation: "What shall be done?" Can we respond to evil effectively without becoming evil ourselves? I use the words "bear on" in place of "answer," for, as should be clear by now, there will be no simple solutions to the problem of evil. I can promise no spiritual exercises for opening pathways to empowerment. Our goal must be the more humble one of attending to how the paradoxes just mentioned are *written,* and thus how they can occasion hope – hope being the precursor of sustained political action.

As inspiring as the examples cited in the last three chapters are, the deconstruction of enemies is not simply practical social work. It is equally a theoretical labor, or praxis – theoretically informed practice. What peace activism urgently requires is a careful thinking through of what routinely, hence unconsciously, is said about peace, the enemy, war, evil, and heroism. This in turn necessitates our attending to the "two-wayness" of these words, to their richness of connotation. Heidegger once said that "language is the house of our being in the world." If we truly wish to be in a world of peace, we must choose our words thoughtfully and utilize a language appropriate to our goal.

War/Peace Language

As we have seen, political violation begins with concern about the fate of our world. It is born from passion, a sense of personal pain, and what we suffer for others sympathetically – our compassion. It is hardly necessary to recount the threats to our world today: ecological disaster, population distress, militarism. It is only important in citing these to reflect on the multiple occasions (excuses) for taking up arms heroically to redeem the world from "the enemy." For ours are the End Times, proclaim prophets from across the earth.

Such a prophet is Rev. Sun Myung Moon, the Korean founder of the Unification Church and its right-wing political arm CAUSA. Today, he tells us, "great tragedy is constantly striking America and the world." This is God's warning that we have deviated from His mission. To rectify the situation, the church must find individuals willing to sacrifice (and be sacrificed). "If we can't give up our little things: our privacy, our apartments, our record players, all the big things will go." If, furthermore, "say that 10,000 people would be killed so that . . . we can set up the right kind of government, the right kind of world, it's better that that should happen."[2]

Such a prophet too is the self-proclaimed Japanese Messiah, Ryuho Okawa, originally dismissed as just another fringe evangelist, but now head of a two million member cult, the wealthiest ($45 million in annual revenues) and largest of several to crop up in postwar Japan. In his book *Nostradamus: Fearful Prophecies,* Okawa asserts that only Japan will survive the imminent apocalypse, this after first devising a "utopia" modeled after his own doctrine and then destroying the United States and Russia.[3]

Such a prophet, too, is the American Black Muslim As Sayyid Issa al Haadi al Mahdi. He would dismiss Okawa's samurai saviors and Reverend Moon's Anglo-Saxon puritans alike as "palemen," both cursed by God with leprosy and whose ancestors sought refuge in northern climes and in dark caves to protect their weakened albino eyes from the sun. "Once the salts in their bodies reached a dangerous low," according to al Mahdi, "the palemen lost the ability to reproduce. It was at this point that they came down from the mountains, kidnapped, and raped clean Nubian [black] women." The results of this miscegenetic "bestiality" are seen in the decline of the world since the golden age. This decline cannot be reversed, insists al Mahdi, until the blackman reclaims his rightful place and "cleans them [the palemen] up."[4]

In these final pages we shall attempt to break through this style of unthinking thought, of this logic which even if variant in detail – that is, in the identification of who exactly is to blame for our pain – nevertheless has all the marks of a robotic cant. For however much Moon, Okawa, al Mahdi, and the countless other military prophets differ in race and religious creed – Okawa, for example, is Buddhist – they inhabit a similar world, one laid out on the same Manichaean dimensions of "us and them."

The first step in breaking through the logic of enemies is to posit a now widely acknowledged fact: The world of radical dualism, of us and them, is in crisis, its splitting evident in a series of contradictions. There is the contradiction between military security and domestic (national) security, as exploding military expenditures to defend ourselves from "them" consume the wealth of our common household. There is the contradiction between the survivability of weapons systems – "survivability," a term in technostrategic jargon referring *only* to weapons systems – and the viability of the "collateral resources" (us), whose lives these systems were originally devised to protect. There is the contradiction between individual freedom and the legions of priests, therapists, and moral entrepreneurs (which is to say, us) poised and armed to correct, "heal," order, regiment – in a word, "militarize" – the bodily orifices of "them": their mouths, their anuses, their pores, and ears, and their endlessly "perverted" tastes, hungers, appetites, drippings, and effusions.[5]

Out of these contradictions – emerging from the mortally fractured world of us and them – is a space, a clearing, an opening for the bringing forth of what before was hidden. This is what Heidegger calls "the turning," the moment of "in flashing" (*Blitzen*), when conversion to a new, perhaps less thoughtlessly violent world view becomes possible.[6]

"Where danger is, grows the saving power also," Heidegger quotes the poet Hölderlin as saying.[7] For while the apocalypse of dualism shatters what heretofore has provided immeasurable meaning and comfort, it is also an occasion for the "presencing of the saving power," its revelation and disclosure (from the Greek *apo* "reversal," *kalyptein* "to cover"). Indeed, says Heidegger, the danger – the apocalyptic fracturing – *is* the saving power "inasmuch as it brings the saving power out of its . . . concealed essence."[8]

To finally be loosed from the bondage of a world that has cost so much in treasure and human life to sustain should be welcomed with gratitude. But this is not the case. In reality, our first, perhaps instinctive, reaction to the apocalypse is fright, flight, or fight. After all, the very sensibleness and significance of my personal existence is bound up with the continuation of a "them" against whom to compare myself. The end of "us and them" is thus tantamount to a kind of death, with all the terror and absurdity this implies. For this reason Heidegger tells us that surrender ("releasement") to the turning requires the utmost moral and intellectual courage. That is, it requires virtues celebrated in the ancient myths of warrior heroes. Let us see how this is so.

A newspaper headline tells us: "U.S. Earthmovers Bury Iraqi Soldiers Alive."[9] Here now for us is a wound, shocking and searing: dread, anger, sorrow, and more than that – shame and guilt. How is it possible that our own sons and daughters, so clean and bright, could commit such atrocities, which even military authorities agree go against American army doctrine. Yet they did: "No American was killed in the operation. The Iraqi body count was estimated in the thousands. . . . They were buried under tons of sand in 70 miles of trenches." This is the moment referred to above: the moment when the old world shatters and a new world emerges from the shadows. Have we the courage to release ourselves, to surrender ourselves to the apocalypse of our world, to suffer a "circumcision of the heart," as Saint Paul calls it? Or will we resist: attacking the news reporter, excusing the crime, or simply numbing ourselves psychically to the fact of our own willing complicity in evil? On this decision depends the perpetuation of an existence of calculated murder or our "salvation" (from this fate).[10]

It was Arthur Schopenhauer who, in "The Foundations of Morality," first argued that to be psychically wounded with sorrow for our victims, and shame and guilt for our crimes against them, was "proof" of our interconnection, that we are all cells of the same living organism. Likewise, ecologists say that the dread we endure when witnessing a logging clearcut or upon reading about the extinction of still another animal species is an "instinctive" recognition, re-knowing, of our ontological union with the earth. Cultivate that feeling; don't repress it! For in the pain comes the insight to save ourselves.[11] Max Scheler expands on these themes in his phenomenology of sympathy (from *syn* "together," *pathos* "suffering").[12] The apathetic individual, he says, incapable of sympathy, thereby isolates himself from his fellows. Sympathy is an act of "remembering." Through it the human organism (the We) that was previously *dis*-membered, taken apart and severated, is *re*-membered, put together and healed. The American activist and counselor Joanna Macy teaches the same lessons in her "despair workshops."[13]

The Hero's Fight

A legend enjoyed by Occidental peoples for centuries relates the story of the killing of a fire-breathing monster by a fearless knight. In some versions the act wins him the hand of a virginal princess; in others a stupor is lifted from the kingdom, allowing it to flourish once again; in still others a grand jewel chest is bequeathed him.

If we attend to this legend metaphorically, it can provide insights into Heidegger's concept of releasement; and we may be positioned intellectually to transcend Reverend Moon's, Ryuho Okawa's, and al Mahdi's self-defeating dualistic logic.

In the standard Indo-Aryan variant of the hero myth, Defender of the World goes by the name of Indra, Zeus, Jupiter (Zeus plus *pater,* hence god the father), Thor, or Beowulf.[14] He may be armed with a thunderbolt, a blazing hammer, or a razor-edged short sword. The Enemy, sower of confusion and deceit, although sometimes born with wings, has neither legs nor arms, hence must slither along. It is none other than the archetypal Mercurius in its swamp-dwelling, chthonic (and, we should add, female) aspect: Vritra the serpent, the man-snake Titan called Typhon, the Grendel Worm, or the green-scaled and many-eyed Midgard.

As invincible as her countenance seems to ordinary mortals, the poison-dripping dragon is defeated nonetheless, her arrogance rendering her susceptible to the hero's telling blow. Read esoterically as a psychological symbol, the slaying of the monster mother may be seen as the de(con)struction of conventional moral illusions. The most blinding of these concerns the enemy's ineradicable difference from ourselves: we are pure and blameless; the enemy filthy and diabolical. This is a phantasm so powerfully seductive and so seemingly "natural" that only a weapon of divine proportions is equal to its dispatching. Such an instrument, we might venture, is what theologians have called grace, an insight granted gratuitously, beyond human will and ken. The female association may be considered a typical masculine representation of unconsciousness, with its womblike security. With the magical thunderbolt of intuition, the heroic soul slays what is in the shadow about itself, what is too terrifying for the ordinary person to consciously acknowledge: its own diabolism.[15]

There is a pivotal sidelight to the myth, conveniently forgotten by most modern bards. In putting an end to the monster of moral fantasy – in shattering the always beguiling division between us and them – the champion himself is lacerated grievously. Beowulf in fact dies; Thor too, after turning from Midgard's body and walking nine paces. As for Indra, the Mahabharata describes his fate this way:

> [There] came forth from the body of [Vritra] with teeth projecting terribly, of an aspect furiously contorted, tawny and black, with disheveled hair, and appalling eyes, and a garland of skulls around her neck, bathed in blood. . . . And she went after [Indra] . . . seized him, and from that moment Brahminicide was stuck to him.[16]

Vritra is sustainer of conventional moralism, *maya*. In destroying her, Indra the hero is forcibly thrust out of the wonderfully consoling illusion of his own benevolence into cognizance of his criminality. He is made at one with his own evil. Wounded by this realization, he seeks solace in a lotus stalk, residing there for generations. But the dark knowledge continues "clinging to him still." In the end, Indra surrenders to Brahma the Creator, who until the end of time "ponders [unsuccessfully] the question of how [Indra] might be set free." The night vision of the Pandu brothers recited in chapter 2 merely reiterates the tale of Indra's painful enlightenment. In struggling against the enemy "out there" (the black-skinned and deceitful Kurus), the Pandus are forced to confront the excruciatingly humiliating lesson that behind the mask of their righteousness they are kinsmen to the enemy. Like the Kurus, they themselves are dishonorable, murderous, black. No wonder, we might say, that Heidegger recommends something along the lines of military virtues to make us capable for releasement, surrender, to the turning, to the apocalypse of dualism: courage, clearsightedness, perseverance.

Conclusion

We opened these comments with a story; let us end with another.

One fine summer day the pious boy Carl Jung, son and nephew of rigid Lutheran parsons, was walking home from school. "The world is beautiful," he thought to himself, "and the church is beautiful, and God made all this and sits above it far away in the blue sky on a golden throne and . . ." At this moment he was struck with a choking sensation and the realization that he should quickly discontinue thinking along these lines lest he commit a terrible sin, which would send him to hell for all eternity. For the next three days he tried to occupy his mind otherwise, but the original thought kept returning, each time more insistently "like a powerful electric shock." By the third night the torment had grown so unbearable that Jung was sweating with fear. "Now it is coming, now it's serious! I *must think!* . . . I don't want to, by God, that's sure. . . . Who wants to force me to think something I don't know and don't want to know?" He was aware that conventional morality demanded that sin be avoided at all costs. Yet the distress was unbearable; it could not go on. He knew then that God had arranged a decisive test of his obedience by imposing upon him the task of doing something against his own moral judgment and the teachings of his religion. Gathering his courage he let the thought come: "I saw before me the cathedral, the blue sky. God sits on his golden throne, high above the world – and from under the throne an enormous turd falls upon the sparkling new roof, shatters it, and breaks the walls of the cathedral asunder."[17]

At once Jung felt "an indescribable relief." Instead of damnation he experienced "unutterable bliss" and wept for hours in gratitude. This was his secret knowledge, which his moralistic elders could never grasp, having acquired their religion from books instead of from direct, unpleasant experience: "God forces me to think abominations in order to experience His grace." While at first the paradoxical secret isolated Jung from his parents and peers, after years of reflection it would come to form the basis of his now honored notion of the psychological salience of the hero's fight with his own shadow.[18]

As Ernest Becker has convincingly shown, the call to heroism still resonates in modern hearts. However, we are in the habit of either equating heroism with celebrity ("TV Actress Tops List of Students' Heroes") or caricaturing the hero as a bluff-and-swagger patriot/soldier making the world safe for, say, Christian democracy. In these ways heroism is portrayed as a rather happy if not entirely risk-free venture that earns one public plaudits. Toady we are asked to learn that, in the deepest and truest sense, heroism is really none of these things, but a largely private vocation requiring stamina, discipline, responsibility, and above all courage. Not just the ascetic courage to cleanse our personal lives of what we have been taught is filth, or even less to cleanse society of the alleged carriers of this filth, but, as Jung displayed, the fortitude to release our claim on moral purity and perfection. At a personal and cultural level, I believe this is the only way to transcend the logic of enemies.[19]

In saying this, two points should be kept in mind. First, just as Thor's defeat of the ogress Midgard is never final, so we can never call a truce in our battle against righteousness. In Thor's first confrontation with the cosmic serpent of moral illusion, his companion Hymir cut the fishline at the gunwhale prematurely and Midgard sank away. Thor threw his hammer at the last moment and thought he saw Midgard's head lopped off. If true, this would have solved the problem of evil permanently. Others, however, thought they saw the Worm safely swim away. Sure enough, later in the age that the Edda calls War with the Wolf – "ax-time, sword-time, wind-time, wolf-time, 'ere the world falls" – Midgard is observed swimming at Hymir's side as his armed host sails to death ground from the East for the battle of the apocalypse. Thor must once again confront the dragon; the habit of negative projection cannot be annihilated with a single deed. It is a temptation about which we must be vigilant and work daily to control, particularly during moments of hysteria when things break down and we seek to give them meaning by falling back on old patterns of unthinking thought.

Second, it can never be emphasized enough that sociology, even phenomenological sociology of great psychological import, is not theology. In other words, elucidating the possible psychological meanings of winged, fire-breathing fiends, warrior heroes, and their conflicts is not to deny the ontological existence of Evil (or, by the way, of Good), and of the tragic possibility of having someday to engage in actual, not merely metaphorical, combat. However, it may also be that if we are shielded by the golden armor earned in earlier confrontations with our own private demons, the propensity to violate our antagonists, if not entirely eliminated, will at least be tempered.

Here, too, we grasp a sobering answer to the question of whether in our struggles against evil we can avoid becoming infected with it ourselves. If we can believe what the ancient texts relate, this is simply impossible. We cannot engage in political fighting without tasting the bitter fruit from the tree of knowledge and losing our innocence. Max Weber once referred in his writings to the biblical warning that those who live by the sword shall perish by the sword (Matt. 26:52), commenting that "fighting is everywhere fighting." But there is a big difference between going into battle either clearly recognizing our family resemblance to the opponent or blindly denying it, rendering us automatically into the malleable tools of what Weber calls "the diabolic forces lurking in all violence."[20]

Nor is consciousness of our own evil important in just a negative sense. A close reading of the hero myths reveals that the champions all acknowledge the futility of attacking the monster mother directly. Rather, they are advised by an elfin helper to employ wiliness, to sneak up on her as she sleeps or in some other way is distracted, searching for the chink in her armor. In other words, to defeat the serpent the hero must become serpentlike himself: slippery and mercurial. The proud refusal to do so would only render him the enemy's victim. This is consistent with the ancient Chinese military admonition that acknowledgment of one's *own* envy, vengefulness, lust, dishonesty, and greed is the very precondition of victory. For without this wounding self-knowledge, one is defenseless against the enemy's traps and ploys. "Know the enemy *and know yourself,*" says Sun Tzu, the fifth century B.C. military theorist, and "in a hundred battles you will never be in peril."[21] The question raised at the outset of this chaper, therefore, of whether we can fight effectively against evil without becoming evil ourselves – that is, without becoming conscious of our own shadow – is not merely a moral issue, but a very practical political one: No, we cannot.

Notes

Introduction

1. James A. Aho, *Religious Mythology and the Art of War* (Westport, Conn.: Greenwood, 1981).

2. James A. Aho, *The Politics of Righteousness: Idaho Christian Patriotism* (Seattle: University of Washington Press, 1990).

3. For a detailed characterization of the style of sociology employed here, see Peter Berger, *Invitation to Sociology* (Garden City, N.Y.: Doubleday-Anchor, 1963).

4. Cf. Sam Keen's eminently readable and lavishly illustrated *Faces of the Enemy: Reflections of the Hostile Imagination* (San Francisco: Harper and Row, 1986). A more academic approach to the subject is *The Psychology of War and Peace: The Image of the Enemy*, ed. Robert W. Rieber (New York: Plenum, 1991).

5. Keen, *Faces of the Enemy*, p. 12.

6. For a classic statement of the moral obligations of sociology, see C. Wright Mills, *The Sociological Imagination* (New York: Oxford University Press, 1959), especially pp. 3–24, entitled "The Promise."

1. The Problem of the Enemy

1. Jussi Vähämäki, "What Are the Common Values that Europeans Share?" TAPRI Workshop on European Values in International Relations, Helsinki, Finland, September 1988, pp. 11, 9, 5–6.

2. These words may be compared to the active-voice *occidio* (complete slaughter, extermination). *Occidio* comes from a word that has the same spelling as *occido* but a different pronunciation and, more important, a different meaning. Specifically, it derives not from *ob* + *cado* (to fall) but from *ob* + *caedo*, which means to cut or hew.

3. Matthias Finger, "European Values After the Euromissile Crisis," in *European Values in International Relations*, ed. Vilho Harle (London: Pinter, 1990). Michel Serres, "Trahison: La thanatocratie," *Hermes III* (Paris: Minuit, 1974). E. P. Thompson, "Notes on Exterminism, the Last Stage of Civilisation," in his *Beyond the Cold War*, pp. 41–79 (New York: Pantheon, 1982), and "Exterminism Reviewed," in *The Heavy Dancers*, ed. Thompson (New York: Pantheon, 1985). Paul Virilio, *Pure War* (New York: Foreign Agent Series, 1983).

4. This philosophy of history first found academic formulation in the writings of the nineteenth-century sociologist Herbert Spencer. Today variations are found in the work of the preeminent American social theorist, the late Talcott Parsons.

5. Gil Elliot, *The Twentieth Century Book of the Dead* (New York: Charles Scribner's Sons, 1972), p. 1.

6. Ruth Leger Sivard, *World Military and Social Expenditures, 1987–88* (Washing-

ton, D.C.: World Priorities, 1990). Liberal estimates add another 20 million to this figure.

7. For an attempt to forge a new language and legend of death appropriate to the modern world, see Edith Wyschogrod, *Spirit in Ashes: Hegel, Heidegger, and Man-Made Mass Death* (New Haven: Yale University Press, 1985).

8. Adolf Hitler, *Mein Kampf,* trans. Ralph Manheim (Boston: Houghton Mifflin, 1943), pp. 249 and 65 (Hitler's emphasis).

9. William I. Thomas, *On Social Organization and Social Personality: Selected Papers,* ed. Morris Janowitz (Chicago: University of Chicago Press, 1966), pp. xl, 154–67.

10. "I see many similarities between Iraqi behavior in Kuwait and the way the death-head regiments behaved in Poland," President George Bush was quoted by the Associated Press as saying November 1, 1990. "I don't think I am overstating it," he added. "I know I am not overstating the feelings I have about it."

11. Marie Louise von Franz, *The Feminine in Fairytales* (Irving, Tex.: University of Dallas Press, 1972), pp. 143–57.

12. Ibid., p. 175 (her emphasis).

13. Joseph P. Martino, *A Fighting Chance: The Moral Use of Nuclear Weapons* (San Francisco: Ignatius, 1988), p. 164 (his emphasis).

14. Ibid., p. 171 (his emphasis); cf. pp. 116–26.

15. Ibid., p. 175.

16. Ibid., p. 176 (my emphasis).

17. Ernest Becker, *Escape from Evil* (New York: Free Press, 1975).

18. Ibid., p. 150.

19. Lewis A. Coser, *The Functions of Social Conflict* (Glencoe, Ill.: Free Press, 1956).

20. Quoted on ABC Nightly News, January 21, 1991.

21. "What a Wonderful Time to Be American!" *Idaho State Journal,* March 15, 1991.

22. James A. Aho, *Religious Mythology and the Art of War* (Westport, Conn.: Greenwood, 1981). For discussion of the nuclear death cult, see Ira Chernus, *Dr. Strangegod* (Columbia: South Carolina University Press, 1986).

23. Rudolf Otto, *The Idea of the Holy,* trans. John W. Harvey (London: Oxford University Press, 1923).

24. Paul Bowles, *A Distant Episode* (New York: Ecco, 1988).

25. For his classic statement, see Emmanuel Lévinas, *Otherwise Than Being: Or Beyond Essence,* trans. Alphonso Lingis (The Hague: Martinus Nijhoff, 1981). For an excellent review of Lévinas's ethics, along with applications to specific cases, see *The Question of the Other,* ed. Arleen Dallery and Charles Scott (Albany: State University of New York Press, 1989).

26. Max Scheler, *Ressentiment,* trans. William Holdheim (New York: Schocken Books, 1972), p. 125.

27. Albert Camus, "Neither Victims nor Executioners," in *Seeds of Liberation,* ed. Paul Goodman (New York: George Braziller, 1964).

2. Heroism, the Construction of Evil, and Violence

1. Friedrich Nietzsche, *Toward a Genealogy of Morals,* trans. Walter Kaufman (New York: Vintage Books, 1969), part 1, sec. 10 (translator's emphasis).

2. Ernest Becker, *The Structure of Evil* (New York: Free Press, 1968); *The Denial of Death* (New York: Free Press, 1973); *Escape from Evil* (New York: Free Press, 1975).

3. James A. Aho, *Religious Mythology and the Art of War* (Westport, Conn.: Greenwood, 1981), pp. 101–26.

4. Becker, *Escape from Evil*, p. 148.

5. Peter Berger and Thomas Luckmann, *The Social Construction of Reality* (Garden City, N.Y.: Doubleday-Anchor, 1967).

6. One of the first uses of reification theory in modern social theory was by Karl Marx to explain what he called "commodity fetishism": our alienated relationship to the products of our own hands. See *Marx's Concept of Man,* trans. Thomas Bottomore, ed. and intro. Erich Fromm (New York: Ungar, 1961).

7. James A. Aho, " 'I Am Death . . . Who Shatters Worlds': The Emerging Nuclear Death Cult," in *A Shuddering Dawn: Religious Studies and the Nuclear Age,* ed. Ira Chernus and Edward T. Linenthal (Albany: State University of New York Press, 1989), pp. 49–68.

8. Representative literature employing this approach includes: Aron Cicourel, *The Social Organization of Juvenile Justice* (New York: Wiley, 1968); Robert Scott, *The Making of Blind Men* (New York: Russell Sage, 1969); Thomas Szasz, *The Manufacture of Madness* (New York: Dell, 1970); Thomas Szasz, *Ceremonial Chemistry* (Garden City, N.Y.: Doubleday-Anchor, 1974); and David Sudnow, *Passing On* (Englewood Cliffs, N.J.: Prentice-Hall, 1967).

9. The first social problems text to use this approach was Jack Douglas, ed., *The Sociology of Deviance* (Boston: Allyn and Bacon, 1984). A more recent text is *Images of Issues,* ed. Joel Best (New York: Aldine de Gruyter, 1989). See also *The Satanism Scare,* ed. James T. Richardson, Joel Best, and David Bromley (New York: Aldine de Gruyter, 1991).

10. Douglas, *The Sociology of Deviance,* p. 13.

11. It should be understood that this is an axiom of phenomenological sociology only. Once the present author takes off his sociological glasses, so to say, he experiences the world as others ordinarily do – as a place wherein, among other things, good and evil are entirely unproblematic and given in the "nature" of things themselves. Following the suggestion of Edmund Husserl, the practice of phenomenological sociology involves the "bracketing" or suspension of belief in the taken-for-granted world. I will have more to say about this in chapter 7.

12. For one of the original accounts of labeling theory, see Howard Becker, *The Outsiders* (Glencoe, Ill.: Free Press, 1963).

13. Harold Garfinkel, "Conditions of Successful Degradation Ceremonies," *American Journal of Sociology* 61 (1956): 420–24.

14. John Irwin, *The Jail* (Berkeley: University of California Press, 1985).

15. Neal Shover, " 'Experts' and Diagnosis in Correctional Agencies," *Crime and Delinquency* 20 (1974): 347–58.

16. For the concept of "indexicality" and rhetorical "documentation," see Harold Garfinkel, *Studies in Ethnomethodology* (Englewood Cliffs: Prentice-Hall, 1967). For a classic application of this idea to deviance, see William Ryan, *Blaming the Victim* (New York: Vintage, 1971).

17. Berger and Luckmann, *The Social Construction of Reality,* pp. 67–72.

18. Gordon Allport and Leo Postman, "The Basic Psychology of Rumors," *Transactions of the New York Academy of Sciences,* series 2 (1954): 61–81.

19. Theodosius Dobzhansky, *Mankind Evolving* (New Haven: Yale University Press, 1962), pp. 10–22.

20. Wesley George, *The Biology of the Race Problem* (New York: National Putnam Letters Committee, 1962), pp. 46–48.

21. Émile Durkheim, *The Elementary Forms of Religious Life,* trans. J. W. Swain (Glencoe, Ill.: Free Press, 1954).

22. For one of the original statements concerning this subject, see Robert K. Merton, *Social Theory and Social Structure* (Glencoe, Ill.: Free Press, 1957).

23. For the classic sociology of ressentiment, see Max Scheler, *Ressentiment,* trans. William W. Holdheim (New York: Schocken books, 1972 [1961]).

24. For maddening examples of this in a typical hospital for the criminally insane, see Tom Ryan, *Screw: A Guard's View of Bridgewater State Hospital* (Boston: South End, 1981).

25. Jean-Paul Sartre, *Anti-Semite and Jew,* trans. George Becker (New York: Schocken Books, 1965). Frantz Fanon, *Black Skin, White Masks,* trans. Charles Lam Markmann (New York: Grove Press, 1967).

26. René Girard, *The Scapegoat,* trans. Yvonne Freccero (Baltimore: Johns Hopkins University Press, 1986). For an earlier discussion of scapegoating in primitive society, see James George Frazer, *The Golden Bough* (New York: Macmillan, 1951 [1922]).

27. Aho, *Religious Mythology and the Art of War,* pp. 24–26.

28. *The Mahabharata,* trans. Pratap Chandra Roy (Calcutta, India: Datta Bose and Co., 1919–33), *Sauptika-parva,* viii.

29. The quotations are found, respectively, in *The Mahabharata, Salya-parva,* lxiii, and *Sauptika-parva,* x.

3. Reification and Sacrifice: The Goldmark Case

1. Peter Berger and Thomas Luckmann, *The Social Construction of Reality* (Garden City, N.Y.: Doubleday-Anchor, 1967), p. 61.

2. Ludwig Feuerbach, *The Essence of Christianity,* trans. George Eliot (New York: Harper and Row, 1957).

3. The Aztec *Xochiyaoyotl,* so called because its goal was to secure "tuna flowers," human hearts, for the nourishment of the god of light in his struggle against the hosts of darkness.

4. Hugh Duncan, *Communication and Social Order* (New York: Oxford University Press, 1962), pp. 125–26.

5. Howard Becker, *The Outsiders* (Glencoe, Ill.: Free Press, 1963).

6. William L. Dwyer, *The Goldmark Case: An American Libel Trial* (Seattle: University of Washington Press, 1984).

7. Ibid., p. 115.

8. Tamotsu Shibutani, *Improvised News* (Indianapolis: Bobbs-Merrill, 1966).

9. Dwyer, *The Goldmark Case,* pp. 39–40, 74.

10. Ibid., McCarran Act: p. 36; American Heritage Bill: pp. 74–75, 121; ACLU: pp. ix, 68; soft on communism: p. 133.

11. Emmett Watson, *Seattle Post-Intelligencer* columnist, quoted, ibid., p. 16.

12. Ibid., Methow Grange: pp. 126–27, 133; regional library: pp. 30–31; anti-Communist documentaries: pp. 23–26, 28, 40, 68, 126.

13. Ibid., not married: pp. 32, 86–87; flag salute: p. 32; Reed college: pp. 36–37.

14. Ibid., out to kill us: p. 77; Herbert Philbrick: p. 35; Irma Ringe and Victor Perlo: p. 34; Irma Ringe as Sally: p. 36; Goldmark as conspirator: p. 67.

15. In 1948 Canwell, then chairman of the Washington State Joint Legislative Fact-Finding Committee on Un-American Activities, held public hearings on subversion in the state. The conclusion of these hearings was that "the state of Washington is acrawl with trained and non-disciplined Communists." The hearings resulted in three faculty dismissals at the University of Washington. Philosophy professor Melvin Rader, one of the accused, eventually cleared himself of charges by the Committee, the result being public ridicule of Canwell and the end of his short-lived political career. See Melvin Rader, *False Witness* (Seattle: University of Washington Press, 1969).

Canwell returned to Spokane and started an "intelligence service," keeping files on local "subversives," including Mrs. Goldmark. It is possible that he received information on Goldmark either from the FBI or from the House Un-American Activities Committee (HUAC), both of which were pursuing their own investigations at this time. In 1949 two FBI agents interviewed Sally Goldmark, at her home, about her past associations. In 1953 the Navy used the subsequent report in the course of a security clearance investigation of her husband, who was in the Naval Reserve (he was granted the clearance). And in 1956, HUAC subpoenaed her to answer questions in executive session. Canwell claims to have seen a copy of the latter confidential report (Dwyer, *The Goldmark Case*, p. 77). Whatever its source, Canwell published the gossip in his *American Intelligence Service* report and in *Vigilante* articles. He was copublisher of the *Vigilante* with Ashley Holden, who disseminated the same information in his own *Tonasket Tribune*.

16. Dwyer, *The Goldmark Case*, pp. 113, 116.

17. Ibid., pp. 48, 80, 41–46.

18. The defendants: Albert Canwell and Ashley Holden (see note 15); a prominent local businessman and regional antisubversive chairman of the American Legion; the state coordinator for the John Birch Society; the Society itself; Holden's Tribune Publishing Company; and the *Okanogan Independent*.

19. Richard Schwartz and Jerome Skolnick, "Two Studies of Legal Stigma," in *The Other Side*, ed. Howard Becker (New York: Free Press, 1964), p. 111.

20. Ibid., pp. 112–14.

21. But see Edward Sagarin and Robert Kelly, "The Brewster Effect: Political Trials and the Self-Defeating Prophecy," in *Politics and Crime*, ed. Sawyer F. Sylvester and Edward Sagarin (New York: Praeger, 1974).

22. Harold Garfinkel, "Conditions of Successful Degradation Ceremonies," *American Journal of Sociology* 61 (1956): 420–24.

23. In the early 1960s Arnold Rose (now deceased) was libeled as a Jewish Communist by one Gerda Koch, then director of Christian Research, Inc. (Rose, professor of sociology at the University of Minnesota, had assisted Gunnar Myrdal in the preparation of *An American Dilemma*, a major 1944 study that served as a source for the U.S. Supreme Court during the 1950s in decisions concerning

equal rights for minorities.) He won his libel suit and was awarded $20,000 punitive damages. In 1967 the decision was overturned by the Minnesota Supreme Court on grounds that the trial judge had not properly instructed the jury on "actual malice." See Arnold M. Rose, *Libel and Academic Freedom: A Lawsuit Against Political Extremists* (Minneapolis: University of Minnesota Press, 1968).

24. Including John Lautner, ex-Communist Party security chief; Karl Prussion, party counterspy for the FBI; Barbara Hartle, ex-party Northwest regional director; and nationally celebrated Herbert Philbrick.

25. Cf. Robert Scott, "On Doing Good," in *The Sociology of Deviance,* ed. Jack Douglas (New York: Allyn and Bacon, 1984).

26. Analogously, when Arnold Rose was vindicated in Minnesota civil court (see note 23), his success paradoxically only strengthed the conviction of the defendants' supporters that the court was biased (Rose, *Libel and Academic Freedom,* pp. 213–4).

27. Personal interview no. 2, December 16, 1987.

28. Phillip Finch, *God, Guts and Guns* (New York: Seaview/Putnam, 1983), pp. 132–35.

29. John Lofland and Rodney Stark, "Becoming a World-Saver," *American Sociological Review* 30 (1965): 862–75.

30. Psychological report no. 1, January 2, 4, 6, 7, 9, and 13, 1986.

31. Ibid.

32. Ibid.

33. Personal interview no. 1, December 16, 1987.

34. Personal interview no. 2.

35. Psychological report no. 1.

36. Ibid.

37. Psychological report no. 2, August 12, 1985.

38. Psychological report no. 1.

39 Psychological report no. 2.

40. Psychological report no. 1.

41. Psychological report no. 2.

4. Standoff on Ruby Ridge

1. Robert Mathews, "Last Letter," quoted by Vicki Weaver in one of her personal letters. Mathews was founder of the *Bruders Schweigen,* or Order. He died in a shoot-out with federal marshals in Washington, November 1984. For the full transcript of his last testament, written while under fire, see James A. Aho, *The Politics of Righteousness* (Seattle: University of Washington Press, 1990), pp. 246–50.

2. Eldridge Cleaver, "The Black Man's Stake in Vietnam," in *Soul on Ice* (New York: Delta, 1968), pp. 121–27.

3. Austin D. Sarat and Malcolm M. Feeley, *The Policy Dilemma: Federal Crime Policy and the Law Enforcement Assistance Administration, 1968–1978* (Minneapolis: University of Minnesota Press, 1980).

4. Andrew Kopind, "The Warrior State: Imposing a New Order at Home," *Nation,* April 8, 1991.

5. Personal interview no. 4, November 3, 1992.

6. James Gibson, "American Paramilitary Culture and the Reconstitution of the Vietnam War," in *Making War/Making Peace*, ed. Francesca Cancian and Gibson (Belmont, Calif.: Wadsworth, 1990), pp. 86–99. See also H. Bruce Franklin, "The POW/MIA Myth," *Atlantic*, December 1991, pp. 45–81.

7. Anti-Defamation League of B'nai B'rith, *Extremism on the Right* (New York: Anti-Defamation League of B'nai B'rith, 1983), pp. 54–55.

8. Louis Beam, "Vietnam: Bringing It on Home," *Essays of a Klansman* (Hayden Lake, Idaho: AKIA Pub., 1983), pp. 35–41. The theme of "bringing it on home" is the basis of a novel by Andrew MacDonald, *The Hunter* (Hillsboro, W.V.: National Alliance, 1989). The main character is a disillusioned Vietnam veteran who murders interracial couples in his off-hours from work. MacDonald is also author of *The Turner Diaries*, the so-called bible of neo-Nazi terrorism.

9. Richard Cockle, "Survivalist Refuses to Come in From Cold," *Oregonian*, March 30, 1992.

10. Ken Fuson and Marie McCartan, "After the Showdown," *Des Moines Register*, September 13, 1992.

11. Ibid. Cf. Jess Walter, "Warning Shot: The Lessons of Ruby Ridge," *Spokesman-Review*, November 19, 1992.

12. Associated Press laser-photo, "Fugitive Ends Siege," *Idaho State Journal*, September 1, 1992.

13. Fuson and McCartan, "After the Showdown."

14. "We hereby make a public notice on this date that we, a married couple, Randall Claude and Vicki Jordison Weaver, believe our physical Lives to be in Danger. . . . I believe I may have to defend myself and my family from a physical attack on my life. . . ." (Associated Press, "Weaver Wrote of Fear for Life in 1985 Affidavit," *Idaho Statesman*, August 29, 1992).

15. Personal interview no. 2, September 17, 1992.

16. Associated Press, "Relatives Fear Hoodoo Mountain Family Feud Could Become Bloody," *Idaho State Journal*, July 29, 1991.

17. David Jordison, Vicki's brother, quoted in John Wiley, "Family: Beliefs Evolved Over Decade," *Idaho Statesman*, August 29, 1992.

18. Michael Weland, "Fugitive: No Surrender," *Coeur d'Alene Press*, May 3, 1992.

19. Ibid.

20. Ibid.

21. John Snell and Stuart Tomlinson, "Religion Prompts Weaver to Defy US Government," *Oregonian*, August 30, 1992. For other documents concerning the Weaver's beliefs, see Weland, "Fugitive: No Surrender," and Richard Cockle, "Letters Indicate Wife Shares Beliefs," *Oregonian*, August 26, 1992. These letters were all written in 1991 and are addressed to the "Aryan Nations: Our Brethren of the Anglo-Saxon Race." See also Walter, "Warning Shot."

22. Bo Gritz, "Randy Weaver Story," taped transcription of speech, Boise, Idaho, September 1992.

23. Personal interview no. 4.

24. These claims are cited in Snell and Tomlinson, "Religion Prompts Weaver to Defy Government," and in Peter Harriman, "What Are You Going to Do?" *Daily News* (Pullman, Wash./ Moscow, Idaho), September 5 and 6, 1992.

25. Snell and Tomlinson, "Religion Prompts Weaver to Defy Government." Vicki added, however, "what the whole thing is, this [race-mixing] is Satan's way of destroying the Yahweh people, the white race" (ibid).

26. Ibid. See Associated Press, "Standoff Draws Both Pro, Con Responses in Northwest," *Idaho State Journal*, August 26, 1992. The distinction between two kinds of racist styles in America – dominative (or supremacist) and aversive (or separatist) – is recognized in sociology. Cf. Joel Kovel, *White Racism: A Psychohistory* (New York: Pantheon, 1970).

27. For assertions from neighbors that the Weavers were not white supremacists, see Melanie Threlkeld, "Friends Say Weaver Separatist, Not White Supremacist," *Idaho Statesman*, August 27, 1992, and also Melanie Threlkeld, "Friends Call Weavers Close, Religious Family," *Idaho Statesman*, August 27, 1992. My interview with Randall Weaver's closest friend confirms this (Personal interview no. 2). Randall's presence at Aryan Nations-sponsored conventions does not necessarily prove that he adhered to any particular doctrine. My own field observations of such get-togethers reveals that they are attended by persons representing a wide diversity of ideological persuasions, from the merely curious to libertarians, from jack-booted SS-uniformed weekend Nazis to wilderness survivalists, from robed and conically hatted Klansmen to confused teenagers, and from buttoned-down Mormon John Birch racists to law-abiding FBI informants.

28. Weland, "Fugitive: No Surrender." See also Associated Press, "Cabin Offers Glimpse into Fugitive's Life," *Idaho State Journal*, September 1, 1992.

29. Weland, "Fugitive: No Surrender."

30. Personal interview no. 2. For more on the Weaver library, see Walter, "Warning Shot."

31. Jack Killorin, AFT agent, quoted in James Coates (*Chicago Tribune*), "Idaho Standoff Enters 2nd Year," *Sacramento Bee*, March 18, 1992. See also the interview with U.S. Marshall Jack Cluff in Harriman, "What Are You Going to Do?"

32. Coates, "Idaho Standoff Enters 2nd Year." When asked to justify this extraordinary surveillance, a U.S. marshal, requesting anonymity, said "we're going to do anything we can do to make the safest possible arrest . . . for both us and the violator" (Personal interview no. 4).

33. All information on Cluff is from Harriman, "What Are You Going to Do?" and Personal interview no. 5, November 10, 1992.

34. For information on Degan, see Associated Press, "Slain Marshal Highly Decorated," *Oregonian*, August 24, 1992, and Tom Coakley, "Agent Recounts Shootout Near Cabin," *Idaho State Journal*, August 27, 1992.

35. Tom Coakley, "Thousands Attend Services for Marshal Shot in Standoff," *Idaho State Journal*, August 27, 1992.

36. Cockle, "Letters Indicate Wife Shares Beliefs."

37. Fuson and McCartan, "After the Showdown." See also Snell and Tomlinson, "Religion Prompts Weaver to Defy US Government." Says Randall's father: "He [Randall] always believed in God, always did right by Him. We didn't stand for anything else" (Walter, "Warning Shot").

38. Hal Lindsey, *The Late Great Planet Earth* (Grand Rapids, Mich.: Zondervan, 1970).

39. Personal interview no. 3, October 21, 1992.

40. Lindsey, *The Late Great Planet Earth*, p. 141.

41. Fuson and McCartan, "After the Showdown." Cf. Walter, "Warning Shot."

42. Cockle, "Letters Indicate Wife Shares Beliefs."

43. Harriman, "What Are You Going to Do?"

44. Considerable controversy revolves around what exactly transpired during the shoot-out. For Weaver's version, see *Idaho Statesman,* September 2, 1992. For the law enforcement version, see Associated Press, "Feds Dispute Weaver's Story," *Lewiston Tribune,* September 7, 1992. See also Richard Cockle, "Shots Exchanged," *Oregonian,* August 24, 1992.

45. "I was praying that if they were going to kill us, they'd take us all at once, because I couldn't stand to see any more of my family hurt," says Sara. "I couldn't watch them pick us off one at a time. I was praying that they would just firebomb us" (Associated Press, "Daughter Can't Believe She's Alive," *Idaho Statesman,* September 2, 1992). Cf. John K. Wiley, "Weaver Comes Down from the Mountain," *Lewiston Tribune,* September 2, 1992, and Associated Press, "Weaver's Daughter Tells of Life Under Siege," *Oregonian,* September 3, 1992.

46. Harriman, "What Are You Going to Do?"

47. Ibid.

48. This information is from "Bo Gritz for President," America First Coalition, n.p., n.d.

49. ". . . There is a repugnant anti-Semitic undertone to Gritz's presidential campaign that appeals to fringe hate groups such as the Aryan supremacists, skinheads and Ku Klux Klanners. . . . What everyone must remember is that he was in his element and preaching to the choir when negotiating with a man of Weaver's ilk. That is a pathetic claim to fame" (Editorial, *Idaho State Journal,* September 2, 1992).

50. Tom Paulson, "Gritz Gets Credit for Saving Day," *Seattle Post-Intelligencer,* September 2, 1992. Gritz says this in regard to his refusal to run with David Duke, a long-time Klan leader, on the Populist Party ticket in 1988: "I don't like David Duke and I don't like what he stands for. . . . Anyone who is a racist, anyone who is a bigot . . . I don't want their support" (quoted in Seattle P-I Staff, "Gritz Makes Life's Work of Being in Hot Situations," *Seattle Post Intelligencer,* August 30, 1992). Gritz reiterates his stance against white supremacy in "The Randy Weaver Story." See also Bette Tomlinson, "The Warrior Who Would Be President," *Missoula Independent,* April 17, 1992.

51. Lt. Col. James "Bo" Gritz, "A Nation Betrayed" (Santa Barbara, Calif.: Prevailing Winds, n.d.). Cf. Gritz's "A Message from Bo Gritz," *Scriptures for America,* vol. 2 (1990), pp. 3–5. For a more balanced discussion of this issue, see Alfred W. McCoy, *The Politics of Heroin in Southeast Asia* (Brooklyn: L. Hill, 1991).

52. Lt. Col. James "Bo" Gritz, "POWs, MIAs and Drugs" (Santa Barbara: Prevailing Winds, n.d.).

53. Seattle P-I Staff, "Gritz Makes Life's Work of Being in Hot Situations."

54. *Idaho Statesman,* September 17, 1992. Weaver's lawyer, Gerry Spence, believes this is the first time in American history that a ten-month old child has been charged with a felony.

55. Melanie Threlkeld, "Gritz Asks to Talk to Weaver," *Idaho Statesman,* August 29, 1992.

56. Scriptures for America Ministries, "Special Report on the Meeting of Christian Men Held in Estes Park, Colorado, October 23, 24, 25, 1992 Concerning the

Killing of Vickie and Samuel Weaver by the United States Government" (Laporte, Colo.: 1992).

57. Richard Cockle, "North Idaho Siege Produces No Winner," *Oregonian*, September 6, 1992. I agree with the title of this article, but disagree with the facile conclusion quoted.

5. A Library of Infamy

1. Sergey Nilus, *The Protocols of the Learned Elders of Zion*, trans. Victor Marsden (n.p., 1905), quoted from the commentary on protocol number five.

2. James A. Aho, *The Politics of Righteousness* (Seattle: University of Washington Press, 1990), pp. 138–46.

3. For a third case supporting this claim, see ibid., pp. 72–73.

4. Richard Cockle, "Survivalist Refuses to Come in from Cold," *Oregonian*, March 30, 1992.

5. The myth of the Aryan (Christian) peoples, as distinct genealogically from the "Jewish race," identifies them as having descended from Adam; the Jews, blacks, and Asians from other Fathers. The classic scholarly account of this myth is Léon Poliakov's *The Aryan Myth* (New York: Basic Books, 1971). For a recent update of this myth in what today is known as Identity Christianity, see Aho, *The Politics of Righteousness*, pp. 83–113.

6. Elizabeth Dilling, *The Plot Against Christianity* (n.p., 1952). Cf. Dilling's *The Jewish Religion: Its Influence Today* (Torrance, Calif.: Noontide, 1983).

7. Norman Cohn, *Warrant for Genocide* (New York: Oxford University Press, 1967), p. 162. The fullest discussion of Ford's role in the authorship of this book is Leo P. Ribuffo, "Henry Ford and *The International Jew*," *American Jewish History* 69 (June 1980): 437–77. For Hitler's positive appraisal of *The International Jew*, see *Mein Kampf*, trans. Ralph Manheim (Boston: Houghton Mifflin, 1943), p. 639.

8. Pauline Rosenau, *Post-Modernism and the Social Sciences* (Princeton: Princeton University Press, 1992).

9. Hayden White, quoted ibid., p. 39.

10. J. Baudrillard, quoted ibid., p. 77. Cf. p. 90.

11. Dilling, *The Plot Against Christianity*, p. 5.

12. Ibid., p. 6.

13. Dilling, *The Jewish Religion*, p. 4.

14. Ibid., exhibit 70. All exhibits from *The Babylonian Talmud*, trans. Jacob Shachter and H. Freedman (London: Soncino Press, 1934–48).

15. Ibid., incest: exhibits 54–55, 81–82, 136–37, 152, 156, 159; bestiality: exhibits 157–58; necrophilia: exhibit 89; adultery: exhibit 53; murder: exhibits 60, 85–92; theft: exhibits 57–58.

16. Ibid., exhibits 285–92.

17. Ibid., exhibits 277, 166–67, 117, 277.

18. Ibid., exhibit 112.

19. Ibid., exhibits 46, 48, 52, 75, 114, 151, 274.

20. Ralph Roy, *Apostles of Discord* (Boston: Beacon, 1953), pp. 37–39.

21. For the influence of Eisenmenger on Rohling, Ludoph Holst, Alexander Lips, and Sebastian Brunner, see Jacob Katz, *From Prejudice to Destruction: Anti-Semitism, 1700–1933* (Cambridge: Harvard University Press, 1980), pp. 139–40, 152, 286.

22. For example, see Rosemary Ruether, *Faith and Fratricide: The Theological Roots of Anti-Semitism* (New York: Seabury, 1974), or Malcolm Hay, *The Roots of Christian Anti-Semitism* (New York: Anti-Defamation League of B'nai B'rith, 1981 [1950]).

23. Katz, *From Prejudice to Destruction,* pp. 13–22.

24. Adin Steinsaltz, *The Talmud: The Steinsaltz Edition, A Reference Guide* (New York: Random House, 1989), p. 2. Cf. pp. 3, 5.

25. These observations are based on personal correspondence with Michael Barkun, Syracuse University, April 29, 1992. He is not responsible for how I have used his comments.

26. Sanhedrin, chap. 17, Mishnah 7:187–89, in *The Babylonian Talmud,* p. 437. For the analogous selection in an earlier translation of the Talmud, see *New Edition of the Babylonian Talmud,* trans. Michael L. Rodkinson (Boston: New Talmud Pub. Co., 1918), vols. 7–8 (15–16), pp. 187–89.

27. Ibid., pp. 437–39; in Dilling, *The Plot Against Christianity,* exhibits 66–69.

28. Katz, *From Prejudice to Destruction,* pp. 18–19.

29. Ibid., p. 21.

30. Léon Poliakov, *The History of Anti-Semitism,* vol. 3, trans. Miriam Kochan (New York: Vanguard, 1975), p. 421.

31. Max Weber, *On Law in Economy and Society,* trans. Max Rheinstein (New York: Simon and Schuster, 1954), pp. 244–55.

32. Unless otherwise specified, the following account is based primarily on Cohn, *Warrant for Genocide.*

33. Poliakov, *The History of Anti-Semitism,* 3:221.

34. Jean-Paul Sartre, *Anti-Semite and Jew,* trans. George Becker (New York: Schocken Books, 1965).

35. Poliakov, *The History of Anti-Semitism,* 3:275–85. Cf. Katz, *From Prejudice to Destruction,* pp. 139–44.

36. Joseph Shulim, "Napoleon I as the Jewish Messiah: Some Contemporary Conceptions in Virginia," *Jewish Social Studies* 7 (n.d.): 275–80.

37. Poliakov, *The History of Anti-Semitism,* 3:283.

38. For a concise history of Smith, Coughlin, and others, see Laird Wilcox and John George, *Nazis, Communists, Klansmen and Others on the Fringe* (Buffalo, N.Y.: Prometheus, 1992), pp. 304–11.

6. Who Shall Be the Enemy?

1. Georgi Arbatov, member of the Communist Party Central Committee, USSR, quoted in Richard Barnet, "After the Cold War," *New Yorker,* January 1, 1990, pp. 65–76.

2. Allan Bloom, "Response to Fukuyama," *National Interest,* Summer 1989, pp. 19–21.

3. Owen Harries, "Is the Cold War Really Over?" *National Review,* November 10, 1989, pp. 40–45.

4. Quoted in *Nation* editorial, October 9, 1989, p. 369.

5. Francis Fukuyama, "The End of History?" *National Interest,* Summer 1989, 3–18. An expanded book version of this paper, *The End of History and the Last Man,* was published by the Free Press in 1992.

6. Including: *Fortune, New Perspective Quarterly, Current, Harper's, National*

Catholic Reporter, New York Times Magazine, Economist, Time, Newsweek, Nation, Insight, Commentary, National Review, New Yorker, Progressive, Bulletin of Atomic Scientists, U.S. News and World Report, Barrons, and *New Statesman and Society.*

7. Fukuyama, "The End of History?" p. 18.

8. Ibid.

9. Georg Simmel, *Conflict and The Web of Group-Affiliations,* trans. Kurt H. Wolff and Reinhard Bendix (Glencoe, Ill.: Free Press, 1955), pp. 87–89, 98–107. See also Lewis A. Coser, *The Functions of Social Conflict* (Glencoe, Ill.: Free Press, 1956), pp. 33–38, 87–95.

10. Simmel, *Conflict,* p. 106.

11. Heinrich von Treitschke, *Politics,* trans. Blanche Dugdale and Torben De Bille (New York: Harcourt, Brace and World, 1963), p. 59.

12. Ibid., p. 245.

13. Quoted in *Nation* editorial, December 25, 1989.

14. Barnet, "After the Cold War," p. 70. Cf. Joan Chittister, "Life Liberty and the Pursuit of Enmity," *National Catholic Reporter,* March 30, 1990, pp. 1, 14.

15. Simmel, *Conflict,* p. 98. Cf. Coser, *The Functions of Social Conflict,* pp. 104–10.

16. Richard Barnet, "Reflections: The Uses of Force," *New Yorker,* April 29, 1991, pp. 82–95.

A 70-page classified Pentagon document leaked to the press in 1992 elaborates on these plans, envisioning seven possible post–cold war regional military scenarios in the following decade. See Patrick Tyler, "Pentagon Imagines New Enemies to Fight in Post-Cold War Era," *New York Times,* February 17, 1992. Cf. the companion piece, "7 Hypothetical Conflicts Foreseen by the Pentagon," *New York Times,* February 17, 1992.

17. Arthur M. Schlesinger, Jr., *The Cycles of American History* (Boston: Houghton Mifflin, 1986), p. 16.

18. Quoted in Albert K. Weinberg, *Manifest Destiny: A Study of Nationalist Expansionism in American History* (Chicago: Quadrangle, 1963 [1935]), p. 107. The term "manifest destiny" was first invoked in an article appearing in an 1838 edition of the *Democratic Review:* "The far-reaching, the boundless future will be the era of American greatness. In its magnificent domain of space and time, the nation of many nations is *destined to manifest* to mankind the excellence of divine principles; to establish on earth the noblest temple ever dedicated to the worship of the Most High – the Sacred and the True" (quoted in Weinberg, *Manifest Destiny,* p. 107, his emphasis).

19. Coser, *The Functions of Social Conflict,* pp. 93–94.

20. For further discussion and documentation of this proposition, see Albert O. Hirschman, *Shifting Involvements* (Princeton: Princeton University Press, 1982); Herbert McClosky and John Zaller, *The American Ethos* (Cambridge: Harvard University Press, 1984); and Schlesinger, *The Cycles of American History.*

21. For the standard sociology of right-wing movements in American history, see Seymour M. Lipset and Earl Raab, *The Politics of Unreason: Right-Wing Extremism in America, 1790–1970* (New York: Harper and Row, 1970). The following discussion has profited greatly from Richard Hofstadter, *Anti-Intellectualism in American Life* (New York: Vintage, 1963), pp. 117–41, and his *The Paranoid Style in American Politics* (New York: Vintage, 1965).

22. Schlesinger, *The Cycles of American History,* p. 44.

23. Richard Hofstadter, *The Age of Reform: From Bryan to FDR* (New York: Knopf, 1955).

24. William E. Leuchtenberg, "Progressivism and Imperialism: The Progressive Movement and American Foreign Policy, 1896–1916," *Mississippi Valley Historical Review* 34 (1952): 483–504.

25. Lipset and Raab, *The Politics of Unreason,* pp. 62–67.

26. Stanley M. Elkins, *Slavery: A Problem in American Institutional and Intellectual Life* (Chicago: University of Chicago Press, 1959), pp. 27–28 (his emphasis).

27. R. C. Buley, *The Old Northwest Pioneer Period: 1815–1840,* 2 vols. (Indianapolis: Indiana Historical Society, 1950), 2:60.

28. Cf. Eckard V. Toy, Jr., "Right-Wing Extremism from the Ku Klux Klan to the Order, 1915 to 1988," in *Violence in America,* ed. Ted Gurr (Newbury Park, Calif.: Sage, 1989), pp. 131–52.

29. James A. Aho, *The Politics of Righteousness* (Seattle: University of Washington Press, 1990), pp. 216–18.

30. Karl Mannheim, "The Problem of Generations," *Essays in the Sociology of Knowledge* (London: Routledge and Kegan Paul, 1952), p. 29.

31. Arthur Schlesinger, Sr., "Extremism in American Politics," *Saturday Review,* November 17, 1965, pp. 21–25.

32. Robert K. Merton, *Social Theory and Social Structure* (Glencoe, Ill.: Free Press, 1957), p. 129 (his emphasis).

33. Cf. Walter H. Capps, *The New Religious Right* (Columbia: University of South Carolina Press, 1990). See also Perry Deane Young, *God's Bullies: Power Politics and Religious Tyranny* (New York: Holt, Rinehart and Winston, 1982).

34. For one of many articles commenting on this, see Steven Weisman, "Japan's Scorn for Americans Rising," *New York Times,* October 25, 1991.

35. Barnet, "After the Cold War," p. 74.

36. For discussion of the emerging Russian superstate in the twenty-first century, see the series of articles in *National Interest,* Spring 1991.

37. "End's in Sight, Group Insists," *Idaho State Journal,* September 3, 1991.

38. Milton Viorst, "Report from Baghdad," *New Yorker,* June 24, 1991, pp. 64–68.

39. Michael Klare, "Stopping the War Against the Third World," *The Progressive,* January 1989, pp. 14–16.

7. A Phenomenology of the Enemy

1. Investiture hymn for a traditional tribal king in what is now Zaire, quoted in René Girard, *Violence and the Sacred,* trans. Patrick Gregory (Baltimore: Johns Hopkins University Press, 1977), p. 107.

2. For standard statements laying out the discipline of phenomenology, see Edmund Husserl, *Cartesian Meditations,* trans. Dorian Cairns (The Hague: Martinus Nijhoff, 1960); Martin Heidegger, *Being and Time,* trans. John Macquarrie and Edward Robinson (New York: Harper and Row, 1962); Alfred Schutz and Thomas Luckmann, *The Structures of the Life-World,* trans. Richard M. Zaner and H. Tristam Engelhardt, Jr. (Evanston, Ill.: Northwestern University Press, 1973); Alfred Schutz, *Collected Papers,* 3 vols. (The Hague: Martinus Nijhoff, 1962–66).

3. Sam Keen, *Faces of the Enemy* (San Francisco: Harper and Row, 1986).

4. Although neither can be held responsible for the following analysis, the inspiration for a sociology of colonics comes from Norman Brown, *Life Against Death* (Middletown, Conn.: Wesleyan University Press, 1970), and Ernest Becker, *The Denial of Death* (New York: Free Press, 1973).

5. Northrop Frye, *Words With Power* (San Diego: Harcourt Brace Jovanovich, 1990), p. 263.

6. C. B. Baker, "Alien Terror Over America," *Youth Action News*, September 1985.

7. John Gerassi, *The Boys of Boise* (New York: Macmillan, 1966), pp. 3–4.

8. Girard, *Violence and the Sacred*, pp. 286–90. For the original study of the scapegoat in Greek civilization, see James G. Frazer, *The Golden Bough* (New York: Macmillan, 1951 [1922]), pp. 670–75.

9. Girard, *Violence and the Sacred*, pp. 98, 288.

10. From Gisar, *Luther*, 5:324, quoted in Brown, *Life Against Death*, p. 225.

11. For further amplification of this equation in German folklore, see Alan Dundes, *Life Is Like a Chicken Coop Ladder* (New York: Columbia University Press, 1984).

12. The term "excremental assault" is borrowed from Terrance DePres, *The Survivors: An Anatomy of the Death Camps* (New York: Oxford University Press, 1976).

13. Edith Stein, *On the Problem of Empathy*, trans. Waltraut Stein (The Hague: Martinus Nijhoff, 1964).

14. Georg Simmel, *The Problems of the Philosophy of History: An Epistemological Essay*, trans. Guy Oakes (New York: Free Press, 1977), p. 45.

15. Ibid., p. 75. Alfred Schutz's analysis of empathy corresponds to Stein's and Simmel's. Ego, he says, can understand alter's perception of the world only by imaginatively assuming alter's "angle" toward it. "I attribute to him the same perspective which I should have if I were not 'here,' but 'there' [in alter's position], and vice versa" (Schutz, *Collected Papers*, 1:178).

16. Simmel, *Problems of the Philosophy of History*, p. 65.

17. Urie Bronfenbrenner, "The Mirror Image in Soviet–American Relations," in *Psychology and the Prevention of Nuclear War*, ed. Ralph K. White (New York: New York University Press, 1986), p. 81.

18. *Psychology and the Prevention of Nuclear War*, pp. 550–51.

19. Max Scheler, *The Nature of Sympathy*, trans. Peter Heath (London: Routledge and Kegan Paul, 1958).

20. Erich Neumann, *Depth Psychology and a New Ethic*, trans. Eugene Rolfe (New York: G. P. Putnam's Sons, 1969). For a less technical presentation, see Keen, *Faces of the Enemy*. See also *Meeting the Shadow: The Hidden Dark Side of Human Nature*, ed. Jeremiah Abrams and Connie Zweig (Los Angeles: Tarcher, 1991), esp. pp. 195–238, entitled "Enemy-Making: Us and Them in the Body Politic."

21. George Herbert Mead, *Mind, Self and Society* (Chicago: University of Chicago Press, 1934), pp. 144–64.

22. Charles Horton Cooley, *Human Nature and Social Order* (New York: Scribner's, 1902), p. 184.

23. Jean-Paul Sartre, *No Exit*, trans. Stuart Gilbert (New York: Knopf, 1947).

24. Girard, *Violence and the Sacred,* pp. 93–96. For further elaboration, see René Girard, *The Scapegoat,* trans. Yvonne Freccero (Baltimore: Johns Hopkins University Press, 1986), and Frazer, *The Golden Bough,* pp. 633–60.

25. Schutz and Luckmann, *The Structures of the Life-World,* p. 15.

26. Ibid., p. 6.

27. Keen, *Faces of the Enemy,* pp. 168, 13. For a more comprehensive presentation of tactics and therapies concerned with "shadow work," see Abrams and Zweig, eds., *Meeting the Shadow.*

28. Ernest Becker, *Escape from Evil* (New York: Free Press, 1975), p. 103.

29. Heidegger, *Being and Time,* p. 211.

30. Victor Farías, *Heidegger and Nazism,* trans. Paul Burrell, Dominic Di Bernardi, and Gabriel R. Ricci (Philadelphia: Temple University Press, 1989). See also Karl Moehling, "Heidegger and the Nazis," in *Heidegger: The Man and the Thinker,* ed. Thomas Sheehan (Chicago: Precedent, 1977).

31. This is not to say that Heideggerianism logically authorizes Nazism, but that it permits Nazi-like cynicism toward death. See Jean-François Lyotard, *Heidegger and "The Jews,"* trans. Andreas Michel and Mark Roberts, ed. David Carroll (Minneapolis: University of Minnesota Press, 1990), pp. 67–68.

32. Ernest Becker, *The Denial of Death* (New York: Free Press, 1973), pp. 279, 264.

33. Ibid., p. 277.

34. Elisabeth Kübler-Ross, *On Death and Dying* (New York: Macmillan, 1969).

35. Erich Fromm, *You Shall Be As Gods* (New York: Rinehart and Winston, 1966).

36. Becker, *The Denial of Death,* pp. 276, 265, 277.

37. Mohandis Gandhi, *Autobiography* (Boston: Beacon, 1957).

38. James W. Douglass, *Lightning East and West* (New York: Crossroad, 1984), pp. 8–9.

39. Husserl, *Cartesian Meditations,* p. 26; cf. p. 19.

40. Girard, *The Scapegoat,* pp. 109–110.

41. Peter Berger, *The Rumor of Angels* (Garden City, N.Y.: Doubleday-Anchor, 1969), p. 82.

42. Husserl, *Cartesian Meditations,* p. 157.

8. Out of Hate

1. Michael Ryan, "Haters Can Change," *Parade Magazine,* September 15, 1991, p. 11.

2. Tarja Seppa, *Peace Research in Finland: Trends, Institutions, Publications* (Tampere, Finland: Tampereen Yliopisto, 1987), p. 4.

3. Ibid., p. 7.

4. Georg Simmel, *Conflict and The Web of Group-Affiliations,* trans. Kurt H. Wolff and Reinhard Bendix (Glencoe, Ill.: Free Press, 1955), p. 34.

5. It is true that the sine qua non of bureaucratized violence is not hatred but cold, emotional detachment and robotic discipline. Indeed, efforts are routinely made to screen out through diagnostic tests those who in premodern times might have been celebrated as berserkers. But this observation applies only at the point of execution of state violence. Having lived in the twentieth century, we know

that mass hatred is not only compatible with "cost-effective" military violence, it is one of its preconditions.

6. James A. Aho, *The Politics of Righteousness* (Seattle: University of Washington Press, 1990).

7. M. Green, "Greg Withrow's Nazi Past Returns to Inflict the Ultimate Scourge: Crucifixion," *People Weekly*, September 21, 1987, pp. 41–45.

8. Richard Mauer, "Violence Plagued Ex-Aryan Ally," *Idaho Statesman*, September 17, 1980.

9. Coplon, "Skinhead Nation," *Rolling Stone*, December 1988, pp. 54–65, 94.

10. See, however, David G. Bromley, ed., *Falling from the Faith: Causes and Consequences of Religious Apostasy* (Newbury Park, Calif.: Sage, 1988).

11. James T. Richardson, Jan van der Lans, and Frans Derks, "Leaving and Labeling: Voluntary and Coerced Disaffiliation from Religious Movements," *Research in Social Movements, Conflicts and Change* 9 (1986): 97–126.

12. Armand Mauss, "Dimensions of Religious Defection," *Review of Religious Research* 10 (1969): 128–35; Merlin B. Brinkerhoff and K. L. Burke, "Falling from the Faith," *Sociological Analysis* 41 (1980): 41–54.

13. Rodney Stark and William Sims Bainbridge, *The Future of Religion: Secularization, Revival and Cult Formation* (Berkeley: University of California Press, 1985), pp. 314–15.

14. Peter Berger and Thomas Luckmann, *The Social Construction of Reality* (Garden City, N.Y.: Doubleday-Anchor, 1967).

15. John Lofland and Rodney Stark, "Becoming a World-Saver: A Theory of Conversion to a Deviant Perspective," *American Sociological Review* 30 (1965): 862–75.

16. On the Mormons see Stark and Bainbridge, *The Future of Religion*, pp. 316–20. On the Children of God see James T. Richardson, "Experimental Fundamentalism: Revisions in Orthodoxy in the Jesus Movement," *Journal of the American Academy of Religion* 51 (1983): 397–425.

17. Aho, *The Politics of Righteousness*, pp. 185–211.

18. Leon Festinger, Henry W. Riecken, and Stanley Schachter, *When Prophecy Fails* (Minneapolis: University of Minnesota Press, 1956).

19. Roy Wallis, "Network and Clockwork," *Sociology* 15 (1982): 102–7.

20. Bert Klandermans, "Mobilization and Participation: Social Psychological Expansions of Resource Mobilization Theory," *American Sociological Review* 49 (1985): 583–600.

21. The information on Tarrants is from Patsy Sims, *The Klan* (New York: Stein and Day, 1978). On Withrow: Green, "Greg Withrow's Nazi Past Returns to Inflict the Ultimate Scourge"; D. Vargas, "Love Comes to White Supremacist," *Sacramento Bee*, June 21, 1987; and Nancy Wride, "Reformed Nazi Directs Youth Away from Hate Movement," *Sacramento Bee*, June 17, 1989. On Sipes: C. Marine, "A Klansman Renounces a Life of Hatred," *San Francisco Examiner*, January 17, 1988. On Rollins: "Tommy Rollins Interview," 700 Club, Christian Broadcasting Network, Spring 1987. On Benedict: Personal interview, March 8, 1987. On Lufkin: Personal interview, April 13, 1988. On Waughtal: Ryan, "Haters Can Change."

22. Furthermore, the pattern of affiliation for the sample is the mirror image of their subsequent defection: affiliation with the hate group involved simultaneous pushes from conventional social life and social pulls into the group.

Name	Immediate Social Push from Conventional Life	Immediate Social Pull into Hate Group
Tarrants	High school "loser"	Sam Bowers, a KKK terrorist
Withrow	Isolated, transient, assaulted by blacks	Father and Tom Metzger, founder of WAR
Sipes	Isolated, trouble with law, assaulted by blacks	KKK recruiter
Rollins	?	?
Benedict	Unsatisfied single divorcée with child	"Good Christian man"
Lufkin	High school "loser," teased by blacks	High school teacher
Waughtal	Drop out, marginally employed, unsatisfied	Friends

23. John Snell, "Jury Deals Metzger $12.5 Million Blow," *Oregonian,* October 23, 1990.

24. Ibid.

25. John Snell, "Metzger 'Stupid to Defend Himself,' Says Opposition Attorney," *Oregonian,* October 23, 1990.

26. Snell, "Jury Deals Metzger $12.5 Million Blow."

9. The Cantor and the Klansman

1. The information in this chapter is based on an Associated Press news release, "Rabbi Softens Heart of Former Klansman Trapp," *Idaho State Journal,* November 26, 1991, plus three telephone interviews, the first conducted November 27, the second December 3, 1991, the last, January 13, 1992.

2. Josef Pieper, *About Love,* trans. Richard and Clara Winston (Chicago: Franciscan Herald, 1974), p. 3.

3. Ibid.

4. But see Samuel P. Oliner and Pearl Oliner, *The Altruistic Personality* (New York: Free Press, 1988). This book examines the psychological characteristics and social background of gentile Europeans who, at grave risk to themselves, aided Jews and other persecuted peoples in World War II. The findings of the Oliners may be contrasted with those reported by Theodor Adorno and his associates concerning the sources of the so-called fascist personality, the characterology of Nazi supporters. See Adorno's *The Authoritarian Personality* (New York: Harper, 1950).

5. Pieper, *About Love,* p. 19.

6. Ibid.

7. Evidently, Trapp had grown so tired of hearing from Weisser by this time that instead of programming something like the following into his answering machine – "Hello, this is Larry Trapp, I'm not available at the moment, please leave your . . ." – he simply left a flatulent noise.

8. For the classic statement of this theory, see Leon Festinger, Henry W. Riecken, and Stanley Schachter, *When Prophecy Fails* (Minneapolis: University of Minnesota Press, 1956).

9. See our discussion of Metzger in the previous chapter.

10. Although Hanukkah is considered only a minor Jewish religious feast, it has evolved into a major Jewish family ritual in America because of its proximity to Christmas.

11. Thomas A. Harris, *I'm Ok, You're Ok* (New York: Harper and Row, 1969).

12. Paraphrased from Hebrews 12:8 in Pieper, *About Love,* p. 45.

13. Pieper, *About Love,* p. 54.

14. René Spitz, "Hospitalism," *The Psychoanalytic Study of the Child* 1 (1945): 53–72. Cf. Pieper, *About Love,* pp. 27–28, 30–31.

15. This was also the concern of the Russian-born Harvard sociologist Pitirim Sorokin. With the help of a generous endowment from the Eli Lilly foundation, he established the Harvard Research Center in Creative Altruism in 1949. Among its many publications: Pitirim Sorokin, *Altruistic Love: A Study of Good Neighbors and Christian Saints* (Boston: Beacon, 1950), *Explorations in Altruistic Love and Behavior* (Boston: Beacon, 1950), and *The Ways of Power and Love* (Boston: Beacon, 1954).

10. A Community with a Heart

1. James W. Douglass, *Lightning East and West* (New York: Crossroad, 1984).

2. Laird Wilcox, *1989 Guide to the American Right* (Olathe, Kans.: Editorial Research Service, 1989).

3. James A. Aho, *The Politics of Righteousness* (Seattle: University of Washington Press, 1990), pp. 56–57.

4. For standard journalistic accounts of the Order, see Kevin Flynn and Gary Gerhardt, *The Silent Brotherhood* (New York: Free Press, 1989), and Thomas Martinez with John Gunther, *Brotherhood of Murder* (New York: Pocket Books, 1988). For a more sociological picture, see Aho, *The Politics of Righteousness,* pp. 61–67.

5. Considerable skepticism exists regarding the credibility of the FBI informant, and ex-convict, whose allegations are the basis of this report. See *Seattle Post-Intelligencer,* February 19, 1992.

6. Unless otherwise specified, all the information in this chapter was secured in August 1985 in the course of eleven in-depth interviews (lasting anywhere from one to three hours) with Kootenai County citizens who played pivotal roles in the development of the KCHRTF. I also interviewed three members of the Aryan Nations Church, including a three-hour interview with its pastor, Rev. Richard Butler.

7. For a concise and readable model, see Rodney Stark, *Sociology* (Belmont, Calif.: Wadsworth, 1985), pp. 492–523.

8. A letter sent to Abigail Van Buren in care of the *Coeur d'Alene Press,* April 10, 1985.

9. *Coeur d'Alene Press,* September 5, 1980.

10. Ibid.

11. As reported in "To All Residents Regardless of Race, Creed, or Color," undated, unsigned flyer received by the Coeur d'Alene Chamber of Commerce.

12. The document arising out of Justice Department concern with racism in Idaho is U.S. Department of Justice, *Bigotry and Violence in Idaho* (Washington, D.C.: Government Printing Office, 1986).

13. The following account is based on Alleconda Fort (complainant), "Human Rights Violation," Idaho Human Rights Commission, July 28, 1982. See also U.S. Department of Justice, *Bigotry and Violence in Idaho*, pp. 6–7.

14. In Idaho, if a misdemeanor occurs outside the presence of an officer, the officer has no authority to arrest without a citizen's complaint validated by the prosecutor. At that time there was not complete agreement among northern Idaho authorities that racism was a significant problem. While the Sheriff's Department and County Prosecutor did view it seriously, the Coeur d'Alene Police Department and City Attorney had a more benign view of the situation (see U.S. Department of Justice, *Bigotry and Violence in Idaho*, p. 5).

15. Fort, "Human Rights Violation."

16. Ibid.

17. Ibid.

18. U.S. Department of Justice, *Bigotry and Violence in Idaho*, p. 7.

19. Ibid.

20. For a sensationalized version of this event, see Joshua Hammer, "Trouble," *People Weekly*, August 29, 1983, pp. 44–48.

21. *Idaho Code*, vol. 4, chap. 79, secs. 18-7901 to 18-7904. In 1992 Idaho State Fourth District Judge Gerald Schroeder declared the malicious harassment act an unconstitutional infringement on the right of free speech. The defendant in the case was still tried on misdemeanor charges of assault on a black Boise family, resisting arrest, and obscene conduct. See Martin Johncox, "Judge Abolishes Harassment Law," *Idaho Statesman*, October 29, 1992.

22. Idaho, County of Kootenai, "Certificate of Assumed Name," February 3, 1983, book 124, p. 50.

23. Besides the article cited in note 20, see also Carl T. Rowan and David M. Mazie, "Can the Klan Come Back?" *Reader's Digest*, September 1983, pp. 197–200.

24. Letter received by the Coeur d'Alene Chamber of Commerce, March 10, 1985.

25. Emerson later left the Chamber and now works as a realtor.

26. This phrase is from the editorial "Silence Can Be Eloquent," *Spokesman-Review*, June 1, 1983.

27. Coeur d'Alene Chamber of Commerce, "Human Rights Policy Statement" (memorandum), September 1983.

28. Coeur d'Alene Lions Club, "Human Rights Policy" (endorsement), January 30, 1984.

29. *Spokesman-Review*, October 23, 1983.

30. For coverage of the debate on this issue, see the articles in *Spokesman-Review*, February 11, 14, and 17, 1989.

31. Cf. Colin Greer, "We Must Take a Stand," *Parade Magazine*, April 28, 1991, pp. 4–6.

32. James Coleman, *Community Conflict* (New York: Free Press, 1957), p. 21.

33. *Spokesman-Review*, October 23, 1983.

34. *Coeur d'Alene Press*, February 27, 1985.

11. Apocalypse and the Hero

1. Nathaniel Hawthorne, quoted in Joseph Campbell, *Myths to Live By* (New York: Viking, 1972), p. 168.

2. Dick Anthony and Thomas Robbins, "The Resurgence of Traditional Absolutism in an Age of Anxious Relativism," in *The Sociology of Deviance*, ed. Jack Douglas (Boston: Allyn and Bacon, 1984), pp. 163–81.

3. Associated Press, October 17, 1991.

4. As Sayyid Issa al Haadi al Mahdi, *The Paleman* (n.p.: 1990).

5. Cf. Ruth Leger Sivard, *World Military and Social Expenditures* (Washington, D.C.: World Priorities); published annually since 1974.

6. Martin Heidegger, "The Turning," in *The Question of Technology and Other Essays*, trans. William Lovitt (New York: Harper, 1977), pp. 36–49.

7. Friedrich Hölderlin, "Patmos," quoted in Heidegger, "The Turning," p. 42.

8. Heidegger, "The Turning," p. 42.

9. Associated Press, September 13, 1991.

10. This is the basis of the argument of Robert Lifton and Richard Falk in *Indefensible Weapons* (New York: Basic Books, 1982).

11. Neil Evernden, *The Natural Alien* (Toronto: University of Toronto Press, 1985).

12. Max Scheler, *The Nature of Sympathy*, trans. Peter Heath (London: Routledge and Kegan Paul, 1958).

13. Joanna Macy, *Despair and Personal Power in the Nuclear Age* (Philadelphia: New Society, 1983).

14. The protagonists in the equivalent Semitic myth are Yahweh versus Leviathan and Marduk (Asshur) versus Tiamat.

15. This esoteric interpretation of the slaying of dragons has received considerable attention in clinical psychology. The most recent example is *Meeting the Shadow: The Hidden Power of the Dark Side of Human Nature*, ed. Jeremiah Abrams and Connie Zweig (Los Angeles: Tarcher, 1991). This anthology includes excerpts from the writings of several scholars cited in this chapter and elsewhere, including Ernest Becker, Carl Jung, Sam Keen, and Joseph Campbell. Others excerpted in *Meeting the Shadow* who have influenced the position taken here but who have not been formally cited include M. Scott Peck, Jerome Bernstein, John A. Sanford, and Robert Bly.

16. Quoted in Joseph Campbell, *The Masks of God*, vol. 2 (New York: Viking, 1970), p. 187.

17. Carl G. Jung, *Memories, Dreams, Reflections*, trans. Richard and Clara Winston (New York: Vintage, 1965), p. 39.

18. Cf. Carl G. Jung, "The Fight with the Shadow," in Jung's *Collected Works*, vol. 10, trans. R. F. C. Hull (Princeton: Princeton University Press, 1958), pp. 218–43.

19. Again, this is not my creative idea, but is supported by a growing body of social psychology. See Abrams and Zweig, eds., *Meeting the Shadow*, especially pp. 239–302.

20. Max Weber, "Politics as a Vocation," in *From Max Weber: Essays in Sociology*, trans. and ed. H. H. Gerth and C. Wright Mills (New York: Oxford University Press, 1958 [1946]), pp. 119, 125–26, 118–28.

21. Sun Tzu, *The Art of War*, trans. Samuel Griffith (New York: Oxford University Press, 1963), chap. 3:31 (my emphasis); see also 3:32–33, 10:26.

Bibliography

To facilitate research, the bibliography is presented in two sections: (1) Works Dealing with Conflict, Hatred, Violence, and Related Subjects; (2) Primary and Secondary Sources Concerning Right-Wing Extremism and Nazism. Newspaper articles cited in the text are not listed in the bibliography.

Works Dealing with Conflict, Hatred, Violence, and Related Subjects

Abrams, Jeremiah, and Connie Zweig, eds. *Meeting the Shadow: The Hidden Dark Side of Human Nature.* Los Angeles: Tarcher, 1991.

Aho, James A. " 'I Am Death . . . Who Shatters Worlds': The Emerging Nuclear Death Cult." In *A Shuddering Dawn: Religious Studies and the Nuclear Age,* edited by Ira Chernus and Edward T. Linenthal. Albany: State University of New York Press, 1989.

———. *Religious Mythology and the Art of War.* Westport, Conn.: Greenwood, 1981.

Allport, Gordon, and Leo Postman. "The Basic Psychology of Rumors." *Transactions of the New York Academy of Sciences,* series 2 (1954): 61–81.

Babylonian Talmud, translated by Jacob Shachter and H. Freedman. London: Soncino Press, 1934–48.

Babylonian Talmud, New Edition of, translated by Michael L. Rodkinson. Boston: New Talmud Pub. Co., 1918.

Barnet, Richard. "After the Cold War." *New Yorker,* January 1, 1990, pp. 65–76.

———. "Reflections: The Uses of Force." *New Yorker,* April 29, 1991, pp. 82–95.

Becker, Ernest. *The Denial of Death.* New York: Free Press, 1973.

———. *Escape from Evil.* New York: Free Press, 1975.

———. *The Structure of Evil.* New York: Free Press, 1968.

Becker, Howard. *The Outsiders.* Glencoe, Ill.: Free Press, 1963.

Berger, Peter. *Invitation to Sociology.* Garden City, N.Y.: Doubleday-Anchor, 1963.

———. *The Rumor of Angels.* Garden City, N.Y.: Doubleday-Anchor, 1969.

Berger, Peter, and Thomas Luckmann. *The Social Construction of Reality: A Treatise in the Sociology of Knowledge.* Garden City, N.Y.: Doubleday-Anchor, 1967.

Best, Joel, ed. *Images of Issues.* New York: Aldine de Gruyter, 1989.

Bloom, Allan. "Response to Fukuyama." *National Interest,* Summer 1989, pp. 19–21.

Bottomore, Thomas, trans., introduced with commentary by Erich Fromm. *Marx's Concept of Man.* New York: Ungar, 1961.

Bowles, Paul. *A Distant Episode.* New York: Ecco, 1988.

Brinkerhoff, Merlin B., and K. L. Burke. "Falling from the Faith." *Sociological Analysis* 41 (1980): 41–54.

Bromley, David G., ed. *Falling from the Faith: Causes and Consequences of Religious Apostasy.* Newbury Park, Calif.: Sage, 1988.

Bronfenbrenner, Urie. "The Mirror Image in Soviet–American Relations." In *Psy-*

chology and the Prevention of Nuclear War, edited by Ralph K. White. New York: New York University Press, 1986.

Brown, Norman. *Life Against Death: The Psychoanalytic Meaning of History.* Middletown, Conn.: Wesleyan University Press, 1970.

Buley, R. C. *The Old Northwest Pioneer Period: 1815–1840.* 2 vols. Indianapolis: Indiana Historical Society, 1950.

Campbell, Joseph. *The Masks of God.* 4 vols. New York: Viking, 1970.

———. *Myths to Live By.* New York: Viking, 1972.

Camus, Albert. "Neither Victims Nor Executioners." In *Seeds of Liberation,* edited by Paul Goodman. New York: George Braziller, 1964.

Chernus, Ira. *Dr. Strangegod: On the Symbolic Meaning of Nuclear Weapons.* Columbia: South Carolina University Press, 1986.

Cicourel, Aron. *The Social Organization of Juvenile Justice.* New York: Wiley, 1968.

Cleaver, Eldridge. "The Black Man's Stake in Vietnam." In *Soul on Ice,* edited by Cleaver. New York: Delta, 1968.

Coleman, James. *Community Conflict.* New York: Free Press, 1957.

Cooley, Charles Horton. *Human Nature and Social Order.* New York: Scribner's, 1902.

Coser, Lewis A. *The Functions of Social Conflict.* Glencoe, Ill.: Free Press, 1956.

Dallery, Arleen, and Charles Scott, eds. *The Question of the Other.* Albany: State University of New York Press, 1989.

Dobzhansky, Theodosius. *Mankind Evolving.* New Haven: Yale University Press, 1962.

Douglas, Jack, ed. *The Sociology of Deviance.* Boston: Allyn and Bacon, 1984.

Douglass, James W. *Lightning East and West.* New York: Crossroad, 1984.

Duncan, Hugh. *Communication and Social Order.* New York: Oxford University Press, 1968 [1962].

Dundes, Alan. *Life is Like a Chicken Coop Ladder: A Portrait of German Culture Through Folklore.* New York: Columbia University Press, 1984.

Durkheim, Émile. *The Elementary Forms of Religious Life,* translated by J. W. Swain. Glencoe, Ill.: Free Press, 1954.

Elkins, Stanley M. *Slavery: A Problem in American Institutional and Intellectual Life.* Chicago: University of Chicago Press, 1959.

Elliot, Gil. *The Twentieth Century Book of the Dead.* New York: Charles Scribner's Sons, 1972.

Evernden, Neil. *The Natural Alien: Humankind and Environment.* Toronto: University of Toronto Press, 1985.

Fanon, Frantz. *Black Skin, White Masks,* translated by Charles Lam Markmann. New York: Grove Press, 1967.

Festinger, Leon, Henry W. Riecken, and Stanley Schachter. *When Prophecy Fails.* Minneapolis: University of Minnesota Press, 1956.

Feuerbach, Ludwig. *The Essence of Christianity,* translated by George Eliot. New York: Harper and Row, 1957.

Finger, Matthias. "European Values After the Euromissile Crisis." In *European Values in International Relations,* edited by Vilho Harle. London: Pinter, 1990.

Franklin, H. Bruce. "The POW/MIA Myth." *Atlantic,* December 1991, pp. 45–81.

Franz, Marie Louise von. *The Feminine in Fairytales.* Irving, Tex.: University of Dallas Press, 1972.

Frazer, James George. *The Golden Bough.* New York: Macmillan, 1951 [1922].

Fromm, Erich. *You Shall Be As Gods.* New York: Rinehart and Winston, 1966.

Frye, Northrop. *Words With Power: Being a Second Study of "The Bible and Literature."* San Diego: Harcourt Brace Jovanovich, 1990.

Fukuyama, Francis. "The End of History?" *National Interest,* Summer 1989, pp. 3–18.

Gandhi, Mohandis. *Autobiography.* Boston: Beacon, 1957.

Garfinkel, Harold. "Conditions of Successful Degradation Ceremonies." *American Journal of Sociology* 61 (1956): 420–24.

———. *Studies in Ethnomethodology.* Englewood Cliffs, N.J.: Prentice-Hall, 1967.

Gerassi, John. *The Boys of Boise.* New York: Macmillan, 1966.

Gibson, James. "American Paramilitary Culture and the Reconstitution of the Vietnam War." In *Making War/Making Peace,* edited by Francesca Cancian and Gibson. Belmont, Calif.: Wadsworth, 1990.

Girard, René. *The Scapegoat,* translated by Yvonne Freccero. Baltimore: Johns Hopkins University Press, 1986.

———. *Violence and the Sacred,* translated by Patrick Gregory. Baltimore: Johns Hopkins University Press, 1977.

Harle, Vilho, ed. *European Values in International Relations.* London: Pinter, 1990.

Harries, Owen. "Is the Cold War Really Over?" *National Review,* November 10, 1989, pp. 40–45.

Harris, Thomas A. *I'm Ok, You're Ok.* New York: Harper and Row, 1969.

Heidegger, Martin. *Being and Time,* translated by John Macquarrie and Edward Robinson. New York: Harper and Row, 1962.

———. "The Turning." In *The Question of Technology and Other Essays,* translated by William Lovitt. New York: Harper, 1977.

Hirschman, Albert O. *Shifting Involvements.* Princeton: Princeton University Press, 1982.

Hofstadter, Richard. *The Age of Reform: From Bryan to FDR.* New York: Knopf, 1955.

———. *Anti-Intellectualism in American Life.* New York: Vintage, 1963.

———. *The Paranoid Style in American Politics.* New York: Vintage, 1965.

Husserl, Edmund. *Cartesian Meditations,* translated by Dorian Cairns. The Hague: Martinus Nijhoff, 1960.

Irwin, John. *The Jail.* Berkeley: University of California Press, 1985.

Jung, Carl G. "The Fight with the Shadow." In Jung, *Collected Works,* vol. 10, translated by R. F. C. Hull. Princeton: Princeton University Press, 1958.

———. *Memories, Dreams, Reflections,* translated by Richard and Clara Winston. New York: Vintage, 1965.

Keen, Sam. *Faces of the Enemy: Reflections of the Hostile Imagination.* San Francisco: Harper and Row, 1986.

Klandermans, Bert. "Mobilization and Participation: Social Psychological Expansions of Resource Mobilization Theory." *American Sociological Review* 49 (1985): 583–600.

Klare, Michael. "Stopping the War Against the Third World." *The Progressive,* January 1989, pp. 14–16.

Kopind, Andrew. "The Warrior State: Imposing a New Order at Home." *Nation,* April 8, 1991.

Kübler-Ross, Elisabeth. *On Death and Dying.* New York: Macmillan, 1969.

Leuchtenberg, William E. "Progressivism and Imperialism: The Progressive Movement and American Foreign Policy, 1896–1916." *Mississippi Valley Historical Review* 34 (1952): 483–504.

Lévinas, Emmanuel. *Otherwise Than Being: Or Beyond Essence,* translated by Alphonso Lingis. The Hague: Martinus Nijhoff, 1981.

Lifton, Robert Jay, and Richard Falk. *Indefensible Weapons.* New York: Basic Books, 1982.

Lofland, John, and Rodney Stark. "Becoming a World-Saver: A Theory of Conversion to a Deviant Perspective." *American Sociological Review* 30 (1965): 862–75.

Lyotard, Jean-François. *Heidegger and "the Jews,"* translated by Andreas Michel and Mark Roberts. Edited by David Carroll. Minneapolis: University of Minnesota Press, 1990.

McClosky, Herbert, and John Zaller. *The American Ethos: Public Attitudes Toward Capitalism and Democracy.* Cambridge: Harvard University Press, 1984.

McCoy, Alfred W. *The Politics of Heroin in Southeast Asia.* Brooklyn: L. Hill, 1991.

Macy, Joanna. *Despair and Personal Power in the Nucelar Age.* Philadelphia: New Society, 1983.

Mahabharata, translated by Pratap Chandra Roy. Calcutta, India: Datta, Bose and Co., 1919–33.

Mannheim, Karl. "The Problem of Generations." In *Essays in the Sociology of Knowledge,* edited by Mannheim. London: Routledge and Kegan Paul, 1952.

Martino, Joseph P. *A Fighting Chance: The Moral Use of Nuclear Weapons.* San Francisco: Ignatius, 1988.

Mauss, Armand. "Dimensions of Religious Defection." *Review of Religious Research* 10 (1969): 128–35.

Mead, George Herbert. *Mind, Self and Society from the Standpoint of a Social Behaviorist.* Chicago: University of Chicago Press, 1934.

Merton, Robert K. *Social Theory and Social Structure.* Glencoe, Ill.: Free Press, 1957.

Mills, C. Wright. *The Sociological Imagination.* New York: Oxford University Press, 1959.

Neumann, Erich. *Depth Psychology and a New Ethic,* translated by Eugene Rolfe. New York: G. P. Putnam's Sons, 1969.

Nietzsche, Friedrich. *Toward a Genealogy of Morals,* translated by Walter Kaufman. New York: Vintage Books, 1969.

Otto, Rudolf. *The Idea of the Holy,* translated by John W. Harvey. London: Oxford University Press, 1923.

Pieper, Josef. *About Love,* translated by Richard and Clara Winston. Chicago: Franciscan Herald, 1974.

Richardson, James T. "Experimental Fundamentalism: Revisions in Orthodoxy in the Jesus Movement." *Journal of the American Academy of Religion* 51 (1983): 397–425.

Richardson, James T., Joel Best, and David Bromley, eds. *The Satanism Scare.* New York: Aldine de Gruyter, 1991.

Richardson, James T., Jan van der Lans, and Frans Derks. "Leaving and Labeling: Voluntary and Coerced Disaffiliation from Religious Movements." *Research in Social Movements, Conflicts and Change* 9 (1986): 97–126.

Rieber, Robert W., ed. *The Psychology of War and Peace: The Image of the Enemy.* New York: Plenum, 1991.

Rosenau, Pauline. *Post-Modernism and the Social Sciences*. Princeton: Princeton University Press, 1992.

Ryan, Tom. *Screw: A Guard's View of Bridgewater State Hospital*. Boston: South End, 1981.

Ryan, William. *Blaming the Victim*. New York: Vintage, 1971.

Sagarin, Edward, and Robert Kelly. "The Brewster Effect: Political Trials and the Self-Defeating Prophecy." In *Politics and Crime*, edited by Sawyer F. Sylvester and Edward Sagarin. New York: Praeger, 1974.

Sarat, Austin D., and Malcolm M. Feeley. *The Policy Dilemma: Federal Crime Policy and the Law Enforcement Assistance Administration, 1968–1978*. Minneapolis: University of Minnesota Press, 1980.

Sartre, Jean-Paul. *Anti-Semite and Jew*, translated by George Becker. New York: Schocken Books, 1965.

———. *No Exit*, translated by Stuart Gilbert. New York: Knopf, 1947.

Scheler, Max. *The Nature of Sympathy*, translated by Peter Heath. London: Routledge and Kegan Paul, 1958.

———. *Ressentiment*, translated by William W. Holdheim. New York: Schocken Books, 1972 [1961].

Schlesinger, Arthur M., Jr. *The Cycles of American History*. Boston: Houghton Mifflin, 1986.

Schutz, Alfred. *Collected Papers*. 3 vols. The Hague: Martinus Nijhoff, 1962–66.

Schutz, Alfred, and Thomas Luckmann. *The Structures of the Life-World*, translated by Richard M. Zaner and H. Tristam Engelhardt, Jr. Evanston, Ill.: Northwestern University Press, 1973.

Schwartz, Richard, and Jerome Skolnick. "Two Studies of Legal Stigma." In *The Other Side: Perspectives on Deviance*, edited by Howard S. Becker. New York: Free Press, 1964.

Scott, Robert. *The Making of Blind Men*. New York: Russell Sage, 1969.

———. "On Doing Good." In *The Sociology of Deviance*, edited by Jack Douglas. New York: Allyn and Bacon, 1984.

Seppa, Tarja. *Peace Research in Finland: Trends, Institutions, Publications*. Tampere, Finland: Tampereen Yliopisto, 1987.

Serres, Michel. "Trahison: La thanatocratie: *Hermes III*. Paris: Minuit, 1974.

Shibutani, Tamotsu. *Improvised News*. Indianapolis: Bobbs-Merrill, 1966.

Shover, Neal. " 'Experts' and Diagnosis in Correctional Agencies." *Crime and Delinquency* 20 (1974): 347–58.

Simmel, Georg. *Conflict and The Web of Group-Affiliations*, translated by Kurt H. Wolff and Reinhard Bendix. Glencoe, Ill.: Free Press, 1955.

———. *The Problems of the Philosophy of History: An Epistemological Essay*, translated by Guy Oakes. New York: Free Press, 1977.

Sivard, Ruth Leger. *World Military and Social Expenditures*. Washington, D.C.: World Priorities, annual.

Sorokin, Pitirim. *Altruistic Love: A Study of Good Neighbors and Christian Saints*. Boston: Beacon, 1950.

———. *Explorations in Altruistic Love and Behavior*. Boston: Beacon, 1950.

———. *The Ways of Power and Love*. Boston: Beacon, 1954.

Spitz, René. "Hospitalism." *The Psychoanalytic Study of the Child* 1 (1945): 53–72.

Stark, Rodney. *Sociology*. Belmont, Calif.: Wadsworth, 1985.

Stark, Rodney, and William Sims Bainbridge. *The Future of Religion: Secularization, Revival and Cult Formation.* Berkeley: University of California Press, 1985.

Stein, Edith. *On the Problem of Empathy,* translated by Waltraut Stein. The Hague: Martinus Nijhoff, 1964.

Steinsaltz, Adin. *The Talmud: The Steinsaltz Edition, A Reference Guide.* New York: Random House, 1989.

Sudnow, David. *Passing On.* Englewood Cliffs, N.J.: Prentice-Hall, 1967.

Sun Tzu. *The Art of War,* translated by Samuel Griffith. New York: Oxford University Press, 1963.

Szasz, Thomas. *Ceremonial Chemistry.* Garden City, N.Y.: Doubleday-Anchor, 1974.

———. *The Manufacture of Madness.* New York: Dell, 1970.

Thomas, William I. *On Social Organization and Social Personality: Selected Papers,* edited by Morris Janowitz. Chicago: University of Chicago Press, 1966.

Thompson, E. P. "Exterminism Reviewed." In *The Heavy Dancers,* edited by Thompson. New York: Pantheon Books, 1985.

———. "Notes on Exterminism, the Last Stage of Civilisation." In his *Beyond the Cold War.* New York: Pantheon Books, 1982.

Treitschke, Heinrich von. *Politics,* trans. by Blanche Dugdale and Torben De Bille. New York: Harcourt, Brace and World, 1963.

Vähämäki, Jussi. "What Are the Common Values that Europeans Share?" TAPRI Workshop on European Values in International Relations. Helsinki, Finland, September 1988.

Viorst, Milton. "Report from Baghdad." *New Yorker,* June 24, 1991, pp. 64–68.

Virilio, Paul. *Pure War.* New York: Foreign Agent Series, 1983.

Wallis, Roy. "Network and Clockwork." *Sociology* 15 (1982): 102–7.

Weber, Max. *On Law in Economy and Society,* translated by Max Rheinstein. New York: Simon and Schuster, 1954.

———. "Politics as a Vocation." In *From Max Weber: Essays in Sociology,* translated and edited by H. H. Gerth and C. Wright Mills. New York: Oxford University Press, 1946; Galaxy book, 1958.

Weinberg, Albert. *Manifest Destiny: A Study of Nationalist Expansionism in American History.* Chicago: Quadrangle, 1963 [1935].

White, Ralph K. "Empathizing with the Soviet Government." In *Psychology and the Prevention of Nuclear War,* edited by White. New York: New York University Press, 1986.

Wilcox, Laird, and John George. *Nazis, Communists, Klansmen and Others on the Fringe.* Buffalo, N.Y.: Prometheus, 1992.

Wyschogrod, Edith. *Spirit in Ashes: Hegel, Heidegger, and Man-Made Mass Death.* New Haven: Yale University Press, 1985.

Primary and Secondary Sources Concerning Right-Wing Extremism and Nazism

Adorno, Theodor. *The Authoritarian Personality.* New York: Harper, 1950.

Aho, James A. *The Politics of Righteousness: Idaho Christian Patriotism.* Seattle: University of Washington Press, 1990.

Anthony, Dick, and Thomas Robbins. "The Resurgence of Traditional Absolutism in an Age of Anxious Relativism." In *The Sociology of Deviance,* edited by Jack Douglas. Boston: Allyn and Bacon, 1984.

Anti-Defamation League of B'nai B'rith. *Extremism on the Right.* New York: Anti-Defamation League of B'nai B'rith, 1983.

Baker, C. B. "Alien Terror Over America." *Youth Action News,* September 1985.

Beam, Louis. "Vietnam: Bringing It on Home." *Essays of a Klansman.* Hayden Lake, Idaho: AKIA Pub., 1983.

Capps, Walter H. *The New Religious Right.* Columbia: University of South Carolina Press, 1990.

Coeur d'Alene Chamber of Commerce. "Human Rights Policy Statement" (memorandum). September 1983.

Coeur d'Alene Lion's Club. "Human Rights Policy" (endorsement). January 30, 1984.

Cohn, Norman. *Warrant for Genocide.* New York: Oxford University Press, 1967.

Coplon. "Skinhead Nation." *Rolling Stone,* December 1988, pp. 54–65, 94.

DePres, Terrance. *The Survivors: An Anatomy of the Death Camps.* New York: Oxford University Press, 1976.

Dilling, Elizabeth. *The Plot Against Christianity.* n.p.: 1952. Reprinted as *The Jewish Religion: Its Influence Today.* Torrance, Calif.: Noontide, 1983.

Dwyer, William L. *The Goldmark Case: An American Libel Trial.* Seattle: University of Washington Press, 1984.

Farías, Victor. *Heidegger and Nazism,* translated by Paul Burrell, Dominic Di Bernardi, and Gabriel R. Ricci. Philadelphia: Temple University Press, 1989.

Finch, Phillip. *God, Guts and Guns.* New York: Seaview/Putnam, 1983.

Flynn, Kevin, and Gary Gerhardt. *The Silent Brotherhood.* New York: Free Press, 1989.

Fort, Alleconda (complainant). "Human Rights Violation." Idaho Human Rights Commission, July 28, 1982.

George, Wesley. *The Biology of the Race Problem.* New York: National Putnam Letters Committee, 1962.

Green, M. "Greg Withrow's Nazi Past Returns to Inflict the Ultimate Scourge: Crucifixion." *People Weekly,* September 21, 1987, pp. 41–45.

Greer, Colin. "We Must Take a Stand." *Parade Magazine,* April 28, 1991, pp. 4–6.

Gritz, Lt. Col. James "Bo" (ret.). "A Message from Bo Gritz." *Scriptures for America,* vol. 2 (1990), pp. 3–5.

———. "A Nation Betrayed" (tape recording). Santa Barbara, Calif.: Prevailing Winds, n.d.

———. "POWs, MIAs and Drugs" (tape recording). Santa Barbara, Calif.: Prevailing Winds, n.d.

Hammer, Joshua. "Trouble." *People Weekly,* August 29, 1983, pp. 44–48.

Hay, Malcolm. *The Roots of Christian Anti-Semitism.* New York: Anti-Defamation League of B'nai B'rith, 1981 [1950].

Hitler, Adolf. *Mein Kampf,* translated by Ralph Manheim. Boston: Houghton Mifflin, 1943.

Hofstadter, Richard. *The Paranoid Style in American Politics.* New York: Vintage, 1965.

Idaho, County of Kootenai. "Certificate of Assumed Name." February 3, 1983, book 124, p. 50.

Katz, Jacob. *From Prejudice to Destruction: Anti-Semitism, 1700–1933*. Cambridge: Harvard University Press, 1980.

Kovel, Joel. *White Racism: A Psychohistory*. New York: Pantheon, 1970.

Lindsey, Hal. *The Late Great Planet Earth*. Grand Rapids, Mich.: Zondervan, 1970.

Lipset, Seymour M., and Earl Raab. *The Politics of Unreason: Right-Wing Extremism in America, 1790–1970*. New York: Harper and Row, 1970.

MacDonald, Andrew. *The Hunter*. Hillsboro, W.V.: National Alliance, 1989.

al Mahdi, Sayyid Issa al Haadi. *The Paleman*. n.p.: n.d.

"Malicious Harrassment Law." *Idaho Code*, vol. 4, chap. 79.

Martinez, Thomas, with John Gunther. *Brotherhood of Murder*. New York: Pocket Books, 1988.

Moehling, Karl. "Heidegger and the Nazis." In *Heidegger: The Man and the Thinker*, edited by Thomas Sheehan. Chicago: Precedent, 1977.

Nilus, Sergey. *The Protocols of the Learned Elders of Zion*, translated by Victor Marsden. n.p.: 1905.

Oliner, Samuel, and Pearl Oliner. *The Altruistic Personality*. New York: Free Press, 1988.

Poliakov, Léon. *The Aryan Myth*. New York: Basic Books, 1971.

———. *The History of Anti-Semitism*, vol. 3, translated by Miriam Kochan. New York: Vanguard, 1975.

Rader, Melvin. *False Witness*. Seattle: University of Washington Press, 1969.

Ribuffo, Leo P. "Henry Ford and *The International Jew*." *American Jewish History* 69 (June 1980): 437–77.

Rose, Arnold M. *Libel and Academic Freedom: A Lawsuit Against Political Extremists*. Minneapolis: University of Minnesota Press, 1968.

Rowan, Carl, and David M. Mazie. "Can the Klan Come Back?" *Reader's Digest*, September 1983, pp. 197–200.

Roy, Ralph. *Apostles of Discord*. Boston: Beacon, 1953.

Ruether, Rosemary, *Faith and Fratricide: The Theological Roots of Anti-Semitism*. New York: Seabury, 1974.

Ryan, Michael. "Haters Can Change." *Parade Magazine*, September 15, 1991, p. 11.

Schlesinger, Arthur M., Sr., "Extremism in American Politics." *Saturday Review*, November 17, 1965, pp. 21–25.

Scriptures for America Ministries. "Special Report on the Meeting of Christian Men Held in Estes Park, Colorado, October 23, 24, 25, 1992 Concerning the Killing of Vickie and Samuel Weaver by the United States Government." Laporte, Colo., 1992.

Shulim, Joseph. "Napoleon I as the Jewish Messiah: Some Contemporary Conceptions in Virginia." *Jewish Social Studies* 7 (n.d.): 275–80.

Sims, Patsy. *The Klan*. New York: Stein and Day, 1978.

Toy, Eckard V., Jr. "Right-Wing Extremism from the Ku Klux Klan to the Order, 1915 to 1988." In *Violence in America*, edited by Ted Gurr. Newbury Park, Calif.: Sage, 1989.

U.S. Department of Justice. *Bigotry and Violence in Idaho*. Washington, D.C.: Government Printing Office, 1986.

Wilcox, Laird. *1989 Guide to the American Right*. Olathe, Kans.: Editorial Research Service, 1989.

Young, Perry Deane. *God's Bullies: Power Politics and Religious Tyranny*. New York: Holt, Rinehart and Winston, 1982.

Index

Croly, Herbert, 96
Crusades, The. *See Peregrinatio pro Christi*

Dasein (being there), 107
Death. *See* Becker, Ernest; Kübler-Ross, Elisabeth; Nazism: death in; Necrology; War: costs and casualties
Deconstruction, textual, 70–71. *See also* Enemies: deconstruction of
Defamation. *See* Labeling
Defection from hate groups: causes of, 125–28; ineffectiveness of mass media for, 138; joining as "mirror image" of, 126, 130, 200–1*n22*; pushes and pulls in, 127, 136–38, 146; types of, 125. *See also particular individuals*
Degan, William "Billy," 50; demonization, 61; funeral, 60; killing, 63, 65; military career, 60; reputation, 60–61
Degradation. *See* Public degradation ceremony
Delta Force, 53
Demonization. *See* Mythologizing enemies
Derrida, Jacques, 71
Desert Storm, 14, 101, 147; atrocities in, 179; causes of, 102–3; costs and casualties of, 95; justifications for, 12, 18; support for, 16; unifying result of, 15–17
Despair workshops, 180
Detente from below, 83, 139
Dialectics: of heroism, 25–26; of social reality, 35
Dilling, Elizabeth, 69, 72, 74, 75, 76, 77; Henry Ford and, 73
Distant Episode (Bowles), 18
Dix, Dorothea, 98
Dobler, Norma, 162
Dobzhansky, Theodore, 31
"Doublecross," 59
Douglas, Jack, 28
Douglass, James, 119
Dragon slaying, 204*n15. See also* Heroism: in Occident
Dualism, 4, 69; crisis of, 178; as illusion, 33–34, 180
Duck Book, 44
Duck Club, 44, 45, 46

Duke, David, 193*n50*
Duncan, Hugh, 35
Durkheim, Emile, 14, 86
Dwyer, William, 40

Eagleburger, Lawrence, 84
Eagle Forum, 102
Ecological movement, 33
Edda, The, 25, 183
Editorial Research Service, 152
Edomites, 61
Eisenhower, Dwight D., 92
Eisenmenger, Johann, 74, 77, 78
Elkins, Stanley, 97
Emerson, Sandy, 155, 166, 167, 168–69, 170, 172, 174, 203*n25*
Empathy, 112–13
Emry, Sheldon, 59, 70. *See also* America's Promise
"End of History?" (Fukuyama), 84–85
End of the world. *See* Apocalypse
Enemies, 176; deconstruction of, 6, 11; dual nature of, 18, 103–4, 140; experience of, 108–12; historical significance of, 85; in Indo-Aryan myth, 180–81; locating, 86–87, 88–89, 98–100, 101; mutual construction of, 50, 66–67; psychological projection and, 87, 99, 114, 117; social construction of, 5–6, 11, 18, 20, 28–32, 112–13, 114–15, 150; social sciences and, 17; transcending, 117–20, 183; treatment of, 31–32, 92; unifying function of, 15–16, 85–87; wiliness in defeating, 184. *See also* America: enemies in; *particular enemies*
Entdeckte Christentum (Bauer), 78
Entdecktes Judenthum (Eisenmenger), 74
Essays of a Klansman (Beam), 71
Ethical theory: altercentric, 18–20; evil in, 4, 176; Ground Zero and, 119; impossibility of innocence in, 183–84; hope in, 176; nonfetishistic, 33–34; phenomenology and, 117–21 passim. *See also* Evil; Love
Europe. *See* Occident
Evil, 6, 176; duality of, 183; enemies as fetishes of, 17, 25, 33; as illusion, 34, 180–81; as reality, 20, 104, 120–

21; salvation from complicity in, 179; synonyms for, 61. *See also* Ethical theory; Psychic wounding
Excremental assault, 111
Excremental symbolism of enemies, 108–12
Exterminism, crisis of, 8, 14

Faces of the Enemy (Keen), 108, 117
Fanon, Frantz, 32
Fascism, 24, 28, 85, 101, 131; defined, 13. *See also* Authoritarian personality
Fasel, Ed, 45–46
Fatima Crusade, 164, 165, 168
FBI. *See* Federal Bureau of Investigation
Federal Bureau of Investigation, 51, 189*n15;* 192*n26;* 202*n5;* Bob Mathews Brigade and, 155; Hostage Rescue Team, 58; the Order and, 154; SWAT teams, 52
Federalist Party, 89–90, 91, 93, 95
Federal Reserve System conspiracy, 45, 59
Feminism, 33
Fetishism, 25, 33, 187*n6*
Feuerbach, Ludwig, 35
Flowery war. *See Guerra florida*
Force X, 69, 92. *See also* Communists
Ford, Henry, 81, 82; Hitler and, 70; Dilling and, 73
Fort, Connie, 160–61, 163, 165, 168
Fort, Lamar, 160
"Foundations of Morality" (Schopenhauer), 179
Franz, Marie Louise von, 13
Freemasonry, 11, 26, 61, 79, 91
Freemen Institute, 102
Freud, Sigmund, 6
Fukuyama, Francis, 84, 85
Frye, Northrop, 109

Gandhi, Mahatma, 119, 152
Garfinkel, Harold, 29, 41
Generations: cycle of, 98–100; defined, 99
George, Wesley, 31
Gibson, James, 53, 54
Gilbert, Keith, 163, 173–74. *See also* National Socialist Aryan Peoples Party
Girard, René, 115–16
Gissel, Norm, 170

Goldmark, Annie, 48, 150; alleged Communist, 45; murder, 36, 171
Goldmark, Charles, 48, 150; alleged Communist, 45–46; education, 37, 38; murder, 36, 171
Goldmark, Irma "Sally": education, 37; FBI record, 189*n15;* mythologizing of, 43–44; not Jewish, 37; one-time Communist, 37, 39; public degradation of, 40, 41, 42, 43
Goldmark, John: ACLU member, 38, 39; anti-Communist, 37, 39; education, 37; legislator, 37, 38; mythologizing of, 43–44; not Jewish, 37; public degradation of, 40, 41, 42, 43; rumors about, 38–39; security clearance, 189*n15*
Goldmark, Peter, 37
Goldwater, Barry, 100
"Gook," 111–12
Gorbachev, Mikhail, 84, 102
Gospel of Christ Kingdom Church, 172
Gray, Gen. A. M., 87
Great Society, 90, 93, 95, 98
Grendel Worm, 180
Gritz, Col. (ret.) James "Bo," 50, 51, 54, 66; alleged racist, 64, 193*n49;* on David Duke, 193*n50;* intervention in shoot-out, 63; military career, 63, 64, 65; model for Rambo, 65; not white supremacist, 64; presidential candidacy, 64
Ground Zero, 119
Guerra florida (flowery war), 24, 35
Gulf War. *See* Desert Storm

Hajime, Tanabe, 34
Hansen, George, 41
Harris, Kevin, 50; indictment, 65–66; trial and innocence, 66; wounding, 63
Hart, Edgar, 157–58, 159, 172
Hartle, Barbara, 190*n24*
Harvard Center in Creative Altruism, 202*n15*
Hate: and violence, 199–200*n5;* causes of, 122–23. *See also* Defection from hate groups; Enemies; *particular hate groups*
Hate groups. *See particular group names*
Hegel, G. W. F., 25; Fukuyama and, 84–85

Heidegger, Martin, 107; on language, 176; Nazism and, 117–18, 199*n31;* "releasement," 179, 180, 181; "the turning," 178, 181

Heroism, 14, 32, 85, 127, 151, 176; dialectic of, 25–26; in Jung, 182; in Occident, 24, 180–81; in Orient, 24; sociology of, 23–25; true, 155, 181, 182–83; wiliness in, 184

Hidden Hand, 69, 92

Hinduism. *See* Bhagavad-Gita; Indra; *Laws of Manu;* Mahabharata

Hineinversetzen (reflexive empathy). *See* Projection, psychological

Hiss, Alger, 42

Hitler, Adolf, 81, 131; Aryan Nations and, 154, 169; Henry Ford and, 70; on Jews, 12

Hoax of the 20th Century (Butz), 72

Holden, Ashley, 43, 46, 189*n15*

Hölderlin, Friedrich, 178

Holocaust, Jewish, 42, 72, 138

Homosexuals, 28, 92, 99, 101, 109, 155

"Hooking," 126

House Un-American Activities Committee, 42, 189

Hughes, Bob, 159

Hussein, Saddam, 12, 14, 15, 18, 102–3

Husserl, Edmund, 107, 120, 121, 187*n11. See also* Phenomenology

Hymir, 183

Idaho Human Rights Commission, 162

Identity Christianity, 59, 64, 112, 136, 154, 158; defined, 194*n5. See also* America's Promise; Aryan Nations

"I Led Three Lives," 39

Illuminati, 80, 91–92

I'm OK, You're OK (Harris), 145

Indians. *See* Native Americans

Indo-Aryan mythology. *See* Mahabharata; Heroism: in Occident; *particular deities*

Indra, 180, 181

Insiders, 69, 92

International Jew (Ford), 70, 81

Iraq. *See* Desert Storm; Hussein, Saddam

Iron Eagle, 53

Islam, 24, 102. *See also* al-Mahdi; *Jihad*

Japan, 101–2

Jefferson, Thomas, 90, 93, 94–95, 133

Jewish Peril. See Protocols of the Learned Elders of Zion

Jewish Religion Today. See Plot Against Christianity

Jewish Ritual Murder (Leese), 70

Jews, 142, 143, 144, 153–54; altruism toward, 201*n4;* as alleged archetypal enemy, 30, 91; as alleged Christ killers and satanists, 30, 57, 70, 92; as alleged conspirators, 11, 12, 30, 43, 45, 61, 69, 72, 79, 80, 91, 97; as victims, 35–36; ZOG and, 62; function of, for Nazism, 26; in nineteenth-century Europe, 79–80. *See also Plot Against Christianity; Protocols of the Learned Elders of Zion;* Talmud

Jihad, 24, 35

John Birch Society, 59, 70, 93, 102, 171, 189*n18,* 192*n27*

Johnson, Lyndon, 95

Judenreinmachen (Jew-cleansing), 111

Judeophobia. *See* Anti-Semitism

Jung, Carl, 140, 181–82, 183, 204*n15*

Jupiter, 180

Katharma (scapegoat), 110

KCHRTF. *See* Kootenai County Human Relations Task Force

Keen, Sam, 108, 117, 204*n15*

Kenbei (dislike of America), 101

Kennedy, John F., 52, 94, 95

Kentuckian, 47, 48, 49, 68, 70, 82

Khomeini, Ayatollah, 102

KKK. *See* Ku Klux Klan

Klassen, Ben, 154

Know Nothings, 94

Know Your Enemy (Mohr), 70

Koch, Gerda, 189*n23*

Kootenai County Human Relations Task Force, 153, 155, 162, 202*n6;* conciliatoriness of, 173–74; Connie Fort incident and, 161; conservatism of, 169–70; constituency for, 156; founding of, 160; incorporation of, 164, 165; national recognition of, 153, 157; social networks and, 156, 171–73; structure of, 166–67

Korean War, 90, 91, 96, 97, 98; casualties and costs, 95

Krishna, 34

Vaughan, Peter, 166, 172
Vengeance. *See* Violence
Vietnam War, 51, 90, 111–12, 147; effect of, on American culture, 52–53; "Bring it on home," 51, 191n8; costs and casualties, 95; Special Forces in, 52
Vigilante, 39, 189n15
Violence: in American wars, 95; in modern European wars, 9; hatred and, 199–200n5; and heroism, 14; and insanity, 12, 46–47, 48; justifications for, 13–14; love as possible answer to, 151; racial and religious, in Idaho, 159; as ritual, 31–32, 115, 150; and social integration, 171–72, 174; tragedy of, 12–13, 66–67; sense of victimage and, 11–12, 177; Weber on, 183–84
Voluntary associations: defined, 156; institutionalization of, 166; paradox of success in, 169; recruitment to, 156, 171
Vritra, 180, 181

Walker, Glen, 155, 161–62, 163, 172
Wallace, George, 98
WAR. *See* White Aryan Resistance
War, 32, 176; costs and casualties of American, 95; casualties of modern, 10; defined, 23; heroism and, 14, 24, 25; as sacred, 17; unifying function of, 15–17, 86. *See also particular wars*
Wassmuth, Bill, 164, 172, 172; attempted assassination of, 155, 169; community organizer, 165; leader of KCHRTF, 166, 169
Waughtal, David, 129, 201n22
Weaver, Elisheba, 58, 65, 193n54
Weaver, Randall "Pete," 50, 82, 193n49; charges against, 56–57; death premonition, 191n8; demonization of, 57, 58; education, 54, 55; employment, 55; family life, 58–59; guns of, 56; indictment and

trial, 65–66; military career, 53, 54; neighborliness of, 68; religion, 57–58, 61, 62, 192n37; sheriff's candidate, 56; not supremacist, 192n27; surveillance of, 59, 192n32; toughness, 54
Weaver, Sammy, 50, 63, 66
Weaver, Sara, 56, 193n45
Weaver, Vicki, 57, 66, 82; death premonition, 55, 191n8; employment, 55; family head, 58, 63; killing of, 63; racial separatist, 58, 192n27; religion, 57–58, 61–62
Weber, Max, 183–84
Weishaupt, Adam, 80, 91
Weisser, Julie, 144–45, 148
Weisser, Michael, 139, 141–50, 151, 201n7; philosophy of, 149
Western civilization. *See* Modernization; Occident
Westmoreland, General William, 64
White, Robert, 44
White Aryan Resistance, 53, 66, 130, 133, 137, 144
White Man's Bible, 154
White Student Union, 133–34
White supremacy. *See particular groups*
Wilcox, Laird, 152
Wilson, Woodrow, 96
Winrod, Gerald, 74, 81, 82
Withrow, Greg, 129, 130, 133–34, 135, 149, 201n22
World Anti-Communist League, 123
World citizenship movement, 33
World Council of Churches, 62
World War I, 95, 96

Yahweh Believers, 57
Yugoslavia, 86

Zeus, 180
Zionists. *See* Jews
ZOG (Zionist Occupation Government), 62. *See also* Jews: as alleged conspirators